PRISONER OF THE OGPU
Four Years in a Soviet Labor Camp

GEORGE KITCHIN

First published by Longmans, Green and Co. in 1935.

This edition published in 2017.

"Why should we hope? Our lives are wholly blasted,
And all of us are damned by destiny?"

[From the prisoners' song at the OGPU Northern Penal Labor Camps]

Table of Contents

Penal Camp Area in North European Russia

PREFACE

Stories of prison experience in Soviet Russia are not new. In fact the sordid details of nocturnal searches, incarceration in filthy jails, midnight inquisitions, and executions without warning have been made known to English readers through many personal accounts. But the narrative of the present author is unique in several respects and deserves a special place in literature descriptive of Russian conditions.

In the first place it gives the only first-hand authentic account of the penal camps of the Far North that has yet appeared. Two or three of those condemned to penal servitude in these camps have, it is true, escaped or been released, but in these cases their stay was brief and came at a time when for special reasons the severity of the regime was relaxed. The present author is the only man, so far as I am aware, who has undergone the actual experiences of these penal camps and lived to tell the tale.

George Kitchin is a gentleman of education and culture and an able and successful business executive. His social standing and business reputation were above reproach. The authenticity of his account is implicit in the narrative.

As will be seen in his story, he had the good fortune after a time to be assigned clerical work in the office of the penal camp administration. This undoubtedly saved his life and it also gave him a unique opportunity to observe the inner workings of the OGPU organization.

Perhaps the most noteworthy feature of Mr. Kitchin's vivid narrative is the absence of violent partisanship. Despite the injustice of which he was a victim and the hardships to which he was subjected, the author in describing conditions in Russia and the operation of the Soviet system, treats the subject objectively and without bitterness. His attitude is that of a man caught up accidentally in the meshes of a vast impersonal machine, the operation of which he can observe and describe without rancor.

Mr. Kitchin, whose mother was English, was born in Finland. His English and American connections together with his Russian experience fitted him especially for his work in Russia as the representative of an American company, and at the same time enabled him to view conditions broadly and without the strong partisanship of the native Russian. As a citizen of Finland, his case was a matter of concern to the Finnish government, whose efforts finally obtained for him permission to leave Soviet Russia.

His physical condition after four horrible years can well be imagined. A year and a half were spent in convalescing, and another year in preparing his notes and writing the present volume. It is now offered to the public as a vivid narrative of personal experiences and as a contribution to the understanding of conditions in the Soviet Utopia.

Jerome Landfield

CHAPTER ONE: THE NET

The doorbell rang in the dead of the night. It was an agent of the OGPU calling. He was accompanied by armed soldiers. The agent was polite, but taciturn. The soldiers stood there like statues.

The agent presented a warrant for search and arrest. The warrant had been issued by the counter-espionage department of the OGPU. What were they looking for? What did they want? The search was on. It lasted five hours.

I was in the living room, sitting by the fireside, while the search was being made. A soldier stood at the door and watched every move of mine. Luba was nearby, her eyes filled with terror. On my knee was our new-born baby, a tiny little being with violet eyes. A pink coverlet was wrapped around her, and she slept tranquilly through all those anxious hours.

Finally the search was over. Nothing incriminating had been found, as was to be expected. The OGPU agent stepped to the telephone.

"Hello, hello. Is this the OGPU? Extension 76, please. Is that you? There is a new-born baby here, what am I to do? What? Six weeks old. What? His wife? But she is a foreign subject. What is it? Yes, yes, all right."

Luba's lips were pale, her hands trembled.

"Will they take me, too? But how about Baby?" she whispered almost inaudibly. There was something unforgettable in the expression of her eyes. I tried to calm her, to assure her that she had nothing to fear.

The agent hung up the receiver. There was a long pause.

"Citizen," he turned to my wife, "we shall leave you in peace, for the time being."

What a relief! The agent made out his report and we quickly signed it. I packed a few things. I lifted the little being that I had already learned to love.

"Good-bye, little one."

The moment of parting came. There was Luba. And here was the dark stairway. I turned back for a last glimpse. Her silhouette was in the lighted doorway.

"Good-bye, my darling."

The steel-shod boots of the soldiers echoed as they struck the stone steps:

"Good-bye, good-bye."

The clock in the prison office pointed to a quarter past five. In half an hour I had passed from freedom to jail, leaving behind me a series of grilled and locked doors. Here I was thoroughly searched. My necktie, belt, shoe-laces and towels were taken away. It was the routine, to guard against attempts at suicide.

I was then led to a damp and dreary cell on the "special" fifth floor of the notorious Shpalernaya prison. Attached to the wall of my cell were a bunk and a small iron table with a seat. There was a window beneath the ceiling. Under the window was a toilet seat, and adjoining it an iron basin with a faucet.

I sat down on the bunk and tried to collect my thoughts. I was in the Shpalernaya, on the special floor where the OGPU kept only grave offenders. What did it mean? Why had they arrested me?

It was March 26, 1928. The seven years I had spent in Soviet Russia raced past me in swift review. I was a citizen of Finland, a business man, lured by the promises of the NEP (New Economic Policy) proclaimed by Lenin in 1921. I had started out as the representative of a Finnish group seeking a concession in Russia, and within a year developed an import business on a large scale.

My offices were then in the Finnish Government Building in Leningrad which housed many foreign firms. It was a building kept under special observation by the OGPU, which suspected every foreigner of being a spy. That did not worry me, as I had no connection whatever with espionage.

I recalled my first contact with the OGPU. It was in the summer of 1921. A modestly dressed young man called on me at my office. He introduced himself as Troitsky, an official of the OGPU in charge of the Finnish section, and openly proposed that I become informer on all the activities of the Finnish Trade Delegation. He said that he had selected me because his agents had described me as cool and careful in my work. I thanked him for the honor and unceremoniously showed him the door.

"We shall meet again," was his parting remark.

At the time I reported the incident to my headquarters, but forgot about it in the following years. It was not until after the death of Lenin in 1924 that my next contact with the OGPU occurred. There was a British consul in Leningrad, Mr. Preston, who occasionally entertained both foreigners and Russians at tea. Mr. Preston was a thorn in the flesh of the Soviet officials. He wore a monocle in the land of the Soviets, donned a silk hat when driving out on official visits, and his English manner irritated the comrades exceedingly. Moreover, he consistently ignored the local representatives of the Commissariat for Foreign Affairs whenever he sent out invitations to a reception.

My fiancée, Luba, frequented the Preston five-o'clocks. One day, there came an end to the fashionable receptions. There were wholesale arrests among the Russians who had attended them. Luba was one of the prisoners.

It was Luba's second experience with the OGPU. She had been arrested two years earlier, together with her first husband, and had left the prison a widow. Now she was taken to the OGPU headquarters at the Gorokhovaya. Here she received a flattering offer to serve the OGPU as an informer on the British consulate. It was her duty as a loyal Soviet citizen, she was told, to accept the offer.

"Think it over carefully," the examining official said to her. "Consider it well before you decide. If you do not consent, you will not leave these walls. It is not prudent to quarrel with the OGPU."

Luba refused point-blank and was taken to the Shpalernaya, where I was now confined. At the time we sought the intervention of the higher Soviet authorities, but in vain.

Within a week after her arrest, I had my next direct encounter with the OGPU. I was having supper alone in a restaurant when Troitsky suddenly appeared at my table. He was the young OGPU official who had called on me two years before.

I got up and made a move to leave, but he stopped me. He had business which concerned my fiancée.

"Don't you really want to help her?" he asked. I stayed.

Troitsky offered to release Luba in exchange for my services. It was the same proposal that he had made two years earlier. He sought information on the Finnish Consulate General.

"Say the word and this very evening a telegram will be sent ordering the release of your fiancée," he concluded.

I refused the offer. He began to threaten me. He was vexed by his failure to enlist my services. He left in anger.

I went away filled with disgust. The threats were not to be taken lightly, but I would not be dragged into the net.

The Finnish consul advised me to leave the country at once, but I could not even think of leaving without Luba.

She was condemned, after five months in solitary confinement, to three years in Siberia. I continued my efforts to secure her freedom, but without avail.

It looked as if I would have to wait until Luba had completed her term in Siberia. Then something happened. There was an upset in the OGPU headquarters. A number of officials were dismissed or punished. Many of their victims were rehabilitated. Troitsky was among the banished officials. Luba was one of the fortunate prisoners to be set free.

We were married immediately upon her return to Leningrad. Two months later we received from Moscow the precious document canceling her Soviet citizenship. She was now the wife of a citizen of Finland. This was no mean achievement.

During Luba's exile in Siberia, a New York firm, the Lidgerwood Manufacturing Company, appointed me as its representative in Russia. I had also established a plant for the manufacture of oil and candles for churches. There were sixty thousand churches in Russia at the time and I enjoyed a virtual monopoly of the business.

There was a quiet interlude. I was happy at home. Business was good. Luba was on the eve of becoming a mother.

It was January 1928. The shadow of the OGPU suddenly appeared again. I heard that Troitsky was back. He had been reinstated as chief of the Finnish counter-espionage section.

"Let us leave the country immediately," pleaded Luba.

"Leave everything and go?" I retorted. "Don't let the thought of this scoundrel get on your nerves. We are foreigners and he will not dare to start anything."

"But suppose he lays a trap for you with his agents-provocateurs?" she insisted.

Well, here I was in the Shpalernaya. If I had only heeded Luba's warning! But why did they arrest me? It was useless to seek the reason. I had simply fallen into the second category of Soviet citizens. According to a popular saying in Russia, the population of the U.S.S.R. is divided into three categories, those who have been in prison, those who are in prison, and those who will be in prison.

My reflections were interrupted when the light went out in my cell. I threw myself on my bunk and sank into oblivion.

During the two following days I had all the time to consider my situation. I waited in vain to be taken before an examining official. I worried about my wife and child. Were they arrested, too?

They came for me in the night of the third day. I followed the armed guard who led me to the examination. In a small office, a man in the uniform of an OGPU official sat at his desk, bent over papers. He raised his head and smiled.

It was Troitsky. My worst apprehensions were confirmed.

Four years had passed since our last meeting but he had changed little. He greeted me sarcastically as an old acquaintance and proposed that we have a quiet little talk. He asked me to keep in mind that I would face grave consequences in the event that we did not arrive at a satisfactory agreement.

I brushed all this aside and demanded that I be presented with a formal charge for my arrest.

"Don't you worry," he smirked, "a charge will be found, but that will be so much the worse for you. Let us settle matters amicably. Some important considerations demand that we be fully informed of everything that is going on in your consulate. Our present sources of information are not satisfactory and you will have to help us."

He said that his department had caught a group of spies whom they had long suspected and that all the evidence pointed definitely at the consulate. It was imperative, he repeated, that they receive positive information as to whether it was the consul or his assistant who was directing this espionage.

This turn of events was utterly unexpected and I realized that even had I been willing I would not have been able to assist him.

"Do not forget," said Troitsky, "that when we arrest a foreigner we do not fail to have on file enough evidence to justify such action."

He supplemented this statement with the assertion that he was in possession of a signed confession by one of the arrested spies to the effect that the latter had called on me in connection with his work.

This was ridiculous. Never had I had any connection with any foreign intelligence department and no spy had ever called on me.

In order to dispel my doubts Troitsky then produced and showed me the confession of the arrested spy, which stated plainly that the latter had delivered to me a locked brief-case and a package of letters from the Finnish Intelligence Department.

This was such a preposterous lie that I expressed doubt of the very existence of the man who was supposed to have signed the confession. Troitsky offered to confront me with him and a few minutes later a man who was a total stranger to me was brought into the room. On Troitsky's request he repeated the statements made in his confession. He spoke in a low voice and was afraid to look me in the eye.

Troitsky's face bore a satisfied smile and seemed to challenge any further objections on my part. He dismissed me but said that he would call me again in a day for my final answer. He counseled me to weigh my decision carefully, for it would determine my whole future.

"If you make a wrong step," he said, "you will be sure to regret it. Remember, we mean business."

Two hours were left before the morning call and I spent them pacing my cell and thinking. I was now fully aware of the danger of my situation. I was sure that my consulate would intervene on my behalf, I also knew the value of such intervention. Undoubtedly there would be lengthy correspondence, conferences, numerous demands and a like number of refusals. I was a citizen of little Finland, and the U.S.S.R. pays scant attention to the protests of small unimportant countries.

"But there must be some way out," I thought. "While I am in prison I am cut off from the rest of the world. Prisoners are not allowed to see an attorney and I know only too well the worth of a petition to the attorney-general. So what can I do?"

In desperation I ran about my cell considering various courses of action. Some definite course had to be adopted. Toward morning I had arrived at a decision.

The following night I faced Troitsky again. I told him that I would comply with his request. He jumped up and made several quick steps about the room. He was excited and obviously pleased.

"Good!" he exclaimed. "You should have done it long ago. Well, here are three documents, all ready for you. Sign them and you will be home tomorrow."

The first document was an agreement whereby I became an informer of the OGPU; in the second I pledged secrecy concerning the first; the third was a report divulging some incriminating actions on the part of the consulate.

"As to the report, you will have to copy it in your own handwriting and sign it," said Troitsky.

There was a limit to what I had been willing to do. I had never intended to bear false witness against anybody.

I explained to Troitsky that my consent was not entirely unqualified and that I could not sign such a report. I would sign the first two papers and a report incriminating myself, but no one else. All of this I would do on one condition, only upon receipt of a postmarked message from my wife that she was safe in Finland.

"You do not need my wife," I said. "Besides, she has a young baby. You cannot arrest her anyway. The moment I receive the message from her I am at your disposal."

The all-important thing was to get my family out of the danger zone. I had laid my plan with that in view. If my services were badly needed, I would at least be enabled to ascertain the OGPU intentions regarding my wife. Of course, I had no idea whatever of acting as an informer. I felt that once my wife and child were safe, it would be an easy matter to slip out of the country.

"Take the prisoner back to his cell," Troitsky called to the guard. He had listened to me in silence and with a frown.

"Tomorrow morning I shall have your wife arrested also," he turned to me.

Had I unwittingly caused the arrest of my wife? The next forty-eight hours were full of torment. I was again brought before Troitsky on the third morning. To my surprise his manner was extremely pleasant. Apparently all was not yet lost.

"Listen here," he said, and renewed his proposals. I firmly maintained my position. "Perhaps you distrust me personally," Troitsky added. "I shall have you discuss the matter with my chief. It may be easier for you to settle things with him. And so far I have not disturbed your wife," he concluded, "but beware, it will go badly with her if you persist in your obstinacy."

Peterson, Troitsky's superior, was present at the next examination. This time they received me cordially, asked me to sit down, offered me cigarettes and drinks. We argued the matter for a long time and in the end I understood that my game was lost. They did not need me at all for obtaining information, but wanted to use me for manufacturing evidence to enable them to instigate a sensational court action against the Finnish consul.

When I saw their purpose I knew that we had reached an impasse. But they did not wish to give up without playing all their trumps. Evidently they could do nothing without the evidence they hoped to obtain from me.

After a whispered conference with his superior, Troitsky stepped to the telephone and in my presence gave the order for the arrest of my wife. "This is your last chance to reconsider," he said, as he took the receiver off the hook.

I shook my head in refusal. I still had hope that they would not dare to carry out their threats. It seemed so monstrous and improbable, considering the baby.

But in another minute my hopes were dashed. I shook like a leaf as I arose from the chair. A guard entered.

"We shall see both of you rot away in prison, together with your brood," snapped Troitsky, as I left to go.

The blow they had aimed at me had struck its mark. Back in my cell my nerves gave way. All night and all of the next day I was in the state of mind which makes men commit suicide in the cells of the OGPU, as Luba's first husband had done.

Like a drowning man clutching at a straw I sent a petition to the attorney-general demanding his intervention. What naivete!

I handed my petition to the guard. From him it went to the chief of our section, then to the warden, and from the latter to ... Troitsky, who then forwarded it to the attorney-general with his notations. He told me all of this himself at the next examination and openly laughed at me.

"You may be sure," he said, "that all legal formalities will be complied with, but remember that it is the attorney-general's first duty to facilitate the inquest."

Two weeks after my arrest I was handed a formal charge accusing me of espionage in behalf of the Finnish General Staff and the British Naval Staff. Not only had I no connections whatever with either one of these institutions, but I was even ignorant of the existence of the latter.

For five months I remained in solitary confinement in a cell on the "special" floor of the Shpalernaya prison. The first month was especially hard because of the intermittent examinations, always in the middle of the night, and the constant worry about my wife and child. I had had no news of them whatever and all my inquiries were answered by the stereotyped reply that "they were feeling fine."

I was not allowed books or newspapers, was never taken out for a walk. Absolute silence was maintained on the "special" floor. I was completely isolated in my stone box, shut in with my sad thoughts. My nerves went back on me and I could not eat, getting dreadfully thin and feeling as helpless as a lamb in a slaughterhouse. But I would not give in.

After the first month the regime suddenly changed. I was allowed to receive parcels from outside, was given books and newspapers, and was taken out for a walk in the prison yard. It was due to the efforts of our consul on my behalf.

The very first parcel brought me great relief. My wife, who had had her own experience with Soviet prisons, wrote my name with an ink-pencil on the napkin in which she had wrapped the food. I recognized her handwriting and knew that she was safe at home. A heavy weight was lifted from my mind.

In another parcel Luba had very ingeniously contrived to hide a message apprising me of the fact that the consulate was fighting for me and insisting that my case be brought to trial in court. If these efforts were successful, it would mean that the principal danger would be averted, namely, a sentence by the board of the OGPU, reached behind closed doors. I was looking forward to the court trial, never doubting that it would be an easy matter to confute the false evidence brought against me.

CHAPTER TWO: THE RED MILL OF JUSTICE

My wife and child were safe in Finland! What thrilling news! The consul's efforts were bearing fruit. The guard handed me a copy of an order of the OGPU transferring my case to the jurisdiction of the court. That evening I was brought before Peterson, who advised me to plead guilty at the trial.

"Just think about it a bit," he said, "you will have plenty of time to consider my advice. In a few weeks the examiner of the military tribunal will take your testimony. If you do not plead guilty, it will go badly with you and you will regret it."

But encouraged by the favorable turn in my affairs I decided to ignore this advice, thinking that once my case went to court, it would be difficult for the OGPU to influence it further. So I quietly awaited the trial. But I had a longer wait than I had expected. After waiting for five months in my solitary cell I was finally brought before the examiner of the military tribunal.

He looked like a decent young man. Inasmuch as I thought him to be independent of the OGPU I seized this opportunity to tell him all about Troitsky and how the OGPU was persecuting me.

"I have already written a petition about this to the attorney-general," I said, "but without result. Now I shall write to the military prosecutor, for it is not conceivable that the latter should also be working hand in glove with the gentlemen of the OGPU."

The examiner frowned.

"Let me tell you something," he said. "If you should address such a petition to the military prosecutor, he would probably have to take some action, but it would result only in the OGPU insisting that the whole case be handed back to it for revision. I have studied your case and cannot conceive of your receiving a sentence exceeding a year in prison. Besides, the trial is very near, so why risk any further delays? This is my honest opinion and I wish you to believe me and not make any further fuss."

I looked at this man who was giving me his "honest opinion" and tried to decide whether he was to be trusted. Could you trust any Soviet prosecutor? But the argument was plausible. The military prosecutor evidently could not be independent of the OGPU and would not pick a quarrel with them on my account. Judging by the words of the young examiner the latter was not personally predisposed toward the OGPU, but he too preferred to maintain pleasant relations with the all-powerful institution. I decided to take his advice. He told me that I would be brought to trial in three weeks and issued instructions to have me transferred from my solitary cell to a double one, which is of the same size as a solitary one, but is shared by two, three, and sometimes even four prisoners.

But again I was doomed to disappointment. Three weeks, and three months passed, and there was no further mention of the trial.

Finally I was again called for an examination. I had expected to see the examiner of the military tribunal, but instead was greeted by Troitsky.

"Ah, you did not expect to see me?" he chuckled. "Very foolish of you. We are destined to meet each other many more times. Perhaps you have made good use of your time and have reconsidered your decision? No? As you like. You thought that your case was now in the right channel and would soon be brought to trial?" He laughed again. "No honorable citizen, no. It is not all as simple as it looks. Your case, for instance, has been handed back to us for revision."

I was stunned. "Haven't you had ample opportunity for a very complete investigation during these eight months?" I asked.

He rubbed his hands with a satisfied air and informed me of the death of Pukkila, the Finnish spy to whom my case had been linked by the perjured evidence.

"Think of it, he died, yes, died," he repeated again and again, snickering and taking great delight in the telling. He concluded with the statement that owing to Pukkila's death the court trial had been canceled and my fate would be decided by the board of the OGPU.

I returned to my cell in a rage. This was too much. To have waited for eight long months and then to have to start it all over again from the very beginning. There is an end to patience! But what could I do? As before, I was cut off from the outside world and utterly helpless. Should I resort to a hunger strike and demand an interview with our consul? Such action would be futile and would only further undermine my already weakened constitution. The OGPU does not interfere with hunger strikers until they are thoroughly starved. Then it sends them to the hospital, where they are artificially fed.

It was now clear to me that they were dragging out my case purposely. I came to the conclusion, however, that all necessary steps would be taken

19

without any effort on my part. The consulate would be advised of Pukkila's death and this news would rouse my wife's anxiety. Since she was now in Helsingfors she would immediately bring pressure on the Finnish Ministry of Foreign Affairs.

Ten months from the day of my arrest I was informed that my case had been removed from that of the Finnish spies and was transferred to the Supreme Court.

"What are they up to now?" I pondered. The fact that my case had been transferred to the Supreme Court signified that unusual importance was ascribed to it. Unfortunately, it also meant that I would have to wait in prison six to twelve months longer before my trial.

One more month passed. A special prosecutor, Halperin, arrived from Moscow. It was clear that he was thoroughly versed in the details of my case. He smiled when I tried to explain to him that I had been framed, and politely suggested that I address a protest to the attorney-general.

"Of course," he added, "if you do that, it will take several months for your case to get back to me, but you have the privilege of filing such a protest. In the ordinary course of events your case would come up for trial in three weeks, but if it should go first to the attorney-general, you would have to wait until October at the earliest. It is for you to choose."

He then proceeded to make out the report of the examination. Toward the end he asked me casually whether I remembered when I had registered the names of the foreign firms I had represented. I told him I had never registered any such thing.

He nodded. Then he briefly finished the report and passed it to me for signature. After locking it up carefully in his brief-case, he contentedly told me that in view of my confession the evidence was now complete.

"What confession? What are you talking about?" I asked.

With a cunning smile he read to me a copy of a decree published in 1923, instructing all foreigners to register the firms they represented in the U.S.S.R. I had violated this decree and was subject to a punishment of one to ten years in prison, and the confiscation of all my property!

I was stupefied. Never had I heard of any foreigner registering his firm. I protested that it was too unreasonable to keep a man in confinement for almost a year and then to present to him the insignificant charge of having transgressed an old decree that had never been enforced and was now well-nigh forgotten. But he placidly interrupted me:

"Don't let us argue," he said. "Better consider the facts as they are. I have dropped the idea of charging you with espionage, as the evidence seems quite unsubstantial, but please consider for yourself, how could we possibly let you go free now after having kept you a year in prison? It is imperative that you be legally convicted and this is exactly what we propose to do. For a whole year we have been trying to get under your skin, all in vain. But now we've got you where we want you. Have you any further questions?"

A few minutes later I was back in my cell. During the eleven months in prison I had learned one thing — not to be surprised at anything. All I could do now was to wait. I had already become hardened to being in prison. After the news that my wife had left the country the desperation of the first period had given way to apathy. I had reconciled myself to the fact that I was powerless, in captivity.

During the long time of my confinement in the double cell all kinds of prisoners had passed before me in kaleidoscopic procession: a former social-revolutionary, a baker, an old railroad employee, a bandit murderer, a Red Army soldier, a speculator, two communist workingmen, a Trotskyist student, a professor of history, an officer of the Red Army, the managing director of an industrial plant who had risen to this position from a simple worker. With all of these men I lived for several weeks at a time, talked to them at length and tried to encourage them. The other bunk was never left unoccupied for more than a few hours. One after another my cell-mates left me to be taken to other cells or prisons, to be set free, to be sent into exile, or to be shot. But I saw them all go and remained there, waiting and hoping for a change.

Every morning I awoke at the signal, swept the floor of my cell and received my cup of hot water. At noon I received a plate of nauseating soup and a dish of porridge without butter or milk. The evening meal consisted of another dish of the same porridge.

Once a week we were allowed to receive food parcels from without, but of course I could not gorge myself on the food I received while my hungry cell companions looked on. Hence, my food parcels lasted only one or two days.

Another three months went by. At the end of May 1929, I was finally transferred to a general cell. This apparently signified the approach of some decision in my case.

After the quietness of the single and double cells, the noise that greeted me in the general cell made it seem like a madhouse. It housed thirty-two prisoners from all walks of life, beginning with a bishop and ending with a city bum.

I did not remain long. At the end of June, I was ordered to pack up my belongings and was taken to Moscow, where I was to appear before the Supreme Court. Another prisoner travelled with me. It was Fabrizius, a Finnish journalist, who had been ordered to Moscow for the same reason as I.

In Moscow I first spent two weeks in the Lubianka — the well-known prison of the OGPU headquarters in Moscow — in a general cell which was first filled with some forty members of the clergy and later with a heterogeneous crowd from all trades and professions. After three weeks I was transferred to the old Butirsky prison. This probably would rank first among prisons the world over in the amount of filth and vermin in it.

The general cell intended for thirty prisoners held over seventy. They slept on boards spread on the concrete floor, lying closely side by side. It was dreadful and the stench was awful.

The clergy were again represented by a bishop and several priests, and the lay professions all the way from composer to thug. The horrible living conditions in the cell made the prisoners irritable and hostile to each other. They quarreled and sometimes even fought. A loud din constantly filled the air.

These were very trying conditions for me with my shattered nerves. I sharply protested and demanded to be taken to a solitary cell. My demand was granted, probably thanks to the violent tone of my protest.

After sixteen months in prison I was finally handed a copy of the decision of the Supreme Court with reference to my case.

It was scheduled for a hearing at a closed session of the military tribunal, without prosecuting or defending attorneys. Not a very pleasant surprise.

The second surprise consisted in the news that my case had been joined to that of Fabrizius, the journalist whom I had met *en route* to Moscow, and the third surprise was the information that I was charged with violating Statute 58, which meant a charge of espionage.

Why espionage again, and why the hearing before the military tribunal? I was bewildered and alarmed. Again, as in the first days in prison, I kept pacing my cell from corner to corner. They were playing with me like a cat with a mouse.

There was only one consolation. Some definite decision was near. I had waited for the trial so long that I was indifferent as to which court should pronounce judgment, whether a justice of the peace, a judge of the Supreme Court or the military tribunal. All I wanted was a definite verdict and then I was sure an exchange could be arranged for some Soviet citizen convicted and held prisoner in Finland.

Nevertheless I wrote a protest, demanding an explanation. Though physically weak, I managed to keep alive the spirit of courage.

"But what are you making all this fuss for?" asked Halperin, who summoned me several days later. "Didn't I tell you that we shall not charge you with espionage? Pay no attention to the slip of paper you received, it has no bearing on the matter at all. I joined the two cases together for purely technical reasons, so that's that."

He was vexed that he had been disturbed on such an insignificant matter. It seemed strange to him that a man should have been imprisoned for sixteen months and still be worrying about something; he should have had ample time to get used to things as they were.

The military tribunal held its session in modest surroundings, in the private office of Cameron, the chairman, without pomp or ostentation.

I sat next to Fabrizius, opposite the three men who were to decide our fate.

After a few formalities the chairman asked me whether I had known Fabrizius before. I said no, and Fabrizius confirmed my statement that we had first met in the train that brought us to Moscow.

The members of the tribunal whispered a little and decided to consider my case separately from that of Fabrizius.

While I was waiting and sadly musing on the further delay, the tribunal reached a verdict in the case of Fabrizius. He was sentenced to be shot. Then we were both taken back to prison in our respective cells.

The military tribunal had brought me more disappointment. I had hoped that the matter would be finally settled, but apparently they were in no hurry and all I could do was to wait patiently, as I had waited all these long months.

The days succeeded each other in tiresome uniformity. My only diversion consisted in observing the regular morning aeroplane passing over the prison on its way to Berlin. It was hard to realize that the current of life moved on and that some human beings were free to fly away, while others in prison cells awaited trial or prepared themselves for execution.

Two weeks later I was unexpectedly brought before the military tribunal again. The same three men were in session at the desk of the chairman.

After the preliminary formalities had been complied with, I made the extraordinary request that the Court grant me the right to ask several questions pertaining to the law in my case. I pointed out that since I was a foreigner and unacquainted with Soviet law, and since I had been denied the privilege of having an attorney to defend me, I needed some information to enable me to formulate my defense.

"The Supreme Court does not consider it necessary to give you any explanations," Cameron decided bluntly. Why then did they bother to have this comedy of a trial? It would have been much simpler to send a copy of the verdict to me in my cell.

I was asked if I had anything to say. The legal formalities evidently required this and the comrades followed them implicitly.

"I request you to set me at liberty at once," I said.

"Is that all?" asked Cameron in surprise.

"Yes, that's all," I said. Any further arguments would evidently be a mere waste of time.

The trial lasted exactly twenty minutes and the verdict was, "Four years in prison and confiscation of all property."

"Commandant, take the prisoner out," ordered the Court, and I made my exit from a court of justice probably the most severe and the most original in the world. Perhaps the same sort of justice might have been meted out with even less ceremony in darkest Africa. As to the confiscation of my property, the court order came post factum, as my plant had been confiscated and sold by the OGPU long before.

A week later I was transferred to the Lefortovsky prison, which was a decided improvement. It seemed that the worst had been left behind. I had passed out of the jurisdiction of the OGPU to that of the Prison Department of the People's Commissariat of Justice. My new abode served as a model for purposes of exhibition to foreign delegations visiting the U.S.S.R. Conditions were quite acceptable, as prisons go. In any event, in comparison with the prisons of the OGPU, it might be called a paradise.

It housed only the most important prisoners, such as famous bandits, engineer "wreckers," counter-revolutionaries, etc. Convicted foreigners were also usually kept there.

During the first few days I was assigned the task of chopping wood. Then I was transferred to the spinning mill and from there, because of the breakdown of some machinery, to some work in the library.

For the first time in eighteen months I was allowed to correspond with my wife, and to receive a whole series of photographs of my growing child. I lived quietly in prison, outside the sphere of the OGPU. All the past seemed a bad dream. No matter how dismal my life at that time might have seemed to an outsider, I accepted it almost without murmur. A man can get used to almost anything. Eighteen months in the OGPU prisons had transformed me physically to a mere shadow of my former self.

November came. The monotony of prison life was interrupted only by the frequent visits of foreign and native delegations, to which we had become thoroughly accustomed. But toward the end of the month some sinister rumors spread among the prisoners about a transfer to the jurisdiction of the OGPU and to the penal labor camps. Several days later the rumors were confirmed when the news came that three hundred of our prisoners were to be sent to the northern penal camps in the middle of December.

The details soon became known. The OGPU had simply made an agreement with the People's Commissariat of Justice whereby the latter was to transfer to it all able-bodied prisoners. The OGPU was to receive as remuneration one ruble and thirty kopecks per day for each prisoner.

The reason behind this transaction was evident. The Five-Year Plan had just been embarked upon and there was an acute shortage of hands in some of the remote districts. As a way out, the OGPU had undertaken some construction contracts. It did so on condition that it be allowed to employ the prisoners held in its penal camps and organize other camps wherever necessary. New penal camps were opened, but the OGPU had not enough convicts at its disposal. Therefore, it made a new agreement with the Commissariat of Justice and the transport of prisoners began at once. We had been bought like slaves.

The day before our departure a special commission for the examination of the "goods" arrived. It was to examine all prisoners as to the state of their health and ability to work. There was not even a doctor on the commission. Five men who knew nothing of medicine sat at the table and determined the fate of the prisoners. One prisoner out of ten was subjected to a cursory examination of lungs or heart by a medical attendant. The prisoners stood in line, naked, called out their names and stepped up to the table. "Ready, next; ready, next," in quick succession, was all that one heard. The examination of three hundred prisoners was finished by five o'clock, an average of one man per minute, an example of splendid non-bourgeois efficiency.

My cell companions were gloomy. They had been at the Lefortovsky prison for a long time and did not want to leave. One of them was the Ukrainian Pevny, a representative of a Swedish firm manufacturing separators, convicted as an "economic spy." Another was Timofeyich, an embezzling cashier. In the adjoining cell the consumptive financial inspector Granovsky uttered his denunciations of the Bolsheviks with renewed bitterness.

On the morning of departure our cells were not opened. At noon we received our last meal and two kilograms of black bread each. After the meal the cells were opened and the prisoners with their bundles went downstairs into the lower corridor. There they were searched by the prison guards. The latter were polite and even kind, as they had lived with some of the prisoners for several years. After the search, we were marched to the end of the corridor and delivered to the OGPU.

A different atmosphere was immediately noticeable. The OGPU agents were dressed in the uniforms so well known to me and were armed with revolvers; soldiers were armed with rifles; all of them were churlish and rough. Our little prison barber who had carelessly boasted of having successfully smuggled a razor, was promptly beaten over the head in compensation. The spinning mill experts had escaped the general fate. Among them was Egorov, who was serving a ten-year sentence merely because he was a friend of the English Charnock family. Prisoners who had access to some influential protection were also left behind.

In the yard we were awaited by several "black crows," as the motor-vans were called which served the OGPU for the transport of prisoners.

"Get into the vans," the command sounded, and we obeyed, passing between lines of soldiers standing with their rifles pointed.

The crowded vans started. We stood there in the dark, packed like sardines. In twenty minutes our van came to a stop. I lifted up my bundles and stepped to the door through which I could see a dimly lighted railway carriage. I followed Pevny out of the van, walking slowly in the dark, floundering ankle-deep through a ditch full of icy water. Convoy-soldiers stood on both sides of the door, hustling the men into the carriage. Other vans had arrived. From all of them emerged prisoners loaded with bundles. They came from the Butirsky, Tagankovsky and Myasnitsky prisons.

CHAPTER THREE: JAIL-ON-WHEELS

Our railway carriage was luckily not a regular prison car but an ordinary third-class carriage with barred windows and steel grated doors. It was but slightly heated. Two soldiers served as our convoy. One of them, rifle in hand, sat at one of the doors inside the carriage; the other, his superior, carried a gun and occupied the service compartment near the other door. The superior kept the keys to both doors, therefore his assistant was as a matter of fact kept under lock and key as much as ourselves.

It was the assistant's duty to maintain order within the car, while the superior was the go-between in all transactions with the outside world. The assistant was periodically relieved while the superior remained on duty to the end and was responsible for all occupants of the car. The assistant ministered to our needs and brought us boiling water for our tea; the superior admitted us to the lavatory by turns. The assistant was a somewhat dumb thick-headed peasant boy, the superior — a shrewd trusty of the OGPU. Both were dressed in good quality overcoats and helmets.

When we came in, the sleeping-shelves were already down. We climbed in and made ourselves at home. Four of us found room on the middle shelf of the second compartment. The shelf was very hard, but we all were badly in need of sleep and conversation soon ceased.

As I fell asleep I could feel the train start, but the fact registered but faintly: all I wanted was — to sleep, to forget everything and sleep. We were lying close to each other: the space designed for three held four, and one of these four was the giant Pevny. My sleep was frequently interrupted by a sort of nightmare: I imagined that a mountain of sand was sliding down upon me and would not let me move. It was Pevny trying to find a comfortable position. I would shove him away and fall asleep again. In a few minutes the same dream would repeat itself. This went on until dawn.

I was one of the first to awake. The candles in the two lanterns had burnt to the end and the gray dawn was just barely visible through the dusty panes. It was early morning and the car was much colder than the night before. Now and then coughing was heard. It was difficult to breathe in the stuffy air mixed with foul tobacco odor. Some glimmering lights of cigarettes indicated that not all of the passengers were asleep. Whispering was heard here and there but the usual noisemakers, the criminal elements, were not yet awake.

The sleepy-headed convoy soldier made his appearance; the noise grew, laughter was heard and soon one could hear only the general drone of voices mingled with the clatter of the rolling car. Nobody gave a thought to washing, as if it were quite natural not to wash. This led to an argument in the other end of the car. Funk, the German shoe-paste manufacturer, boasted that the consumption of soap was greater in Germany than in any other nation; his opponent, a Russian, maintained that the Germans had to use more soap as they were naturally dirtier than all other nations...

We had been duly warned that we would not get any meals en route and that our daily ration would consist of four hundred grams of black bread and of boiling water for tea. Nobody protested except some of the petty criminals. As a matter of fact, prisons accustom one to privations and the majority of us remained indifferent to the announcement. We knew, besides, that it was perfectly useless to protest or to make a row, as experience had taught us that in dealings with the OGPU protests never bear fruit.

Our car held sixty-four prisoners. Some of them were from our Lefortovsky prison and some from other Moscow prisons. The prisoners from the Moscow Myasnitsky prison were convicted of less serious charges, such as non-payment of taxes, graft, embezzling, and other "economic" crimes. This category of prisoners differed materially from us, "State" criminals, both as to their appearance and their state of mind. Their terms of sentence were comparatively short and they were mostly of the well-to-do class, as was evidenced by their clothing and baggage. After the completion of their terms, they could expect full release without any limitations, while the "State" criminals were subject to additional "measures for social protection," such as exile to remote territories, etc. So, for instance, after serving his five years in the penal labor camps, a man was barred from residence in the six principal cities, or was not permitted to live in towns at all, or else, more likely than not, was ordered to settle for good in some distant territory. The government did not assist such exiles financially; on the contrary, the local authorities made all kinds of difficulties when the new settlers tried to find work.

Five of the Myasnitsky prisoners were particularly outstanding in their appearance. Foremost among them was Funk, the manufacturer of shoe-paste, about fifty years old, dressed with great care in a small sealskin cap, a good fur coat with a seal collar, and black felt boots protected by glistening new rubbers. He was smoking a pipe and looked quite un-prisonlike. He wore fur-lined leather gloves, his face was clean-shaven and he smelt of Cologne. His little green, expressionless eyes glittered dimly from under his gray eyebrows.

Next to him was another "economic" offender, Yamiker, who had a vigorous, pleasant smile, bright dark eyes and an active manner. He and Funk were playing dominoes with two other rather well-dressed prisoners sitting opposite them. The fifth one of their company started a conversation with me, we soon found mutual friends and he was happy to be able to gossip and tell me all about his travelling companions.

"Now, take Funk for instance," he chattered. "Of course you have heard the name. His shoe-paste is sold on every corner. He had his name advertised everywhere even before the revolution. He lost his fortune in the revolution, but during the NEP he rented his own confiscated plant from the Bolsheviks and started running it on a shoestring. In another year you could again see his name on fences, house-walls, in papers and magazines. Funk's shoe-paste continued its victorious march and, lacking competition, quickly conquered the Soviet market. Money flowed into Funk's coffers from all parts of the Union, he enlarged his plant and by 1924 had a virtual monopoly of the shoe-paste business. There was no other paste manufactured and its importation was forbidden. He regained his entire fortune and had great plans for the future.

"But man proposes and God disposes or, as we say in Moscow, man proposes and OGPU disposes. The next year brought disappointment to Funk and to all other enterprising men who had placed their faith in Bolshevik promises. First, he was heavily taxed: then, when he paid these taxes, they were doubled and trebled. In 1926 Funk again found himself ruined, this time by the entirely legal procedure of a tax-assessor's arbitrary estimates of his income. And here you have Funk, again a bankrupt and a prisoner bound for the penal labor camps, charged with being a vicious tax-evader and sentenced to five years' imprisonment. Funk is one of the many victims who took the Bolshevik rent agreements seriously. When he finishes his term he will undoubtedly get a job in one of the administration's offices and will be transformed into a useful social worker. But look at his eyes, he is a finished man."

My companion introduced me to the domino players. All of them, except Funk, were jolly and hopeful and were laughing and joking. The conversation turned to the timely subject of penal camps, but I soon came to the conclusion that no one of this crowd knew anything about them.

"It does not pay to think about it; it can hardly be worse than the prisons," said one of them.

"You are wrong there," disagreed another. "It is sure to be worse, but the question is, how much worse?"

Most of the Myasnitsky prisoners were of similar opinions. They had had a fairly tolerable life in prison and few of them were bothered by the eternal question of "what for?" which constantly recurred to most of us Lefortovsky men.

"Wait till we arrive, then you will see," came a voice from an upper shelf. It belonged to our taciturn Lefortovsky bandit, whose cold gray eyes were staring at us significantly out of his pockmarked face.

The meaning intonation of his speech disturbed us, but even he would not tell us anything definite except that he had already finished a three-year term in the Solovetsky camp, had escaped from his transport into exile, had returned to Moscow, and had there again been caught in a "messy" affair. He spoke of the Solovetsky camp with hatred and loathing:

"They beat you there like dogs, the amount of work exacted is beyond all endurance, and the prisoners die like flies," he said. "Prisoners live in tents on swampy ground, the food is nothing but slops, they mock at you and beat you at every occasion. Just wait and see, it will be the same here."

An old priest came up to our group to listen, and the bandit calmed him with the words: "You gents of the clergy have it easy, they make watchmen of you, for you are known to make the very best watchmen." Then our authority disappeared in his shelf, escaping from some of the curious "intelligentsia" who had begun to gather around him and whom he despised thoroughly as a class. Conversation in our carriage soon deteriorated into the usual quarrels of men with ragged nerves and I evaded these by climbing onto my shelf.

My left-side neighbor on the shelf was the architect G., a man who had ranked high in his profession and who had just come from the Butirsky prison. He was tall and thin, his light blue eyes had a bold and cynical expression, and his straight and slightly puffy nose indicated a connoisseur of wine. Even here in this carriage he did not lose a certain show of elegance.

He climbed after me onto our shelf, carefully arranged his silk shirt-cuffs and the creases in his well-tailored suit, pulled out his cigarette case and offered me a smoke. We had just lit our cigarettes when there was a commotion among the passengers caused by the announcement of "boiling water."

"Don't bother, my caddy will bring it to us," the architect said, holding me back.

His "caddy" travelled in the same carriage with us. He was a petty thief from the Butirsky prison and was charged by the architect with certain duties such as to carry his baggage, watch it, look after his patron's comfort and bring him his boiling water. In exchange for these services he received some tobacco, the leftovers of the bread and a little money. Sure enough, in ten minutes or so a dirty paw reached up and handed us a tea-pot.

The board of the OGPU had recently sentenced the architect G. to a ten-year term in the penal labor camps, but in spite of his misfortune he remained true to his usual manner. In a cool and slightly deprecating tone of voice he talked to me on the subject of socialist construction. The even flow of his words and the regular beat of the rolling carriage affected me soothingly; I dozed off and awoke only about five o'clock. We had not had a meal for two days and I was rather hungry.

The architect spread a napkin and brought out various edibles. He said that a full stomach was the best preventative of sad thoughts and advised me to go to it and eat well. We drank some tea and soon finished all our supplies.

In the evening our train passed Yaroslavl. Time was going by easily. The dim candlelight of the lantern lighted the gangway of our carriage. Under the lantern sat a soldier with his rifle: he was tired, his eyes were half shut and he was nodding. Here and there cigarettes were glimmering. Bodies of sleeping men filled all the benches and shelves. The train rolled slowly and made little noise. Now and then it stopped and lights could be seen through the frosted window-panes. Conversation quieted down and soon gave way to snoring. Night had come.

The second, third and fourth day passed in a similar way. Every morning we were given our bread and boiling water and every evening we got some more boiling water. We were not allowed to buy papers and we had no books with us: tediously we whiled the hours away. A faint feeling of hunger would not leave me. We arrived at Viatka in the evening. Kotlas was three hundred kilometers further north, so that we could expect to reach our destination in another two days.

Our little jail-on-wheels was slowly crawling along. It was getting colder as we proceeded northward, but the carriage remained unheated and we resigned ourselves to this discomfort. We were all tired. The further we went, the less laughter was heard. It was replaced by arguments and petty quarrels.

On the eve of our arrival there was a feeling of tension, mingled with curiosity and fear. One thing was certain — it was much colder. The windows were covered with thick frost, coughing increased and the tubercular Granovsky had to clear his throat and spit at more frequent intervals, thus adding to the nervousness of his companions.

When I finally fully opened my eyes, Funk, the shoe-paste manufacturer, was already standing at the window in complete readiness, smoking his pipe. His expressionless little green eyes tried to look out but could not penetrate the frosted, dirty window-pane and wandered over its surface with a tired and indifferent air.

It was getting noisier all the time. Laughter and foul ejaculations came from the gang of common criminals. The clatter of wheels mingled with the conversation and produced a general din. Then the door opened and let in a current of cold air. The din quieted, but was immediately resumed in a more joyful tone: boiling water had been brought in.

The prisoners made a rush for the door where the convoy-soldier had shoved the spout of a large tea-kettle through the grating and was dispensing boiling water, a tin cupful per man. Our precious Timofeyich, with his usual foresight, had worked his way to the grating long before and had been chattering with the soldier on subjects nearest to the peasant's heart; he was now rewarded and brought us a whole tea-kettle of boiling water.

We were told that the penal labor camp was five kilometers from the Kotlas station and that we would have to walk there. Through the frosted windows we could barely see the tops of pine trees, covered with snow. "The very trees which we shall have to cut," drawled the architect G., as the train slowly crawled to the station. Judging by the temperature within our car, it was very cold outside. It would be no joke to cut timber in such weather.

The convoy-chief came in and put an end to our waiting. He slammed the door behind him and cried out in a resonant voice:

"Pack your things, be ready in fifteen minutes. Get out of the car, form in pairs, carry your bundles. Attention to commands, no resistance, otherwise soldiers are instructed to shoot. Understand?"

He disappeared as suddenly as he had come. At the other end of the carriage the junior convoy-soldier was explaining to someone that "you are lucky, citizens, the car will be brought right up to the penal camp. It would have been hard to walk through the deep snow; we would have had to do a bit of prompting with these," and he slapped the butt of his rifle.

My Lefortovsky pupil Baltrusevich, Red commander, cavalier of the Order of the Red Banner and former lieutenant in the Czar's army, remarked amusedly: "Curious, but it sounds just like our barracks; I have been told before that the penal camps are run in the military way, and it seems to be true."

The gangway was filled with prisoners who wanted to be first to alight. The venerable priest resignedly stood in the corridor, murmuring prayers, heaving sighs and crossing himself. Next to him stood his devoted seminarist lad who had insisted on piling all of the priest's bundles on his own immature shoulders. Behind the priest stood a bunch of petty criminals dressed in squalid rags. Right under my shelf stood Funk, in his well-tailored fur coat with raised seal collar. Little Granovsky, the financial inspector from our Lefortovsky prison cut a funny figure. He was terribly overloaded and was grumbling in order to quiet his nerves.

Pevny and Timofeyich urged me to come down from my shelf, but the architect held me back: "There is plenty of time, we do not have to be afraid of missing the show."

Finally the train slowed down and stopped. The door was instantly opened and a command resounded: "Get out." All the sixty-odd passengers scrambled and hurried to the exit, prompted by the cries and commands from the outside. Both inside the car and out there was a loud hubbub of cries, urgings, protests and cursings.

Old Timofeyich was ahead of me in the passage-way. At the door he involuntarily stopped. Right under him, in the snow, sprawled Pevny, who had just jumped out of the car. The soft snow and the heavy box on his shoulders interfered with his endeavor to regain his footing and his mishap accentuated his usual awkwardness.

"Jump, you old fogey," shouted the convoy-soldier.

"But excuse me, can't you see that there is a man down there, how can I jump right on top of him? Generally, how do you expect people to jump from this height; you can break your neck this way..."

His tirade was cut short by a curse and a strong blow in the neck which threw him out of the car and sent him sprawling right on top of Pevny. This was the first ocular demonstration I had of the manhandling methods in the penal camps.

Not waiting for a further invitation I jumped out with my light baggage, trying to land to one side. I landed knee-deep in the snow and narrowly missed my two cellmates. I tried to help them, but a soldier jumped at me and urged me on. The architect landed immediately beside me and dragged me on with him.

Bravely we made our way through the snow, which reached up to our knees. We joined the crowd of bewildered people, overloaded with their bundles, tossing about like men possessed, bawling and cursing, all making their way through the deep snow, lashed on by the shouts and oaths of the soldiers.

People continued to pour out of the cars. They joined the crowd and were irresistibly drawn on with it. Here and there men fell under their heavy loads on the uneven path. Butts of rifles urged them up and in despair they left half their belongings in the snow and trudged on without them. The crowd was milling about much as a herd of sheep does, meeting an automobile at night.

"Go ahead, go ahead, don't stop or we'll shoot," constantly filled the air.

These shouts were effective and the swarm of people steadily rolled onward.

"Two in a row, two in a row," we were ordered.

This command was difficult to fulfill as so many of the men stopped and fell from exhaustion. Close to me, I saw Granovsky's face, convulsed with rage.

He was pushed forward by a soldier who poked his gun in his side. "Move on, you son of a bitch," he bawled at him.

The suddenness of the transition from the quiet of our prison life into this bedlam, the speed of our onward march, the change of emotions and a feeling of dreadful indignation upset me completely. The sardonic voice of the architect brought me back to realities:

"And here is our new 'home,'" he said, pointing his chin at the buildings some two hundred yards ahead of us.

There seemed to be enough housing provision for all of us. The buildings were surrounded by a barbed-wire fence. A sentry-box stood at the high gates and over them was an inscription which I could not read at that distance. Behind the barbed-wire enclosure a group of men in military great-coats seemed to await our arrival.

The tired prisoners and soldiers slackened their pace as they neared the gates. On reaching there we stopped, unburdened ourselves of our bundles, and waited for those behind us. We sat down in the snow, lit our cigarettes and gradually regained equilibrium.

My low brown shoes and Scotch golf-stockings were covered with a crust of ice. The lucky owners of broad coat-collars had raised them and others had pulled their caps over their ears. Time passed but nobody paid any attention to our being there. We were patiently waiting, surrounded by a cordon of convoy.

After an hour and a half of waiting we finally saw a sleigh in the distance approaching us rapidly. When it came alongside of us, it stopped, the coachman jumped off and pulled aside the fur coverlet. A young man of about twenty-five got out of the sleigh first. He wore a khaki woolen helmet, a short black coat and highly polished top boots. He was medium-built, slender and clean-shaven. His dark eyes were unusually bright and accentuated the slightly degenerate expression of his face.

The second passenger got out of the sleigh more leisurely. He wore a large coat, fur outside, and felt boots. He was more corpulent than his companion. His horn-rimmed glasses rather harmonized with his fat face, swarthy complexion and meaty lips. His ears were bulging out from under his Astrakhan cap.

The first passenger was undecided in all his movements, but the second one made up for it by the sureness of his manner. The chief of the convoy jumped up to them and reported while they gave us the once-over. Their smiles, shrugging shoulders and deprecatory gestures made us understand that they were not any too pleased with the merchandise before them.

Some of us they pointed out with their fingers as subjects for especial hilarity. I was among these latter, and I must have really cut a comic figure in my light overcoat with a rope around the waist and with my beaver cap pulled far down over my freezing ears and nose.

Judging by the bright eyes and twitching mouth of the first passenger and by the unsteady gait of the second, they were both slightly intoxicated. Evidently they did not feel the cold, for they were walking about with their overcoats open and seemed to be in no hurry, though it was windy and was getting considerably colder. Smoke came out of some of the camp's chimneys and gave us hope of comfort and warmth. The large sign above the camp gates, in red letters on a white canvas, read: "OGPU Northern Camp of Special Designation. Kotlas Transfer Station."

We soon found out that the two passengers were the actual chiefs of the penal camp. The first was Monakhov, commander of the Kotlas Transfer Station, and the second — Bukhaltzev, manager of the camp's town office.

We formed the general opinion that the commanders did not look so very ferocious. Alas, as far as Monakhov was concerned, we were destined to be severely disillusioned.

The commanders walked once around us and seemed to be making a mental estimate of our capacities; then they left us and slowly walked to the camp. Another hour passed. Time dragged on slowly, we were all terribly hungry and cold. The criminal convicts huddled together in a close bunch and were thus conserving heat like freezing ducklings. Somebody informed us that the temperature was seven below zero, Fahrenheit. This kind communication made us feel even colder and the disagreeable wind increased our discomfort. A fine, dust-like snow was falling and was gradually covering us. We were slowly congealing and tried to get warm by running about the space within the cordon of soldiers, by stamping our feet and imitating the Russian coachmen's well-known method of slapping one's hands crosswise against the front and back of the body.

CHAPTER FOUR: INSUBORDINATION

A group of twenty men came out of the gates. They were dressed in army great-coats and in new-looking felt boots. They took their positions in a line, at intervals of twenty yards. The convoy chief commanded: "Your baggage will be inspected. Come up in groups of twenty-five to each inspector."

There was a quick movement in our crowd. We all wanted to be let into the heated buildings as soon as possible and did not have to be asked twice. Queues formed and the inspection began.

We had to use our teeth in order to unravel the hardened and frosted ropes of our bundles; our benumbed fingers were of absolutely no use to us.

One of the great-coated men I recognized as Vorontsov, a former Lefortovsky prisoner who had disappeared from there after a frustrated attempt on his life. It was strange to find him here among the administrative staff. At that time we did not yet know the system of camp management and could not imagine that Vorontsov was just as much a prisoner as ourselves, but one who had already been promoted to a responsible position. The Lefortovsky criminal convicts recognized him at once and carefully avoided him. There was not one of them in the queue opposite him.

Each inspector had his own method. Some of them merely put a hand into the sack or bundle and rummaged among the contents; others ransacked them more carefully. Vorontsov and a few others ordered all bundles to be completely emptied right there in the snow and inspected each item separately. Here and there I heard protests and entreaties to please leave us our letters and photographs of wives and children.

"You'll get them back later if they are passed," answered the inspectors. But as we saw all these personal treasures thrown together in the snow in a common heap, we had no illusions as to their fate.

Some of the most suspicious prisoners had their clothing inspected as well. They were made to take off their shoes and to undress right then and there and stood shivering in their underclothes while the inspectors took their time examining their clothing. Vorontsov showed particular zeal in this respect.

"Present all your money and valuables," said the inspector to me. "Whatever is not shown will be confiscated."

In a camp one is allowed to carry not over five roubles in currency. Any money above this amount was exchanged for special camp certificates which were good in the camp store for the purchase of goods, but only within the limits prescribed by the official allotment.

I did not want to give up my money and decided to take a chance. My money was well hidden in my shirt-cuffs and was not noticed by the inspector. I was given a receipt for my watch.

My belongings were lying scattered in the snow. I gathered them and shoved them into my basket which I then lifted to my shoulder and carried to the gates. I was led toward the office and took my place at the end of a long-stretched line of prisoners who were required to fill in their questionnaires, an obligatory performance in all Soviet institutions.

Only part of the arrivals succeeded in squeezing themselves into the office; all the others were in the yard jumping from foot to foot, trying to keep from freezing. There was a jam in the 'doorway, everybody struggling to get ahead a little quicker. Those who had filled in their questionnaires returned to the yard and sat down on their bundles. By the barbed wire, gun in hand, walked the sentry.

We were among the last to reach the office. Behind the partition five dirty-looking clerks were busy filling in the questionnaires from our answers. All the same familiar questions: Name, place of birth, party allegiance, offense for which sentenced, etc. The work went fairly fast. The clerks were also prisoners recruited from a party which had preceded us and which had already been assigned various tasks in camp. Having completed the questionnaires, we came out.

"Hurry up, citizens, we are freezing," from those awaiting us in the yard. Men sat huddled close together trying to get warm. They blew into their cupped hands, rubbed their noses, stamped their feet. It was becoming unbearably cold.

Monakhov passed by quickly. He was followed by a clean-shaven assistant dressed in a short calfskin coat, fur outside, who jumped about and bent in a servile attitude behind his superior.

"Have all this rabble placed!" Monakhov shouted. This was significant, for in prison nobody had ever presumed to call us "rabble."

"Immediately, immediately, comrade commander," bustled the calfskin-coated assistant who evidently wished to get rid of his superior.

"How about it, Lyskin, will you have enough room?" queried the chief.

"We shall arrange it somehow, comrade commander," answered Lyskin in a tone intended to mollify him.

"Shall arrange! Always your 'shall arrange,' but where are you going to arrange them? Everything is filled up. Hordes of men are being sent up, but where shall we get room to place them? Well, take the better ones to the bathhouse and put the common criminals in a tent. Quickly, don't delay!" ordered Monakhov and entered the office followed by the bustling Lyskin.

We continued "cooling off" in the yard. After several minutes Lyskin came out of the office with two fellows in army great-coats and felt boots. A command rang out:

"Divide! Criminals right, others left!"

The crowd separated into two groups. There were about two hundred criminals. Our group numbered some three hundred.

"Criminals, follow me," commanded the first great-coat.

The criminals filed by, casting unfriendly glances at us. The unexpected prospect of finding themselves in a tent in midwinter did not please them, but no protest was heard. Even a tent was preferable to the open air.

Our group was moved in the opposite direction. Turning the corner, we entered a large yard bounded on one side by long wooden barracks with several entrances. On the other side of the yard were several smaller buildings. We were headed for one of the latter and were led to a small hut. A sentry stood at the door, gun in hand.

"Hurry up, enter, quickly!" shouted our convoy, pushing the slower ones through the narrow door.

The hut, which was the camp's bathhouse, consisted of three rooms. As to furniture, the first room had only a table and some coat hooks on the walls, the walls of the second were lined with benches, while half of the third room was occupied by a large stove.

"Well, what a place! Where are we to sleep?" voices were heard asking.

Evidently we would have to sleep on the earthen floor. With difficulty I pushed my way into the right corner, set my basket on the ground, put my bedding on top, and sat down on it myself.

People were still coming in, crowding, pushing, arranging themselves. Baskets, boxes, bundles were all thrown on the floor. Men walked over all this while the owners of the bundles protested. Swearing and abuse was heard. The rooms were jammed chock full. With people sitting and standing everywhere, there was not a square foot of empty space.

The little windows feebly admitted the dim light of the dying day. It was a miracle how three hundred people found room in the little hut.

The snow brought in on the clothes and shoes began to thaw and it was becoming wet and damp. The prisoners coughed, sneezed, pushed, noisily remonstrated, swore — a veritable bedlam.

Still, in spite of the terrible closeness, everybody finally settled down. Some took out their bread and were eating it with bits of lard, onion or garlic, a favorite and necessary dish; others dozed off, sitting on their bundles.

In our corner Timofeyich, Pevny and I were joined by a handsome old man with a well-kept gray beard and very live eyes. He introduced himself: "Troitsky."

"A relative of the famous commissar?" we inquired.

"No, only the same name; God saved me from close relationship," he answered with a sigh of relief.

Not far from us sat the old priest who had arrived in our railway carriage; his tired eyes were half shut and he had difficulty fighting off drowsiness. The seminarist Seryozha, a nice lad, did not leave him for an instant and cared for him tenderly.

What need was there to send to the penal camp these two old men? Both were way past fifty. Of what use could they be here?

The calfskin-coated Lyskin appeared at the door.

"Hey there, citizens, listen!" he shouted in a rasping voice, and the noise quieted down at once.

"Today we shall not feed you, there are too many of you, we are not prepared. You will have to sleep here, in any old way. Tomorrow I shall try to arrange you in the barracks. Groups of five or six may fetch their boiling water; bring your tea-kettles. In the yard you will be told where to get it. You will be given a ration of bread now; tomorrow morning you will get porridge and tomorrow evening — a dinner."

Having shouted this out hurriedly he vanished as suddenly as he had appeared.

It was getting darker and hunger was beginning to make itself painfully felt. The air in the crowded bathhouse, mixed with foul tobacco smoke, was becoming unbearable. Drowsiness overcame the weary, hungry prisoners. Here and there some slept on the ground, overlapping each other; from the third room came loud cursing.

Cries were heard: "Give us some light!" Some had fetched their boiling water. Among these was Timofeyich. Drinking cups appeared, dried bread and precious sugar was brought out. It grew noisy.

Suddenly the door opened with a bang. Several men, their great-coats covered with snow and with lanterns in their hands, roughly pushed their way through the crowd to the doorway of the second room.

"Silence! Everybody listen!" bawled a stentorian voice.

The head man jumped on top of somebody's bundle, placed his lantern on a hook and looked us over. Small green eyes looked at us from under his low-fitting helmet. A strong coarse square jaw protruded above the upturned collar of the great-coat.

"Silence! Stop that noise!" he continued in a loud voice. "You forget where you are. Stop it — and listen attentively. Understand?"

The shouting had its effect. The noise ceased, everybody was quiet.

"You are addressed by the warden. Note this and remember once and for all. The penal camp is quite different from what you know as prison. Here you have military discipline and martial law. The smallest disobedience is punished severely. When commanding officers talk to you, you must be silent and listen. Execute all commands immediately. No talk is allowed about disliking one thing or another. Understand? This is not auntie's house party but a penal labor camp. You have idled away enough time in the prisons. No more! Here it is different!"

The introduction was very promising. The warden's shouting voice broke and he continued in a lower tone:

"You have arrived in the Northern Penal Camps of the OGPU. There is no district attorney here, you cannot complain to anybody. Therefore I advise you to work conscientiously and not to make any row. There can be no counter-revolution here. For attempting counter-revolution we line people up against the wall and shoot them. For rows, thieving, insubordination — also to the wall. I advise you to realize this and remember it. Not auntie's house party but a penal camp. Forget all your intelligentsia's grievances and other tricks, otherwise we shall bend and break you, you 'intelligentsia.' More than one of you has already departed for better worlds. For refusal to work — the dungeon, and for a second offense — shooting. Understand?"

"What a remarkable style," the architect whispered to me, nudging me from behind. The style was truly original and it seemed fairly obvious that we had not arrived at an auntie's house party, as he called it.

"Beginning tomorrow," continued the warden, "you will start work. Up at five, drink your tea, receive your porridge and out with you into the yard. Your squad commander will be this comrade — Grigoriantz."

He pointed to a swarthy individual with the face of a convict who was standing next to him.

"You must obey him implicitly and execute all his orders without question. Understand? If you have any questions — speak up."

The crowd was stunned and remained silent. Even the more optimistic now realized where we had arrived.

"May we have a little light, comrade commander?" piped out an ingratiating voice.

"We'll give you that. One lantern to a room. To the lavatory you may go in groups of five to ten, with a lantern. Don't go out without a lantern. The sentry is instructed to shoot anyone who goes without one. And now I advise you to go to sleep. Gather some strength, you will need it tomorrow."

"But where shall we sleep?" came a voice from the second room. "There is no room to sleep."

"Silence! You'll sleep all right. What's the matter with you? This is not a hotel, with pillows and sheets! And not auntie's house party!"

For the third time he mentioned "auntie." Evidently this profound aphorism was his favorite.

"Anybody who is not satisfied come out here!" No sound for an answer.

"Well, then, everybody satisfied? Good. And you had better look out!"

Unceremoniously the warden went out, accompanied by our squad commander and his attendants.

There was an immediate burst of exclamations:

"What can this mean?" "This man is some galley convict." "Have we come to this?" "Never mind, he is just trying to scare us." "What did you expect, did you think you were coming to visit auntie?" "Don't pay any attention." "Remember, this is the OGPU and it's no joke."

Indignant cries came from all sides. Those who protested had just begun to see things in their true light. Why so late?

Men were stunned, insulted, scared. The priest was crossing himself, muttering prayers. Everybody was deeply agitated. Such a reception had not been expected. Apparently life in camp will not be any too sweet. Conversation would not cease. The optimists lost all their nerve. The treatment was more than unusual. The greater number of those confined in the bathhouse were intellectuals, but they were treated as bandits.

The lantern dimly lighted the room. Tired faces, sunken eyes, attested to terrible fatigue. For five days we had subsisted on nothing but tea and we were getting desperately hungry. They promised to feed us on the morrow and the only course open was to continue filling oneself with tea and eating a bit of stale bread.

Gradually the room grew silent. Here and there the light of a cigarette could be seen. Men were falling asleep sitting on their belongings, with caps pulled down over their eyes, with collars raised, with hands shoved together into sleeves. Timofeyich snored loudly and his long nose nodded. Old Troitsky slept with an open mouth showing his gold teeth. The architect in his corner looked more comfortable than any of the others — cold, damp, hungry.

Men were constantly passing through our room, gathering in groups near the door, taking the lantern and going out. Every few minutes the door would open and close again. The cold air rushing in through the door rose to the ceiling in white clouds. Outside the wind howled. One could hear some inarticulate remote cries and at times the sound of a shot.

A light chill came over me. I wanted to sleep but couldn't. Perhaps my nerves were too tense, or was it the beginning of a fever? It was uncomfortable to sit. I longed to lie down and stretch my aching feet.

Sad thoughts twinkled through the brain. Christmas is coming soon. Joy for all the world. Everywhere a holiday spirit, trees are trimmed, presents bought. And I — wouldn't it be simpler to end it all at once? ...

I awoke with a violent cramp. Somebody's boots were poking right into my face. How long had I slept this way on the floor, with my nose stuck into those dirty boots? My whole body ached, I was shaking with chills and fever. The architect, Troitsky and the others were still sleeping in the same positions. The lanterns twinkled dimly as before, silence was broken only by snoring. All were asleep. I stretched until my bones creaked and this seemed to bring relief. The old priest, with trembling hands, was trying to cover the young seminarist, who was lying on the floor at his feet. It was still dark outside.

"Get up, get up!" shouted a big soldier who had come to relieve our watch. "Get up, it is five o'clock."

Of course nobody gave a thought to washing. It was cold and shivery. The heavy air in the room was supplemented by the smell from the dying-out kerosene lanterns.

Timofeyich returned shivering from cold and carrying a tea-kettle of boiling water. We started our morning breakfast of rye bread with salt, and tea to wash it down. The tea warmed us and seemed to comfort the soul. But not for long. The convict mug of "comrade" Grigoriantz appeared in the doorway.

"Out into the yard," he cried, "like a flash, quickly, don't delay!"

"Like a flash!" his voice was heard from the other rooms.

There was a jam in the doorway. A mass of people poured out into the dark. We stopped in the middle of the yard. Here a considerable crowd was already tramping about and was constantly augmented by new arrivals from the bathhouse.

"Silence!" came out of the darkness. "We shall have the roll-call presently. When your name is called, come out here."

The muster-roll started. The voice of Grigoriantz came from the right where a group of gray great-coats could be seen in the light shed by a lantern. One after the other we passed into the group of those called. Dawn was beginning.

An interruption. Grigoriantz was shouting: "Ter, come out, Ter, where are you?" No answer.

"Isn't he there, eh?" our squad commander shouted still louder. "Where else can he be? Ter! Ter!" Ra-ta-ta-ta, followed some obscene cursing.

"Perhaps you mean Stepanov, Ter-Stepanov?" a voice was heard asking.

"I call you Ter, and Ter you will be, you son of a bitch, come out quickly," bawled Grigoriantz.

"My name is not Ter, but Ter-Stepanov. Besides I would ask you to be civil." It was a voice trembling from insult and belonged to a medium-built man of about forty-five in a felt hat covering up the fine features of a pale intelligent face. Stepping out of the crowd he came to our group.

"Silence!" cried Grigoriantz. "Hey, you there, give it to him properly!" he commanded.

One of the great-coats jumped at Ter-Stepanov and hit him over the head. The felt hat flew off into the crowd and was followed by the tripped-up body of Ter-Stepanov.

There was no jesting about this place. The warden's warnings seemed to be justified.

"Whoever contradicts me will get the same. Understand this, yon intelligentsia?" laughed Grigoriantz. Being an Armenian himself he knew very well the name was Ter-Stepanov, a typical Armenian name. He called him Ter simply out of spite, or to amuse himself.

The roll-call continued in silence.

"Now, form in a square, twenty men to a row, military fashion, heads up! Attention to commands!"

We started to form. It was getting considerably lighter. The contours of the immense yard were becoming discernible. We formed in a rectangle consisting of about forty rows. Altogether some eight hundred men, among whom there were many new faces, from other party arrivals. It soon became known that during the night a party of three hundred had arrived from Leningrad. They had been quartered in the stables and had slept less than two hours.

"Attention," came Grigoriantz' voice from the side. "First you must learn to greet your commanders. When you are in formation and a commander greets you, you must answer short, snappy and all together: 'Zdrah' (abbreviated from the greeting 'zdrastvuite'). Understand? You are now in the third disciplinary squadron. Well, let us start. Third squadron, greetings! Well? What is the matter? Why don't you answer?"

"Zdrah, zdrah, zdrah," came from our ranks.

"No good," cried Grigoriantz. "Answer all together, like one man, or you'll regret it."

"Once again: Greetings, third squadron!"

Again some disorderly exclamations: "Zdrah, zdrah, zdrah, zdrah!"

"You rabble, idiots, it seems you do not wish to learn," shouted our squad commander. "Well, then, attention, and march, one two, one two, faster, no stumbling, right, right!"

The squadron came into motion. The front rows increased their pace, those behind tried to catch up.

"Run," commanded Grigoriantz, "one two, one two, faster, faster, get along!"

We started to run. Tramping down the loose snow under foot we ran around the yard once, twice, the third time. Men were getting tired and breathing hard. This exercise was very fatiguing after a five-day journey without food and a sleepless night.

"Mark time," resounded the command.

Young, middle-aged and quite old intelligent men, mixed with bandits, murderers, gangsters, all were doing the trot-in-place without moving ahead.

"One two, one two, faster, all together, don't stop," shouted Grigoriantz, running around the square.

The trot-in-place was followed by rehearsals of the greeting and rehearsals were succeeded by more trots. Thus three hours went by. The voices of the tired prisoners were hoarse, the trot was becoming unbearable, but Grigoriantz, finding the training of the animals to his taste, did not stop. The trot-in-place would be repeated, its tempo accelerated. How long would this nonsense last? One, two. One, two.

"And why aren't you running, Madonna?" I heard from the distance. "You, I am talking to you, you old cheese."

"I am very old and very tired, permit me to stand still a while," our old priest answered in a weak and trembling voice.

"Run, and no excuses. Understand, you old dope? Quickly, get on! Am I speaking to you or not? What?" Grigoriantz' voice was shrill and angry.

One two, one two, we tramped in the snow.

"Ah, you won't?" shouted our commander in a thoroughly inflamed voice and at the same moment a desperate cry was heard:

"Don't dare, don't dare beat the reverend father!"

Everything was in confusion. The running slowed up and stopped entirely.

Afterwards we were told that Grigoriantz had grabbed the priest by the beard and was kicking him in the ankles with his heavy booted feet. The priest fell down. The young seminarist lad came to his defense. But all of this was related to us later.

The hum of voices uttering protests came from all sides: "Don't you dare, you have no right to beat, shame on you, you cad!" shouted the prisoners.

"Silence!" roared the mad voice of Grigoriantz. "To your places!" A shot resounded. Sentries ran out of the doors of the barracks, the prisoners fell back and I could then see what was happening in front.

The priest was half kneeling, half lying in the snow, and, grabbing the seminarist's arm, was vainly trying to rise. Seryozha, aroused and with sparkling eyes, his other arm raised in defense, stood between him and the oncoming Grigoriantz. Five soldiers, guns in hand, surrounded the group.

"You mutinous pup, you forget where you are. Get out of here!" shouted Grigoriantz, grabbing Seryozha by the upraised arm.

"I will not go away and won't allow you to beat the reverend father!" cried Seryozha in despair.

"Well, then, take it, you dog," and Grigoriantz hit Seryozha heavily in the face with his gun. Blood covered the lower part of his face and streamed down his jacket. Seryozha leaped on Grigoriantz, but the forces were unequal. Two soldiers caught him by the arms. Three others, brandishing their guns, rushed toward us.

"Get back, get back!"

By a blow of his heavy boot aimed below the abdomen Grigoriantz felled Seryozha. The boy uttered a loud scream and lay senseless in the snow. Emerging from the corner came a group of soldiers in great-coats, rifles pointed. The camp commander, Monakhov, preceded them. His eyes were restless, his face livid with anger.

"What is the matter here? Who was shooting?" he asked, coming up.

Grigoriantz saluted and reported:

"Insubordination, comrade commander. He rushed me with his fists, doesn't want to obey commands. I had to quiet him down."

Monakhov stared at the prostrate figure.

"A new one?"

"Yes, comrade commander," answered Grigoriantz.

"Undress him, stand him up and pour water over him," cried Monakhov. "Let everybody know that we are not jesting here. Warden, make your dispositions. As to you," he turned towards us, "look, learn and remember!"

Boots, coat and clothing were dragged from Seryozha, who was still senseless. He was lying in the snow in his underclothes and moaned as he gradually regained consciousness.

Two great-coats approached carrying buckets. What a nightmare! Is this really possible?

The priest was weeping: "Seryozha, Seryozha."

They poured water over Seryozha and stood him up on his bare feet in the snow. On both sides stood sentries, rifles pointed. A dread came over us. The biting wind was getting stronger and fine snow flurried about us. Over our heads a great flock of crows was hanging in the air, battling the wind with measured wing-beats. Why did they come here now?

"They are scenting it," somebody whispered. "Look, how many of them."

"Krrr, krrr," their cries sounded above us ominously.

A half-naked boy, covered with blood, stood there before us in the snow. All windows around us were filled with the gray faces of prisoners. Camp Commander Monakhov was strutting about the yard, followed by his attendants. He was pale, his lips were tightly compressed and twitched into a smile when he looked at his victim.

And the crows continued their threatening croak: "Krrr, krrr, krrr..."

Our squadron continued tramping in its place: "One two, one two, one two." Seryozha was jumping from one foot to the other, trying to get warm. He was getting blue and was covered with ice. His underclothes, stiffened with the ice, stuck to his body.

"One two, one two," we continued dancing in our places. Sentries were lurking about us to discover if anybody stopped.

"Stop! Attention! Throw this rascal into the cold dungeon for twenty-four hours! That's where he will come to! All others out to work! Quickly!"

Monakhov left. Seryozha was led away. Grigoriantz stood smiling in front of our squadron in a theatrical pose, seeming to say: "Well, have you seen enough? How did you like it?"

CHAPTER V: HUNGER

A low forehead, protruding ears, a fleshy hook nose with a slight dent in the middle, large, strong, yellow teeth, a powerful jaw and dark "pop" eyes — these were the external clues to the character of Grigoriantz.

He was the son of a small tradesman in Rostov and already as a lad he began to show wilful tendencies. In 1918 he joined the Bolshevik Party, took part in the civil war and then in punitive expeditions of the cheka. Later on he was expelled from the party, and, sinking lower, reached the profession of a hired murderer. They caught him in the sensational affair of the Rostov attorney M.

The attorney had a pretty wife and a renowned Rostov gangster fell in love with her. It was decided to murder the attorney in order to get him out of the way. Grigoriantz, who had a good record in the execution of such commissions, was given the job for five thousand roubles. This time Grigoriantz decided to act as a good business man and hired a smaller bandit for the job, promising him five hundred roubles. The murder was executed, but the gangster was caught and squealed on Grigoriantz. His trial brought to light all his former crimes and he was sentenced to be shot.

By some means he escaped execution and was now commander of the disciplinary squadron in Kotlas, transfer point of the OGPU. He enjoyed excellent standing and was on friendly and familiar terms with his superiors.

"Attention!" he shouted again. "Third squadron, greetings!"

"Zdrah!" came from our square fairly uniformly.

"Not so good, but tomorrow I shall teach you some more. You'll learn it, I assure you. And now to work. Front fifteen rows, march ahead. Rear fifteen rows, step back. Middle rows, stay where you are."

After some confusion we divided into three columns. I found myself in the middle one. What next?

A detachment of armed sentries came up to us and behind them several men in felt boots and short jacket uniforms.

"Foremen, distribute the work, a full job to each, no leniency." Grigoriantz gave these last instructions and stepped aside.

The thirty rows from the front and the rear, surrounded by the convoy, went out of the camp gates. Part of those remaining were assigned to clearing away the snow in the yard, others to construction work on the barracks, some to splitting and sawing firewood. A large group was sent to the river bank to free a large float of timber from the ice. Ten men, among them the unfortunate Granovsky, were allotted the disgusting work of cleaning the lavatories, twenty men were carrying water in buckets, and another twenty were sent to the kitchen to clean fish.

My lot fell with the men shoveling snow in the yard. I soon learned from those who had arrived before us that we were not to remain long at the transfer point. From here we were to be dispatched to our permanent work in one of the camp divisions. Almost daily fresh bands of prisoners arrived in Kotlas from all parts of Russia. The supply was not diminishing in spite of the fact that prisoners in the Northern Penal Camps already numbered over forty thousand.

The Kotlas Transfer Station of the Northern Penal Camps of the OGPU was located five kilometers from the town of Kotlas, on the steep bank of the Northern Dvina at its junction with the Sukhona River. This location, exposed on all sides, offered no protection whatever from the constant disagreeable winds. When there was no wind from the north, it blew from the south; if not from the east, it howled from the west. Only during the summer the weather was comparatively quiet and the summers were very short. Unfortunately we arrived in mid-winter.

The Transfer Station itself occupied some fifteen acres and was surrounded by barbed wire. The long barracks were located near the center and served to house transient prisoners. Partitions divided the barracks into several parts, each one of which was occupied by the so-called squadrons. Besides the barracks the buildings comprised storehouses, kitchen, hospital, dungeon, office and the bathhouse wherein we were temporarily quartered on our arrival.

Our party was theoretically added to the third squadron, which was occupying the central part of the barracks, but as the latter was chock full we were for the time being shoved into the bathhouse. The second and fourth squadrons were housed next to the third. The first squadron consisted of teamsters, load carriers and other prisoners assigned to permanent work at the Transfer Station. It occupied separate barracks. Women prisoners lived in a detached building and so did the office workers, foremen, storekeepers and others. All barracks and other buildings were constructed of green lumber and looked very new.

The Transfer Station was filled to overflowing and therefore three enormous tarpaulin tents were set up in the yard opposite the office. These were intended for not over four hundred and fifty men, but already sheltered about a thousand.

The small second squad consisted chiefly of carpenters, joiners and helpers of the woodworking shop which was furnishing door and window frames, tables and all other household furniture needed in the encampment.

The boss of the woodworking shop was the Finnish communist Karjalainen, carpenter by trade, who was said to have been in command of an entire army of the Reds during the civil war in Finland. For some years he had been active in the Finnish Communist Party in Leningrad. Later he was sentenced to five years' imprisonment in the penal camps for having been in communication with Finland through other than party channels.

He had already served three-quarters of his term in the Solovetsky camp and was transferred to Kotlas to take charge of the woodworking shop.

Prisoners who worked under his command led a better life than the others. This tall, slim, quiet, blond, blue-eyed Finn took care of his men, and though he was exacting, he did not overload them with work.

Several of his countrymen, sentenced for various offenses to longer or shorter terms, were working in his shop. As for himself, he enjoyed some quite extraordinary privileges as a former communist, was allowed outside the barbed wire, and lived with his Finnish wife in an apartment in the town of Kotlas.

He was an incorrigible drunkard and, as a true Finnish carpenter, drank pure alcohol instead of vodka. From time to time he would detail his countrymen to some work in town and they were allowed to go there without escort on his personal responsibility. Such days always ended up with great drinking orgies at his apartment where Finnish national songs were sung and scenes of the Fatherland were recalled. In the morning they would all return to camp and sober up in their shop, consuming large amounts of varnish if no more alcohol was to be found.

Camp Commander Monakhov knew of these escapades, but overlooked them because Karjalainen was an old friend of his while already in the Solovetsky camp, and they would often go on a drinking bout together. Besides, Karjalainen had some important protectors in Moscow. Monakhov himself made personal use of some of the alcohol allocated to the hospital and therefore did not bother Karjalainen about the unwarranted consumption of the state varnish supply.

Camp Commander Monakhov also lived outside the barbed wire, in town. Every morning at eight o'clock a smartly turned out sled with bearskin coverings would be sent to his door from the camp. There it awaited him, sometimes several hours, depending on his condition. Usually he arrived at eleven o'clock and signed the papers which were prepared for him at the office. After that he would immediately return to town for lunch. His useful activity commenced upon his return from town after lunch where his nervous system was reinforced by vodka. Before luncheon he was a totally worn-out man with dim, restless eyes, trembling hands and a twitching face. After luncheon, on the contrary, his eyes acquired an especial sparkle of hardness and cruelty, his mouth would be distorted into a grimacing smile and his paleness became pronounced. In camp he enjoyed an infamous reputation for cruelty.

He was a former chekist and had filled a fairly important position in the OGPU, but got caught in a very ugly affair. Having released a young woman prisoner on condition of cohabitation, his sadistic tendencies finally drove her to suicide. Before killing herself, the unhappy woman wrote a letter to the district attorney describing the whole affair in detail. It was all brought to the knowledge of the OGPU heads. He was arrested and tried by the secret tribunal.

Thanks to influential protection, the OGPU sentenced him to only five years' imprisonment in the Solovetsky camp. In that camp his good connections again aided him in making headway, and after serving a part of his five-year sentence he became the strongest candidate for replacing the former commander of the Kotlas Transfer Station in the new Northern camp district. He was twenty-five years old.

He impressed one as a fairly intelligent man, always clean-shaven and well dressed, dandyish in a manner that smacked of degeneracy. He seemed to take better care of his outward appearance than you would expect from a regular party communist. By origin he belonged to the petty bourgeoisie.

Monakhov's staff consisted of his secretary Skryabin, a convict who was formerly prosecuting attorney of the Rostov OGPU; of the guard commander Ogloblin, a typical soldier type who was an out-and-out drunkard and took little interest in anything around him; of a number of clerks chosen from among the prisoners; of the chief of the station's secret intelligence department, Zakhariantz, who was also a former accredited agent of the OGPU now serving a three-year sentence. Then there was the warden, a coarse, cruel man appointed from among the prisoners; fifty soldiers and the manager of the commissary department, prisoner Lyskin.

In 1917 Lyskin was mayor of one of the smaller towns in the South of Russia. The prisoners liked him and he did not give himself any airs. He always readily granted his assent to any request of the prisoners though he hardly ever fulfilled his promises. He did not know how to work, the management of his department was neglected and his chief concern was the comfortable arrangement of his personal life. He was one of the few non-communist prisoners who were allowed to live beyond the barbed wire. He had one weakness: he loved steam baths and massage. Twice a week the bathhouse was especially prepared for him, floors covered with fresh straw, and two prisoners, professional steam-bath attendants, would wash and massage him.

We worked slowly, the cold penetrated my light overcoat and low shoes. Hunger and fatigue were becoming poignant. We were promised dinner at five, but every minute made it more difficult to await it. The sentry would not admit me back into the bathhouse, the storekeeper in his tiny shop refused to sell anything without a ration card and all my entreaties to let me buy a piece of bread were unavailing.

I was slowly congealing. All thought was directed to the one aim of getting something to eat and warming myself. The pangs of hunger were stubborn torture. The degrading occurrence of the morning was almost forgotten. Now and then a thought would flash through my brain, "poor Seryozha," and immediately it would be superseded by another, more tenacious one, "I must get something to eat."

The group which had been detailed to freeing the frozen float of timber from ice returned to camp at five o'clock. They presented a horrifying appearance, blue from cold, hands swollen, eyes watering, some with frostbitten noses, ears or cheeks.

In another half hour the men who had been sent to the forest returned. All of them were desperately tired, having given their last efforts to the new, unaccustomed work. Since it was their first day, they were allowed to return earlier though many had not completed their assignments, but they were warned that on the next day they would be detained in the forest until the whole task assigned was finished by the group.

At six o'clock we were finally admitted into the unheated bathhouse and, in anticipation of the "dinner," we threw ourselves like wild beasts upon the remains of bread given us in the morning. We had but one thought —

to eat and to warm up. For a whole week we had had no dinner, had not washed and had not slept properly. I felt pangs in the pit of my stomach and was so tired that I would have thrown myself on the dirty floor just as I was, had there been room. But the thought of the promised dinner overcame even this fatigue.

We had not received the morning porridge promised by Lyskin. It appeared that it had to be fetched from the kitchen, but when this was made known to us it was too late as the porridge by that time was all eaten.

More than two hours passed, but no semblance of a dinner. Somebody announced that the newly-arrived prisoners would be fed right out in the open yard. The sentry was constantly approached by questions as to the dinner. But the well-fed cannot understand the famished. First he pretended ignorance which later gave way to abuse. "Go to the devil, don't bother me, you'll gobble it up all right when it's thrown to you, wait." After the morning lesson nobody even dared to think of making any demands and we all humbly waited.

At eight o'clock Lyskin entered. He told us that "dinner" would be served soon and that we would get it in the yard.

"Don't forget your spoons," he advised.

He blamed our own selves for not getting the morning porridge and calmed us by a promise that soon everything would be organized, that we would stay in the bathhouse only one more night and that we would then be transferred to the barracks, which were warmer and roomier.

"This place here is, to be sure, not all that it should be," he added, "but you understand that after all this is a penal camp and there is nothing you can do about it."

Getting ready our spoons, we waited. Time dragged slowly and every minute sharpened our hunger. At last a joyous cry announced dinner. Pushing and shoving, the crowd noisily made for the exit.

It was dark and cold. At the right, near the kitchen, open fires were blazing in the snow. Silhouettes of moving men could be seen against this background. Spoons in hand we rushed to the fires. The architect and I were overtaken by some prisoners from the rear room of the bathhouse. Six blazing piles of wood illuminated the feast. Spread upon upturned empty barrels were large iron washbasins filled with a hot souplike concoction.

"Twenty men to each basin," exclaimed a voice, though it was quite evident that twenty men could not approach one basin.

While we were thinking this over we were almost swept off our feet by a veritable avalanche of running men. It was the gang of criminals from the tents, men who had lost the last vestige of human feeling, hungry like wolves.

Upon being let out of the tents they flung themselves upon the barrels, elbowed and shouldered their way through our privileged crowd from the bathhouse, which was just preparing to eat, and in another minute were complete masters of the situation. Surrounding the barrels in a tight ring, all armed with big wooden spoons, they ate, ate, and ate.

But how they ate! The huge spoons filled with boiling hot liquid were shoved into hungry wide-open mouths, the contents were instantly swallowed, the spoons went back into the basins and out again. Some threadlike shreds of substance were hanging on the spoons and all this was swallowed with incredible speed.

The criminals crowded around the barrels two rows deep. Those in the second row shoved their spoons in between those in the front row, spilling half the contents but catching up the drippings somehow and licking them from their hands and spoons.

Without resorting to brute force there was no way of squeezing oneself up to the barrel and we certainly could not fight them! In a few minutes the entire contents of the basins were devoured and we left as empty-bellied as we had come. It was evident that if there was no change in the service of the camp "dinners," we would have to sustain ourselves on the half-kilogram of bread which was our daily ration.

We returned to the bathhouse in a very depressed state. Our quarters were still as cold and damp as before, there was insufficient light, no room to sleep; knees gave way from fatigue and one's body shook all over with cold.

On the way back I had tried to refresh my face with snow and noticed that the snow melted unusually fast and my face remained as hot as ever. I was feverish, which was not surprising under these circumstances. However, as there was nothing I could do in the way of treatment I decided to pay no attention to the condition of my health. I sat down again upon my basket and quickly fell asleep in this strained position.

I do not know how long I slept. I dreamt that I was falling into an abyss, I cried out and awoke. The room was filled with bodies heaped all over and across each other. Hands, feet, faces, were all intermingled. Men were lying on top of each other, their open mouths breathed heavily, some slept with half-open ghastly eyes.

I perched myself on my basket and lit a cigarette. So this is what is called a penal camp! How long can a man bear up under these conditions?

Dim visions of toothsome dishes swam before my eyes: crystal bowls with salads and lobster, my favorite porter-house steaks with luscious lyonnaise potatoes, salmon and meat, meat in all forms!

All around me men slept like the dead. The architect was all crumpled up in his corner, and on the floor, in distorted positions, were Timofeyich, old Troitsky and the deathly, livid Pevny. I alone had awakened and could not fall asleep again in spite of all my efforts. Time dragged on with oppressive slowness.

So the night would last another four hours or so. And then what? Again the degrading trot-in-place, the disgusting "zdrah," the abominable faces of the guards and the croaking crows overhead?

In some strange manner my thoughts would constantly revert to food. Perhaps it would help if I tried to chew the remnant of a very stale crust of black bread which I still had? Yes, it did.

Two prisoners were standing at the door begging the sentry to let them out to the lavatory. I overheard their conversation:

"You were told no and that's the end of it," from the faithful sentry. "My orders are not to let out less than five."

"But you cannot expect us to go and awaken some others," argued the two prisoners. "Perhaps they do not need to go out?"

"That is your business, but I shall not let out less than five," answered the implacable sentry.

Two more prisoners came up from the rear room. They all continued to beseech the sentry but he would not relent.

"I said no and no it is, understand, intelligentsia?"

Jumping from foot to foot, one of the prisoners turned to me imploring me to make up the necessary number. Judging from his uniform cap, he was a railway construction engineer. In his hand he already held the lantern without which we would be exposed to the risk of being shot by the sentry on watch.

It was not far to the lavatory. The proud name of a "lavatory" did not quite fit this hole in the ground covered by a wooden shed. Thanks to Granovsky, who had worked hard cleaning, chopping and carting away the frozen impurities, conditions were not as bad as they might have been.

When we came back we handed our lantern to the next group which was already awaiting our return. Morning was approaching and men were gradually awakening.

Thirty prisoners were sent out for the porridge and returned carrying washbasins filled with mush. It did not bother us that prior to our arrival these washbasins had been used in the bathhouse. Hunger made us forget such fastidiousness. Armed with wooden spoons we closely surrounded our basins and ate the lukewarm buckwheat mush with no trace of butter in it. Then bread was rationed out and everybody cheered up perceptibly. It does not take much to make man happy.

One hour, and another, passed; nobody came to fetch us. Had they forgotten us?

Then the door opened and the grinning mug of Grigoriantz protruded through it. After him came the warden and the noise quieted down. Their appearance evidently promised some unpleasant surprise, but just what?

"Prisoners of the third squadron, greetings!"

"Zdrah," came from our ranks, in unison. Yesterday's lesson had not been in vain and the majority seemed to have decided not to irritate the commanders.

"Listen attentively," the warden shouted in his clear voice. "We shall presently do a little assorting. All those who have ever worked for the OGPU or the cheka and all former communists will go out into the yard and proceed to the office. Secondly, all former members of the Red Army or Navy or of the town or village militia, go to the armed guard detachment and receive further orders there. Understand? All others, wait here."

One after another, about eighty men left the room. It was getting quite light and I decided to take advantage of the roominess left by their departure to visit some of my old friends in the rear rooms. Very few of the Lefortovsky prisoners had joined the group of eighty, as that prison held only a small number of communists and most of these had already succeeded in Moscow in making better provision for themselves.

Utilizing the free time and space, men gathered in groups and were exchanging ideas and impressions. "What a nightmare!" was one of the constantly recurring expressions. The gray, dirty, unshaven and unwashed faces of the speakers presented not too pleasing an appearance. The unnaturally bright eyes and the heightened color in the cheeks testified that yesterday's experience had left its mark. The clothing of the forest workers was still wet and they could find no way to dry their shoes. There was a stove, but there was no fire in it.

A dreadful stench filled the third room. Granovsky, who had climbed on top of the stove, looked more dead than alive. He was feverish and coughing in spasms, but his eyes were still full of bitter hatred and the harrowing coughing fits were interspersed with streams of cursing. Funk, too, as well as his little company, had found room on the stove. They had lost their former bright unprison-like appearance and were no different from all the others, gray, dirty, unshaven.

Returning to the front room, I saw the architect standing at the door beckoning to me.

"Here is the comrade I spoke of," he said to the guard. "We shall come back presently. Come on."

Out in the yard the architect laughingly informed me that our momentary freedom had cost us five roubles. He was a clever dog.

"All men are human," he laughed, "but I can spot a drunkard instantly. We started chatting, I mentioned vodka, we became friends. He accepted the five-spot. And now, old chap, no loitering, let us reconnoiter the possibilities. If anybody asks us about our business we'll tell them we are looking for the commissary manager. Come on."

CHAPTER SIX: WHO STOLE THE BREAD?

At the gate, rifle pointed, stood a sentry. In front of him, standing barefooted in the snow and dressed only in underclothes, was another victim of Monakhov's educational system, the hardened old thief Troushin from the Lefortovsky prison. The tent occupied by the criminals was surrounded by armed guards in helmets and great-coats. Something unusual was happening.

The warden ran out of the large tent, waving his arms and shouting: "Out with all this rabble, tra-ta-ta-ta-ta," he swore wildly, "and don't let them back in until they confess."

Part of the guards swooped down upon the tent and immediately people started pouring out of it into the yard, some of them half dressed and barefooted. Some were kicked out with a bang, head over heels.

"Form in a square!" shouted the warden. "Come on, Comrade Grigoriantz, take the command, it's your squadron."

Unobserved, we approached a little nearer. The criminals were forming in rows, urged on by fists and rifle butts. Their cruel, insolent and cowardly faces bore a concentrated expression, they were whispering and communicating with each other by a strange sign language.

"Attention! I repeat once more," shouted the warden, "confess and you will be better off. Otherwise I'll keep you here in the cold until you confess. Who stole the bread? Speak up!"

A long pause.

"So you will not speak! All right. Then stand in line until you confess."

Several groups of prisoners who had come from the barracks were standing around the square, which was watched by the armed guards. We joined one of these groups. A kindly-faced long-bearded peasant explained to us that several large containers of bread had been stolen from the storeroom. Troushin, one of the thieves, had been caught red-handed. Two others had escaped into the tent. The warden demanded that they be handed over. The organized underworld gang refused to name the guilty, hence the struggle. Who would win out?

"It's no use, they'll give in eventually," was the peasant's opinion. "It's happened before. After a couple of hours in the frost they will speak all right."

It was an unequal game, the authorities held all the trumps.

Some more soldiers approached, armed with guns and clubs. "It is about to commence," whispered the peasant, and true enough, the fun began.

"Hey, you there, come out, I mean you, can't you hear!" shouted the warden stepping up to the square and pulling out a pale shaky youth by his neck. "Answer me, who stole the bread, eh?"

"Not me, I swear to God it wasn't me," wailed the boy, trying to free himself. The warden began beating him and the boy cried with all his might, trying to protect his face from the blows. Grabbing him by the left wrist the warden started to twist it. The boy fell on his knees and whined louder than ever. Suddenly he threw his legs over the arm that held him and, crying with anger and pain, let go of such a stupendous volley of curses that even the tough warden was floored.

"So that's what you mean, you cur," shouted the warden. Crumpling the boy under him, he choked him by the throat and hit him in the face several times with all his might. The helpful guards, unwilling to be outdone by the warden, were beating the boy as best they could, with fists, feet or rifles.

A humming noise came from the square. "Click, click," sounded the familiar warning of cocked rifles. The hum grew louder, shouts were heard; but pointed rifles made the noise subside. The boy was unconscious, lying in the snow. He was dragged aside and the warden approached the front row.

"How about it now?" he sneered. "Will you speak now?" But there was no response.

"Beat them all, one after the other, beat them hard!" screamed the warden, beside himself with rage. "Give me this one, the redhead," he pointed.

Soldiers rushed in with their clubs and dragged out from the second row a strong, bull-headed, red-haired gangster some twenty-five years of age.

"Don't give in, Lenka," his comrades shouted.

"Not to give in? Well then, knock him dead," shrieked the flushed and infuriated warden.

Clubs quickly went into action, descending with all their might upon the red head drawn in between the shoulders. Then something unexpected happened. The red head was lowered and suddenly shot up like a released spring and struck with terrific force the chin of one of the attacking guards. The latter, unprepared for this typical gangster weapon, let go of his stick and fell into the snow with a moan. Almost simultaneously Grigoriantz jumped into the fray, tripped the unfortunate redhead, hit him over the brow with his gun and threw himself bodily upon him. He hit him several more blows, arose and, breathing hard, threw a furtive glance upon the square of bewildered criminals. He then commanded: "Rifles, attention! Shoot the first man who leaves the ranks."

After a short consultation with the warden, Grigoriantz gave some further instructions to the armed guards and stepped aside. Several more minutes passed. The gangsters remained silent. The ill-starred Troushin still stood there undressed, shivering in the frost. The warden shrugged his shoulders, evidently deciding on some other method. He then joined Grigoriantz and they both went to the office.

"Now they will keep them there for two hours or so," said the peasant, "and then they will talk. It's an old game." We walked away from the unfortunate square of criminals. It was getting much colder and we had to move to keep warm.

Our reception at the camp store was utterly hopeless. It seemed at first as if nothing could be obtained, but the architect refused to leave the store and waited. "We shall arrange something," he whispered to me, "don't leave yet."

The store superintendent, whom some of the servile prisoners near the counter were addressing as "comrade commander," did not bite at the bait which my friend was casting and refused to sell us anything, in spite of the fact that he was making some small sales of herrings, sugar and other edibles to the surrounding prisoners. The store itself presented a very poor appearance. Standing on the floor were several barrels filled with herring, sauerkraut and salt fish. The shelves were embellished by several tins of preserves and some packages of poor tobacco. A few mildewed sausages were hanging on a nail in the wall. These caught the architect's fancy.

But the superintendent again categorically refused my friend's supplication to sell him a half-kilo of sausage.

Just at this moment Lyskin entered the store. Using all his ability as a charmer the architect approached him, introduced himself, and taking him aside into the corner convinced him of our extreme need of sausage. In a few minutes he had Lyskin 's scribbled note in his hand which opened the way to a purchase not only of a sausage but also of preserves, cigarettes and tobacco. The superintendent, himself a prisoner, did not try to hide his dissatisfaction as he threw the goods on the counter. We could not understand his attitude and decided that the next time we would try the old well-known method of offering a bribe. With pockets bulging we came out into the yard.

Troushin was no longer at the gates, but the square was still standing in the cold. The half-dressed people were blue in the face and freezing. A young barefooted boy in the front row looked particularly wretched. He was wailing and huddling his light coat over his naked chest; jumping and folding his feet under him like a freezing pup.

"Permit me to leave, comrades," he appealed to the sentry. "I am not guilty, let me go."

No answer. His wails gave way to cries and sobs, his teeth chattered. The warden, who was promenading in front of the lines, looked at him thoughtfully and beckoned him:

"Hey, boy, come along with me."

"Look out, Filka, no squealing or you'll regret it," came shouts from the ranks of his fellow criminals, who had good cause to fear that the boy would name the guilty. His pitiable appearance warranted this conclusion.

"The boy will squeal all right," said someone, "but it is too bad for him, he is as good as dead now, his own gang will let him have it at the first opportunity. No joking with these fellows!"

The warden entered the office, accompanied by the boy. Ten minutes passed. Finally the warden emerged from the office, briskly stepped up to the square and cried:

"For the last time I am asking you, who stole the bread?" Silence followed.

"Fedor Lomakin and Ivan Knazyov, come here."

Silence again.

"So you won't, you rascals. Fetch the boy," ordered the warden. A guard ran to the office and presently returned urging the boy onwards with the butt of his rifle.

"Point out Lomakin and Knazyov." But the boy hesitated. Grabbing the boy by the hand the warden dragged him towards the square.

"Don't be afraid, they won't do you any harm," he reassured. "Point out the culprits."

The boy, closely following the warden, raised his finger at someone in the square. The guards rushed in and extracted the two thieves.

"Take them to the office; and the boy to the bathhouse; all the rest immediately to work at the river. We'll show you a thing or two."

The incident seemed to be ended. One of our fellow observers explained to us that Monakhov would post the two thieves out in the frost, but that first they would be thoroughly manhandled by the guards.

"God forbid to steal in this place," he added. "And never show resistance! These men were among the recent arrivals, they don't know the customs yet, but we have seen plenty. No monkey business here."

The architect and I decided to follow up the matter to its end and went toward the office. Nobody paid any attention to us. In spite of the strict regulations there was no real orderliness in the camp and nobody checked up on what one was doing. For over an hour we walked about the camp and none of the great-coats we met stopped us.

Upon entering the office we heard wild screams of beaten men coming from one of the doors giving into the corridor. Retribution was being meted out. It was nauseating as well as dangerous to remain in the corridor, so we quickly went out. We were soon followed by the two bread-thieves, all covered with blood, who were kicked and shoved forward towards the gates by a group of guards. Monakhov's pale face appeared at the door.

"Stand them up for half an hour," he cried after them. "And pour water over them."

The group stopped at the gate. First the guards tackled one of the victims, quickly pulled off his boots, trousers and coat; then they did the same with the other who even had no shirt on under his coat. There he stood naked, with nothing on but a pair of drawers, soaking up the blood which flowed from his nose and was smeared all over his chest. A man in a dark short coat and carrying two full buckets of water was hurrying towards the scene and on reaching the victims emptied his buckets over them. Then they were ordered to stand there.

"It's a nightmare," uttered the architect. "Let us go and visit the doctor."

The small reception room of the hospital was filled with people awaiting treatment. The assistant surgeon was standing behind the partition, pouring some liquid into a measuring glass. Near the window the doctor, a tall man with a serious face, was examining a half-dressed woman. We mingled with the waiting patients.

The architect broke the sausage in two, handed me half of it, and we started eating as if it was just the right thing to do. The dread vision of the repugnant scene which we had just witnessed began to disappear. The room was warm and we were so unaccustomed to heat that it made us feel logy. We had enough time; it would not pay to return to our bathhouse before dinner; therefore we decided to sit down for a while on the floor in a corner where we would not be noticed.

It was quiet and peaceful in the reception room. It smelt of carbolic acid. The patients talked in whispers, from time to time the doctor would call out "next!"; then there would be a movement in the crowd and the next patient, another gray-faced exhausted-looking individual, would edge his way to the other side of the partition. Then again all would be quiet.

In a few minutes the architect was asleep. Hard as I tried I could not follow his good example. Some nervous shocks comparable to electric discharges awoke me each time that I dozed off. Through a kind of fog I could perceive the legs of the waiting patients and could hear the low whispering all around me.

"Lock the door," said the doctor. "The reception is over."

The assistant, dressed in his white smock, went to bolt the door. On his way back he stopped before us, looked at the sleeping architect, wanted to say something but changed his mind, shook his head and returned behind the partition. There were now fewer patients left waiting. I started to shake my sleeping friend: "Come on, it is time to go." But he waved me aside insisting that he would take his turn only toward the very end.

The doctor's weary eyes looked at me through his glasses. "You have a temperature," he said.

The assistant stuck a thermometer under my arm. The tired doctor was anything but garrulous; however, after the first few words had overcome the unfavorable impression we created by our unshaven and untidy appearance, he answered our various queries. At the mention of the tragic scene which we had witnessed in the yard he ran his fingers through his thinning hair and drawled:

"But what can I do about it? When they leave the dungeon, I send them to the hospital. Each new arrival brings with it several instances of this mediaeval torture. After twenty minutes out in the cold, pneumonia is almost guaranteed. Remember that after they are brought in they are left in an unheated dungeon for twenty-four hours and there even I have no right to enter. Then they are brought or rather carried in here and I send them to the hospital, which is about a mile from here. And what do they find there? General barracks. No food, no care, no medicine. Patients lie all together, with typhus, scarlet fever, diphtheria, venereal diseases. Doctor R., who is in charge of the hospital, works day and night, does all he can, but he is all alone, without assistants. What can he undertake, being only a poor prisoner, when the authorities are of the general opinion 'let all this rabble croak.' This is not a nightmare, my friends, it is worse."

Again he ran his fingers through his hair in a tired gesture, pulled the thermometer from under my arm, and continued:

"Just below 102. Well, you may choose. If I pronounce you sick I shall have to transfer you to the hospital of which I have just told you; if not, you will be driven out to work in spite of your temperature. But if you take my advice you had better remain here. Maybe your system will succeed in arresting the destructive developments and I will give you some pills which may help."

We inquired the reason why the doctor had been deported to the penal camp.

"Always the same reason," he answered, smiling sadly, "counter-revolution. I was insufficiently polite with the sick communists, did not wish to receive them out of turn, and generally was not careful enough in hiding my convictions. I got three years. Come in again tomorrow to check up on the temperature. By all means. So long, gentlemen. Is Ouspensky from your barracks, this boy who had to stand out in the cold yesterday with water poured over him? Too bad, he will not pull through. And now, good-bye, I must go. Try to avoid the timber-works at Uftug. This is good advice. Good-bye."

We decided then and there to find out all about the Uftug timber-works. Coming out of the doctor's office, we met some of our cohabitants of the bathhouse. From their words it appeared that during our wanderings around the camp the criminals from the tent had been sent to the river to free the frozen timber and part of our crowd was dispatched to the forest. The rest of them were working in the yard. Pevny, Granovsky and a few others were chosen for some special work in the office and they were now sitting in warm contentment. The eighty men who had been ordered out early in the morning had returned later to gather their belongings, and were now transferred to another building. Those who had records of service in the Red Army or in the militia were assigned to the ranks of the armed guards. They were given uniforms and were detailed to sentry duty. Communists and former chekists were dispatched to Archangel to occupy responsible positions in the branch of the penal camps there. The bathhouse had become a little roomier.

There were still a few hours left to be whiled away before dinner. There was no organized control of work whatever. Therefore we grabbed some brooms and tried to appear busy cleaning the yard together with the others. The day was successfully coming to an end. On the other side of the gate a small-sized new party of some fifty men was awaiting reception.

Back in the bathhouse our room-mates were considerably more comfortable, having found room for themselves and their belongings. In a corner by the door, protected by the guard, sat the young boy from the ranks of the criminals who had squealed on his comrades that morning. He was isolated in order to protect him from their vengeance.

Opening our preserves and dumping the contents of all tins into a deep plate we invited some friends to partake of our good fortune. The end of the feast was spoilt by the appearance of the warden.

"You have too much room here," he said. "We shall have to add a few more men to your number and you will have to crowd yourselves a bit. Just look how luxuriously spacious it is in here."

All hopes of arranging oneself comfortably for the night seemed to take flight. We were destined to spend another night all huddled and jammed together.

The new arrivals bolted in on us with a bang. They had come from Orel and to our regret consisted of a gang of typical petty criminals. Without pausing in our room, the torrent of these people rushed on into the inner apartments and only those in the rear established themselves in our midst. Noisy disturbances immediately began in the next rooms, typical Russian curses resounded and we heard such exclamations as "Shove aside, intelligentsia!" "Hit him one over the head!" "Don't waste time on ceremonies!" and so forth without end.

Dinner was a repetition of the experience of the preceding day. It was quite impossible to approach the washbasins and the underworld instantly consumed all the food.

The night dragged on painfully, without sleep. In spite of the pills I had taken, my temperature remained high and a feeling of chaotic absurdity seemed to fill the brain. I could not quite realize whether what I was seeing was actually happening or was an hallucination. At times I would drowse away and then again catch myself sitting there with wide-open eyes, not seeing anything. The light from the lantern would become quite dim or flare up and blind me like the rays of the sun. My head was bursting...

CHAPTER SEVEN: "FOLDING UP"

"Do wake up." Somebody was violently shaking me by the shoulder. Was it possible that it was morning already and that the whole dismal story would begin anew? In our corner everybody was already awake. Gloomy, tired faces.

We came into the yard, formed in a square and it all commenced again: "zdrah," mark time, run around the yard; and so the drill continued. There were fewer of us left now since the criminal gang from the tent was absent. Grigoriantz was in a hurry and not quite as captious. Dawn was coming; a convoy of soldiers and foremen began to appear.

"All hands to work on the hay!" ordered Grigoriantz.

Escorted by the soldiers we left the yard and in another ten minutes we reached our destination. On a railway siding stood a trainload of open cars loaded with baled hay. Our assignment consisted of unloading the hay and piling it up some distance from the train.

"Don't let them off until they finish the job," the convoy was instructed.

But for the cold the work was not difficult. We ourselves distributed the work among us. Old men were keeping count, the middle-aged were throwing the bales from the cars, the younger ones were carrying them a distance of some fifty meters and were piling them.

At first the work progressed well, but the longer we toiled the more difficult it became. Fatigue was making itself felt and it was bitterly cold. That morning the camp thermometer showed ten below zero Fahrenheit and at noon a strong wind blew. Whenever we got too tired, we tried to rest, but to stop meant to freeze. Toward the end of the day we could barely drag our legs behind us.

Finally the job was completed.

"May we go?" But the foremen were discussing something. No, we were not allowed to leave. The criminal division had completed but half their allotment and refused to go on. After a momentary pause the soldiers and foremen set themselves to beating up the criminals. Clubs and fists were freely used but to no avail. Perhaps it was real exhaustion, or only a case of soldiering, but all the criminals flatly refused to go on with the work.

Having stopped work we were slowly freezing. Our convoy warned us that nobody would be allowed to leave until the entire assignment was completed by the squad. We had the choice of either finishing the job for the criminals or of standing and freezing there in the open. We chose the first alternative. The job would require some three hours. It was getting dark.

The guards, who were also freezing, angrily herded the criminals together into a close bunch. Throwing themselves into the snow and hugging each other, these men were trying to keep warm. It was difficult to tell who was better off, they — slowly freezing, or we — fainting from fatigue. The last bales seemed incredibly heavy and took away the last bit of strength. Fewer and fewer men remained working as one after another of us became exhausted and joined the bunch of unfortunates freezing in the snow.

At last the job was finished. It was quite dark already and bright stars sparkled in the sky, foreshadowing colder weather. We started heavily and, dragging our feet, slowly crept toward the camp.

At the gates we were met by Grigoriantz.

"Greetings, third squadron," he welcomed us.

"Zdrah."

"Good fellows! Well done! You have earned your dinner!" he mocked. "But you seem frozen. Let us have a little trot. Attention! Company, run!" came his command.

We started to run around the yard in the dark. We ran around once, twice, three times, but though the exercise was warming, we were hungry and dreamed of nothing but food and a little rest.

The run was followed by marking time. Taking advantage of the darkness, many of us stopped jumping from foot to foot.

"All together," our commander's voice resounded out of the dark. "If you do not run, I shall not let you go."

One two, one two, one two, we resumed.

"Stop," and the squadron stood still.

"Listen here, you stiffs," Grigoriantz turned to the criminals. "Another case of sabotage like today, making others do your work for you, and I shall put you out in the cold and keep you there, just as I did to your fellow dogs from the tent. They will tell you how they paid for the stolen bread. All day yesterday they worked without eating, and a night, and then another day. Four of them croaked," he shouted louder. "Some more sabotage from you and I'll give you the same works. Understand? And now to the bathhouse with you, march!"

At last! Tired to death and famished, we literally crawled to the bathhouse. I had only one thought, to reach my corner, to sit down, to get warm. What a life!

There was more room now in our corner, for Pevny had left it. He was one of the first to improve his lot and could now sleep on a desk in the office where he was assigned to a permanent job.

I noticed to my surprise that my temperature was near normal and that there were no chills and fever. I decided not to attempt to come out for dinner, as there was hardly a chance of reaching the washbasins. Therefore I drank a little tea with some black bread and instantly fell asleep.

An awful noise aroused me. A real battle was raging in the second room. The criminal elements, thoroughly brazen, had pushed the older inmates out of their places and were defending their position with fists and any available weapon. The uproar was terrible. The guard was leaning out of the door, blowing his whistle.

A few minutes later ten or twelve guards, headed by Grigoriantz, broke into the bathhouse.

"Who is rioting? All of you, out into the yard! Quick! Get a move on!" he roared.

Men were bursting out in bunches from the inner rooms, crushing each other at the exit.

"Like a flash, like a flash!" shouted the guards. "No resistance or it will go hard with you."

The bathhouse was emptied in a jiffy.

We found ourselves standing out in the open air, mad with rage. It was dreadfully cold. The sudden transition from sleep and the comparatively warm bathhouse into the snow and frost chilled me through and through and I felt myself getting ill. I do not know how long we stood there. At intervals I would fall asleep while standing there and my sleep would be penetrated by the cries of abuse and swearing of Grigoriantz.

"Move on. Get on in!" I was rudely aroused from my doze. Having lost my bearings I was somewhat late in reaching the bathhouse and was one of the last to enter. A huge gangster, one of the insolent leaders of the bunch, was sitting on my basket and reviling the architect who was trying to dislodge him.

"We have no reserved seats here," he kept on repeating over and over again and it was clear that he did not intend to leave. What could I do? Start a fight and again be driven out into the yard?

Vainly seeking another refuge, I wandered about the room, stumbling against the prostrated bodies. There was no room anywhere. But I was so overcome with fatigue that I leaned against the door and fell asleep in a standing position. I was constantly waking up. My feet hurt, my back ached, my skin itched. I was taken with cold shivers and found it difficult to breathe. "Where is the end of this torture?" I kept thinking. I remembered that our sense of humor is supposed to help us in life's darkest moments, but try as I would, I could find nothing humorous in my situation.

In the morning, before porridge, Grigoriantz turned up.

"The Orel party, come on out!" he commanded.

"But how about our mush, allow us to swallow our mush," came cries from the gang.

"Hurry up, get out of here like a flash!" And out they were jostled. Our remarkable squad commander took an active part in throwing out the slow-pokes. Some of the space in the bathhouse was released. Almost dropping from fatigue I spread my blanket on the ground, placed my basket under my head and half swooned away. Nobody disturbed us and it was comparatively quiet. Near the door some people were talking to each other.

Upon awakening I was told that the commission for determining the vocational qualifications of the prisoners had begun its work. The commission consisted of one semi-literate man who was asking idiotic questions. This comedy lasted a whole day.

After the departure of the "commission of one," it became known that the majority of the prisoners of our contingent would be assigned to the timber-works at Uftug, the very place which the doctor advised us to avoid.

Cutting of timber was considered more important than anything else and the greater proportion of the prisoners were constantly flowing in a steady stream into the neighboring districts of Archangel and Uftug. The Kotlas camp was nothing more than a transfer point for the assorting and preliminary training of the prisoners prior to their dispatch to their permanent destination.

The transfer point was so poorly managed and so crowded that chaos reigned supreme. Cruelty toward the prisoners had become the rule. It had been introduced in the Transfer Station by Monakhov and by other executives who had been sent to Kotlas from the infamous Solovetsky camp.

The headquarters of our camp was located at Ust-Sysolsk, the capital of the Komi territory. The position of chief was held by Boksha, the Lett, but the actual head was his secretary, the drunkard Vaskov, who had become notorious at Solovetsky.

During the time the "commission of one" was determining our vocational qualifications, the Orel criminal gang was cutting timber. The men were driven out to work in spite of the bitter cold and, as a result, a great number of them came back with frostbitten hands and feet, not to mention the damage done to their faces which were almost without exception frostbitten.

Two of the prisoners froze to death and were brought in on a sled. The guard who brought them reported that they had tried to avoid work and had hidden themselves. A search was made for them and finally they were found asleep. They were half dead when they were picked up and placed in the sled. In it, without any covering, they were then transported for eight kilometers through open country, with a strong wind blowing.

"Of course they could not stand it, so they just folded up," he calmly reported.

How simple it was. To "fold up" or to die did not seem to be very complicated in this camp. I was struck by the expression itself, "to fold up"!

The two frozen men were brought into camp at the time when I was in the doctor's reception room. I was allowed to leave the bathhouse, thanks to the doctor's permit, and now he was checking up on my temperature.

"Some frozen men have been brought in," reported the assistant.

Just as he was, dressed in a mere smock, the doctor rushed out of the house. "Bring them in quickly." He hustled the men excitedly.

They brought two crumpled-up bodies into the room. Their necks were bent forward and their heads folded down, as it were. Now I understood the origin of the expression "folded up." I could not look at them without horror.

"They are finished," said the doctor. I went out. This was the worst I had yet seen in the penal camp. According to rumors there were a great many cases of "folding up." One hesitated to give credence to such rumors, but if there was no truth in them, whence came this characteristic expression, "folded up"?

My friends in the bathhouse were struck by the expression of my face. Not wishing to talk I crouched into my corner. The two crumpled-up corpses were constantly before my eyes.

The Orel criminals were transferred to the tent. They came to fetch their belongings and looked wretched and frozen. Were the majority of them, and perhaps of us as well, destined to end up as did those other two?

Once more it was roomier in the bathhouse. The night passed quietly, without incident. We had already become accustomed to the cold and dampness and to the dirty ground under our feet. It seemed that the possibility of lying down decently and sleeping like a human being no longer occurred to anybody. Lyskin, who had promised us better quarters, never showed up.

In the morning some forty prisoners received their orders to proceed to the place of railroad construction. My friend the architect was among them. Taking up their belongings, they left for the railway station. They had to march there in military formation, escorted by armed guards, over five kilometers of a poor and little-used road. The old priest was appointed an orderly in the hospital. He was overjoyed at the prospect of seeing his poor sick Seryozha there and was constantly praying and crossing himself.

Our corner had become quite empty, but it was not as warm as before. In the evening I felt acutely hungry and went out to get some dinner.

This time there was far more room at the fires and I could get near the barrels without much difficulty. I glanced at the washbasin. Uncleaned fish had been boiled together with a small quantity of barley. A sort of thin gruel was the result. The spoon would bring up fish-bones, scales and entrails but none of the meat. It had either all disappeared in the process of boiling or it had been previously consumed in the kitchen. With a great effort I swallowed several spoonfuls. The concoction had a repulsive taste, felt sticky and had a perceptible foul odor.

That night I succeeded for the first time in five days in taking off my overcoat instead of sleeping in it. This was an indisputable sign of progress.

In the morning Lyskin showed up. "Presently you will be transferred into the barracks," he said. "There you will find it less roomy but warmer. You have stayed here in the bathhouse entirely too long; there is no other place to wash in and everybody is complaining." And within an hour we were ordered to get our belongings together and to proceed to another building.

Carrying our bundles, we crossed the yard and entered the quarters of the so-called third squadron, enormous barracks with one entrance, low windows, a double tier of sleeping-shelves and a filthy floor covered with cigarette butts, spittle, shreds of paper and all kinds of trash. A large boiling kettle, resembling a samovar and holding enough water for several hundred cups, was placed near the door.

The room was very large, designed for approximately three hundred and fifty or four hundred people, but it contained a much greater number. All places were occupied. The upper shelves were all taken by the criminal gang, not from our Lefortovsky prison, but total strangers, insolent and brazen as usual.

The problem of settling our party, numbering some two hundred, was solved by Grigoriantz. Stepping up to the boiling kettle he shouted from there in a loud voice, so that he could be heard in all parts of the room:

"Lower tier of the shelves to the right, get out and double up on the left side. Give room to the newcomers. Understand? Hurry up." Not seeing sufficient haste in executing his order, he shouted again: "Quick, like a flash, I am telling you! In ten minutes every place must be cleared!"

In another moment everything was on the move. As fast as the places were cleared they were occupied by the new owners. During the next fifteen minutes the interior of the barracks looked like an ant-hive. But two hundred men with their baskets, boxes and bundles to which tea-kettles and other junk were tied cannot easily be placed in a space suitable for one hundred. Suspicion of the criminals caused most of the bundles to be piled up on the sleeping-shelves; the crowded condition resulting resembled that of the bathhouse which we had just left. Somebody tried to climb up into the upper tier but was rudely thrown down by the criminals.

During the day we found out that the entire third squadron would shortly be sent out to the timber-works at Uftug. So much the better. I welcomed any change.

As we were not being ordered out to work I made use of the doctor's written permit, left the barracks and made the rounds of the entire camp. First to the doctor's, where I was told that my temperature was almost normal. Then to the store, but with no success. In the barracks of the office workers I was treated to a glass of tea by my former friends who had found "soft" jobs there. Leaving the office, I came across two former Lefortovsky inmates who were standing in cringing attitudes and explaining something to Bukhaltzev. The latter was the manager of the Kotlas town office of the penal camp.

This encounter had a decisive influence on my further fate.

"Why do you always wear stockings?" He pointed at my golf hose.

"I have no felt boots."

"But you are to be sent to the forest, if I am not mistaken. How can you go there in these clothes? You will fold up over there," he said, knitting his brow. He puckered his lips, continued scrutinizing me and said: "Perhaps I shall take you into my office. Can you use the typewriter?"

"I can type pretty well," I answered.

"Well then, I shall take you. But you are not illiterate?"

"No indeed," I laughed. "Quite literate."

He made note of my name and, with another curt remark, went away. Bukhaltzev impressed me as a man who is fond of good food and drink. He spoke thickly, slapping his heavy lips. His efforts to appear severe were not successful and one could see that he was really a kindly man.

Of petty Jewish origin from the South of Russia, he engaged in speculation during the NEP period. In a short time he was the possessor of a little capital and concentrated on working with the new Soviet offices. Thanks to his good connections there, he soon became engaged in larger enterprises, most of which were based on bribery.

In 1924, together with many other NEP luminaries, he fell into the clutches of the OGPU and was sentenced to eight years in the penal camps. He was sent to the Solovetsky camp and there he soon gained the confidence of the famous Frenkel, who had organized and was running all the commercial and industrial enterprises of the camp. Bukhaltzev became his invaluable assistant and was finally pardoned, together with his superior. He remained working in the camps and in 1929 was appointed manager of the Kotlas town office of the new Northern Penal Camp.

Bukhaltzev was very influential, both with Monakhov and in the communist circles of Kotlas. Members of the latter were particularly kind to him because of his generosity in supplying them with all kinds of delicacies, such as cakes, chocolates, cocoa and sweets, from the camp stores, while such items were entirely lacking on the shelves of the local cooperative stores.

His method was always the same: a masked bribe would carry the point and all of Bukhaltzev's requests were readily complied with. His office hours were from nine A. M. till noon. At noon he would go out to lunch and if perchance he returned to the office after luncheon he would always be slightly intoxicated. He lived together with Monakhov in a pretty little house which belonged to a tall and corpulent widow. The widow was given to habitual drinking. Her affections were shared by both her tenants.

Rumor had it that on Saturday nights orgies took place in the little house. Besides the widow and her two boy friends, these orgies were said to have been attended by some of the high town officials and also by women prisoners, some of whom came voluntarily and some perforce.

Bukhaltzev was good-natured, especially after luncheon, when he would become slightly sloppy and his thick lips jabber more noticeably than ever. He was quite intelligent, an active executive, not at all petty, though somewhat coarse and cunning. He spoke in an authoritative low voice and could not bear contradiction. After luncheon he loved to be flattered and willingly gave credence to expressions of admiration for qualities which he did not possess in the slightest degree. But before lunch such procedure was dangerous and nobody indulged in it. He was tall and well dressed, with a nice manner about him. In conversation he would stare at his companion through his strong glasses perched on his heavy-set nose; his lips would bulge out in a constant chewing motion.

CHAPTER EIGHT: "WE ARE LAZY LOUTS!"

Upon my return to the barracks I was stunned by the noise and hubbub reigning there. Men were swearing, shouting, abusing each other. The uproar was tremendous. The air was dreadful and the filth disgusting.

We had no definite information as to when we were to be dispatched; we only knew that the criminal gang from the tent was to leave on the morrow. We would come next.

I experienced a peculiar sensation of lightness through my body. I knew that feeling from my experience in the Shpalernaya prison and it was attributable to continued hunger. My feet ached. I was famished but no food whatever was to be had. I sat down on my basket in the corridor and dozed off.

In my sleep I could hear shouting, the noise grew and became an uproar. Finally it was pierced by loud cries of a familiar voice. Grigoriantz again, damn him!

"Everybody out into the yard! Come on! Quickly!"

Men in great-coats, clubs in hand, climbing into the upper tier of shelves, drove out the gangsters. Men tumbled on the floor from the upper shelves in whole bunches like peas out of a sack. The doorway was jammed. The guards continued driving, snooping in the spaces between the shelves, looking under the shelves, poking their clubs into the empty spaces and shouting constantly.

A huge soldier, club in hand, accosted me: "I'm talking to you, citizen, or doesn't this concern you?"

I had to go out. In the yard the prisoners were already formed in a square. A pair of boots had been stolen from someone in the barracks and Grigoriantz was seeking the culprit. Half-dressed, barefooted, sleepy prisoners were jumping out of the doorway, urged on by kicks and pokes of the guards' clubs. It was getting to be unbearable.

"Confess, you sons of bitches, who stole the boots, or I'll keep you here until morning," cried Grigoriantz.

This time it did not take long; the former lesson had not been in vain. For some reason the gang decided to give up the thief and in a few minutes a wretched-looking boy was shoved out of the ranks. Grigoriantz grabbed him by the collar and dragged him into the barracks. Loud wails and cries pierced the air.

We stood and waited. Large flakes of snow were falling, covering our shoulders and caps. It was getting dark. Those who were not dressed were blue with cold.

The hoy, beaten until he was unconscious, was brought out of the barracks and carried to the dungeon. The incident was finished. The system of inquiry adopted in the penal camp had quickly given the desired results. However, the constant beatings had such a jarring effect on my nervous system that I decided to avoid as much as possible spending my time in the barracks.

I went to the office. Pevny and others who had found "soft" jobs in clerical work and were already adopting a slightly superior tone, were drinking tea as if nothing had happened. Having appeased the dreadful emptiness in the pit of my stomach by some hot tea, I returned to the barracks.

Coming up to my bundle I immediately noticed that someone had managed to explore the contents of my basket. Ends of reed were sticking out and the right corner was totally wrecked. All my cigarettes were gone, and the rest of the tea as well. Damn it! But what could I do? Complain and again stand out in the frost?

Thoroughly disheartened, I sat down and lit one of my last remaining cigarettes. I fell into a dismal gloom. What was I coming to? Sitting there on my basket in the loathsome barracks. Horrible!

The dinner call sounded. This time I did not stop to deliberate on whether I should eat or not. I was one of the first to run up to the barrel and defended my position there with the resoluteness of a famished beast. "No, my dear fellows, you may be strong but you can't get the better of me," I thought.

The criminals went to it, working with their enormous spoons. The sticky slops burnt my lips and mouth, it stank of putrefied fish and was dreadfully salty. "Never mind, never mind, anything to appease the hunger!" Spoons were shoved through under my elbows and drippings were left all over the sides of my overcoat.

A huge fellow facing me on the other side of the washbasin was opening his enormous maw, shoving the spoon into it to the very hilt, and belching. He and all the others were spitting out the fish-bones and scales directly back into the washbasin. It was nauseating, but the urge to eat was stronger than the feeling of revulsion. "Never mind," I consoled myself, "just let me get a little food into my belly. This is not the Contant Restaurant and the agreeable Monsieur Francois will not run towards me with a bow and take my order!" It did not take long to empty our washbasin and the gangsters quickly ran over to the adjoining barrel. They were insatiable.

The night passed peacefully. I sat on my basket and dozed, waking up and falling asleep again and again. The pangs in the pit of the stomach had quieted down, but they were replaced by an overwhelming thirst. Each time that my leg was gripped by a cramp I got up to fill my cup with lukewarm ill-tasting water from the kettle and then return to my basket. The entire barracks were snoring. Bodies of sleepers were everywhere, on the shelves, under the shelves, on the floor between the shelves. From time to time the door would open and the sentry would let out a group armed with a lantern. Cold draughts of air came through the cracks between the floor boards, but the breath of some seven hundred sleepers made the air tolerably warm.

In the morning, after porridge, we were all escorted out to the yard. Hard work in the forest awaited us. I was offered the choice of a saw or an axe. It was cold, but there was no wind. It was just dawning. Our mixed company stretched out in a long line. An engineer carrying a saw was followed by a hardened bandit with an axe; after him came two priests in their cassocks, then a group of pickpockets, then three Turcomans in their padded silk gowns, finally Funk in his winter coat. Every species was represented and they were all mixed up together.

We were escorted by foremen and guards walking alongside of us. After an hour's walk we turned to the left and small trees gave way to a forest of fair-sized timber. On reaching our destination we were divided into groups of twenty and each group was given its assignment. The foremen measured the distances, made some hatchet marks on the tree trunks, and drove in some stakes next to which the guards took up their positions.

My group was allotted the job of felling all the trees within a measured space, cutting off the branches and tops, piling up the timber in accordance with the foreman's instructions and cleaning out the cut-off branches. The guards warned us that we would be allowed to leave only upon completion of our assignment.

The work began. My group consisted of several pickpockets who did not count as workers, a former lieutenant of the Denikin army, a monk, two engineers and, luckily, about ten peasants. The latter were not at all disturbed by the assignment.

We started out energetically. Some of us were wielding axes, some were sawing, while others were pulling away the felled logs. The pickpockets pretended to be busy carrying away the small branches. At noon half of the assignment was completed, but all of us except the peasants were thoroughly exhausted. We swallowed the crumbs of bread which we had brought with us and continued our work. The slanting rays of the winter sun were breaking through the tree tops and we could see the pale Northern sky above our heads. To the right and to the left of us axes resounded and voices of the workers were heard from all sides calling to each other.

My low shoes and golf stockings were quite wet from the work in the deep snow. My feet froze whenever I pulled them out of the snow, so I would immediately bury them again in this protective blanket.

A foreman came up. "Well, how are you getting along? Get going, what is the matter with you, you have finished less than half your job."

Our energy was falling off perceptibly. I swapped my axe for a saw, but soon realized that I had made a bad bargain. The peasants sawed methodically, the pickpockets gave up altogether and did not try even to make believe that they were working. The monk and the two engineers were now only carrying branches. The rays of the setting sun now touched only the tree tops and it was getting colder. Our thoroughly chilled guard was provoked and made attempts to drive the pickpockets to work, though he probably feared them a little and was urging them not any too persistently. The Denikin lieutenant could hardly stand and had constantly to sit down for a rest. I felt myself weakening. Alas! After all my tribulations my well-trained muscles had lost their strength and my heart was failing. But the peasants were still sawing as methodically as ever.

We had a good last quarter of the assignment still ahead of us. It was obvious that we could not finish our job until late that night.

The work continued on after sunset. It was getting colder all the time. The moon rose and shed its greenish light over the working area. The blows of the axes sounded hollow. The pickpockets had started an open fire and were warming themselves at it. The freezing guard stood with them. The two exhausted engineers were sitting a little way off. The foreman appeared, axe in hand.

"Well, are you ready? Look out, you will have to stay here for the night."

The remaining portion would take at least another three hours. The peasants were abusing the pickpockets, but could not get them to come back to work. The guard feebly urged them but would presently return to the fire. My endurance was coming to an end. My body was cramped with cold and hunger and my fingers would no longer obey; I prayed for the end of this torture.

The work continued at a slowing pace. After their prolonged rest the two engineers resumed carrying branches but they were as slow as snails. It was evident that at this rate we could never finish our assignment.

Should I not try to have a little talk with the foreman? I remembered the architect and his favorite expression, "All men are human." The work had now come to a complete stop. Even the peasants were done for. All of us were crowding around the fire, trying to get warm, when suddenly a terrible heartrending shriek pierced the air. We all looked at one another questioningly, but there were no explanations.

So another half hour passed. The flickering light of a lantern coming towards us appeared in the distance. It was the foreman. I quickly came to a decision and went to meet him.

"Look here," I said, "the assignment is almost finished, everybody is exhausted. Please let us go. We are all cold and hungry. Perhaps you have some little bit of food with you that I could buy. Here, take this five-spot."

He glanced at me, then at the rest of our group sitting at the fire, took the proffered bill and quickly stuck it into his pocket.

"All right, I shall call you in twenty minutes or so."

The matter was settled. In another half hour he again appeared at the fire. The freezing guard, who evidently was very anxious to return to the camp, talked to him in a low whisper. The prisoners, frozen stiff and dumb, were staring into the fire.

"Come on home," ordered the foreman.

Whence did they suddenly get such energy? The first to jump up were the pickpockets, then came the rest. The foreman came up to me and shoved a small parcel into my hand:

"This is in exchange for your money."

The parcel contained a bit of frozen lard.

The road back to camp seemed endless. Only then I felt my fatigue in full degree and, strange as it may seem, noticed that I had lost considerable weight during the one day. The moon shone brightly and lighted up the road. The foreman had put out his lantern and walked ahead. We crawled along behind him, tired and benumbed. The guard closed the procession. The axes and saws which we carried glistened in the moonlight. My drenched oxfords and stockings were covered with a crust of ice.

Every moment seemed to increase the difficulty of going onward. We were so completely exhausted. Turning the corner we saw the lights of the camp about half a mile ahead of us. Oh, how I wished to get back to the barracks! At the gates our number was checked with the list carried by the guard and we were let in.

It was quiet in the barracks. Everybody was asleep and there was a lot of empty space on the shelves, as half the prisoners were still out in the forest though it was already half past ten. We had missed the dinner call, but nobody thought of food any more; we wanted only to sleep.

I scraped the snow from my stockings and shoes, climbed into the first available space, stretched out my drenched feet and instantly fell asleep. My head rested on some kind of a box, my feet were shoved under somebody's bundle. A doghouse would have been better.

"Citizen, wake up, you're in my place. Kindly clear it."

The tired angry face of the owner of the place bent over me.

"What time is it?"

"It is already after two and we have just returned, damn these torturers," he answered.

I got up. My whole body was in pain. My feet were entirely benumbed with cold and ached frightfully. Everywhere around me sleeping bodies covered the floor and every available foot of space was taken. What could I do? I walked over to my bundle and sat down on my basket. Dear Lord, when will these sufferings end?

I recalled the common cell of the Butirsky prison. What a paradise that was compared with my present life! My aching feet did not allow me to sit still, so from time to time I had to get up and stretch them. I walked about the barracks, trying not to step on the sleepers. After a walk I would sit down again, then walk again. In this way the night finally passed. Towards morning I began suffering sharp pangs of hunger. Bit by bit I swallowed my lard, which had thawed during the night. It was sticky and rancid. At last the porridge was brought in. Sticking the remnants of my bread into my pockets I again took advantage of the doctor's written permit and left the barracks.

A large sled stood at the hospital door. Somebody's bare feet were sticking out from under a covering of burlap. Was it another case of "folding up"?

The tired doctor informed me that it was Filka, the boy who had squealed on the bread thieves. He was killed in the forest by a falling tree trunk. The piercing shriek which we had heard in the forest the night before was his: last cry. The vengeance of his fellow gangsters was obvious, but the authorities preferred to regard the case as an accident, and the doctor, having attested to the death, sent the body to the morgue.

Everybody in Filka's detachment was questioned, but they all testified that he was killed quite accidentally during the guard's absence, not having been quick enough to jump aside when the tree fell on him...

At seven o'clock in the morning we were all driven out into the yard. There we saw some forty prisoners formed in a small square. These men were from two of our forest detachments which had not completed their assignment and who had only just now been brought back to the camp. They were ordered to stand there and shout out in chorus, for the edification of the rest of us:

"We are lazy louts! We are slackers!"

Their emaciated faces had a vicious expression and were blue with cold. Grigoriantz was walking in front of their lines and ordered them alternately to mark time or to shout one and the same sentence. The faces of several educated men could be discerned among these victims. This edifying show continued about half an hour. Then they were gradually released and one by one they returned to the barracks.

Taking advantage of the reigning disorder I left the crowd of onlookers and went toward the office. On the way I met Lyskin. He seemed to notice my exhausted appearance, for he stopped me and said that he might use me to help him out with some special work at the office and ordered me to go there.

There was plenty of activity in the office, people were going to and fro, the telephone rang, typewriters hammered away. A large cast-iron stove in the corner heated the room and was constantly fed with wood. It spread a pleasant warmth through the office. My brain was foggy and refused to work, figures were all jumbled in front of my eyes. I repeatedly fell asleep over my work. It progressed very slowly. Towards two o'clock my job was finished, but I decided to take full advantage of my day of rest and did not hasten to hand over my papers. Instead, I peacefully sat over them smoking the tobacco which I had procured.

That day I again had to use brute force to obtain my dinner. After dinner I felt an imperative need to lie down somewhere, no matter where, just to lie down, stretch out and sleep. I carefully inspected all the shelves, though I knew in advance that I could not find any room on them. Finally I found an empty space under the farthest corner shelf. I crept into it and stretched out. It felt like a coffin. It was dark and damp. Cold air was blowing in through the cracks between the floor boards; consequently I had constantly to turn from one side to the other. When the occupants of the shelf above me turned in their sleep I could feel rubbish, bread-crumbs and dirt fall upon me through the crevices between the loosely-jointed shelf-boards. To add to my misery I was attacked by vermin, which were very plentiful in the barracks. Luckily there were no bedbugs among them, thanks to the low temperature.

But I had no luck even in this remote corner under the shelves. Very soon I was aroused from sleep by a warm liquid dripping down on me. Above me a group of peasants were drinking tea. I knew from experience that tea-drinking in the barracks is a leisurely pastime and decided that the best thing I could do was to leave my new abode.

For half an hour I wandered about the barracks in a sleepy daze, trying to find a little room for myself amidst the sleeping bodies, but with ill success. However, having decided to stretch out and sleep at any cost, I wedged myself in between two sleepers and paid no attention to the abuse which was showered upon me.

I was lying soldier-fashion, on my stomach with my left arm as a headrest. The gangsters on the upper shelves were spitting down freely and were unconcernedly throwing cigarette butts and other rubbish upon the sleepers below. When they had to come down they jumped right on top of me, but I paid no attention, as if it did not concern me at all. All I wanted was to be allowed to stretch out and sleep, sleep under any circumstances...

It was the night before Christmas of the year 1929. It is the lot of but few unfortunates to spend Christmas Eve so dismally. My thoughts sped far away to my wife and daughter, to my old mother, who was preparing for Christmas surrounded by her family in far-away California. She had never been told of my misfortunes, but believed that I was taking part in a profitable expedition to a remote district from which I could send no news.

Then all thoughts vanished. In the morning I was stiff all over, but did not feel the mortal fatigue of the night before.

After porridge we were ordered to get ready "with our belongings." At last. Everything in the barracks came into motion, people dressed, packed, bustled about. We would have to walk about thirty-five kilometers. We were given the choice of carrying our belongings on our backs or else leaving them in charge of the storekeeper and having them sent on at the first opportunity. The majority of us chose the first alternative, afraid to lose our last belongings.

Out in the yard we formed in a square for the roll-call. Those whose names were called had to step out of the gates and form on the other side. About fifty soldiers, who were to act as our convoy, stood around us. The roll-call proceeded slowly, it was more than an hour and a half before it reached me. It was snowing. Our column was standing in the road outside the gates and we were gradually wrapped in a blanket of snow. Finally the last prisoner passed through the gate and the column prepared to depart. We numbered about eight hundred.

The commanders, Monakhov, Bukhaltzev and others, came up to see us off.

"Well, are you ready to start?"

"Everything is in order, comrade commander," reported the chief of the convoy.

"Take care that all reach their destination. If anyone tries to escape, shoot him on the spot!" ordered Monakhov in a loud voice so that all should hear him; and turning to Bukhaltzev, he added: "Pretty low-grade merchandise. I doubt whether Orlov will thank us for it."

Suddenly Bukhaltzev saw me. "Come out, return to the camp, you are to work in my office as I had ordered. Why was this man included in your lists?" he asked one of the prisoners who formed his staff. "Did I not order to have him transferred to my office?"

"It must be a misunderstanding, comrade commander," the cringing assistant excused himself.

"What do you mean — a misunderstanding?" interposed Monakhov. "This is not the way to work, you must attend to the checking-up yourself. One more trick of this nature and out into the forest you go, understand?"

"Yes, sir, comrade commander, excuse me, comrade commander," stammered the scared and cringing manager of the labor assignments.

Later on we came to know the way in which labor was apportioned. If you happened to be on friendly terms with a prisoner who was working in the department of labor apportionment, you had no fear for your future. The apportionment was handled by prisoner-clerks who filled the minor positions in the department. Since I had no friends in the department, I had been included in the detachment leaving for the timber-works, and the position for which I was singled out by Bukhaltzev had been reserved for some friend. The manipulation was frustrated at the very last moment and this decided my further destiny.

I stepped out of the ranks, followed by envious looks. This certainly was a piece of rare good luck. One of the last in line and overloaded with baggage, stood Timofeyich, who waved to me a last farewell. Shall we ever see each other again? The column started. Its head had already disappeared before the rear got under way. Finally even the last lines started forward, three or four men to a row, with bundles or baskets on their backs, some of them with sticks in their hands. They waved farewell to me. Goodbye!

At five o'clock in the afternoon I started for the town of Kotlas, together with Pevny and Granovsky, who were also requisitioned by Bukhaltzev for the "EKO," as his office was called. We walked on the railroad tracks, without escort. It was a strange feeling to be almost at liberty after twenty months of imprisonment.

CHAPTER NINE: HALF FREE

Our baggage was sent on ahead of us and we walked leisurely along the railway-track. Fine snow was falling and the general silence was broken by far-away whistles of locomotives and by the occasional barking of dogs, which I had not heard for a long time. I felt peaceful and relieved. In the distance we saw the lights of Kotlas.

Coming out of the forest we began to encounter the little gray houses of the outskirts. Through some of the little snow-covered windows we could see families having tea around the samovars. We repeatedly stopped to admire the long-missed tableaux of family life: women with infants tugging at their breasts, a thin red-haired cat licking its paws, samovars, bearded heads-of-families sitting under the ikons or under the portraits of communist leaders and sipping tea from their saucers, children of all ages — how utterly different it was from the sights which we had just left behind us in the penal camp!

We reached the station and went into the large lunchroom. At one end of the room was a long counter with a sketchy assortment of edibles, and, as behooves a lunchroom, a huge samovar which, however, had not been polished for ages. A similarly unpolished-looking waiter was dozing behind the counter. In the center of the room was a full-length table covered with spotted gray oilcloth. On the table stood two chandeliers without candles and two dusty decanters without glasses. Strung along the walls were some twenty little tables covered with table-cloths dreadfully neglected by the laundryman. Some of the tables were occupied by dull-looking provincial "comrades" drinking tea. Two homely girls with filthy aprons were waiting on them. In a corner was a news-stand tended by an over-ripe hump-backed saleswoman with a shapeless, extravagantly powdered nose. The room smelt of stale cabbage and some other decaying matter. But in spite of the disagreeable first impression of the place, we greatly enjoyed a glass of beer; the newspapers, which we had not seen since leaving Moscow, seemed particularly interesting.

It was already dark when we passed the market-place, scaring the goats which were pasturing there. We came out on the main street of Kotlas. The town was divided in two parts: new and old. Neither one had paved streets.

In the daytime people walked on narrow sidewalks made of a double row of boards, at night they walked in the middle of the street, for safety.

The town office of the penal labor camp occupied a small two-story building, painted in a gay sky-blue color, and located on the main street of the Old Town commercial section. It bore the abbreviated name of EKO which stood for the Economic Department of the Kotlas Transfer Station. The office was on the lower floor and the upper story contained the clerks' living quarters.

In spite of the late hour, the office was brightly lit and all the clerks were still in it. We became acquainted. In the chief's absence the office was managed by the head-accountant Wahl, a German from the Baltic provinces, who was serving a six-year term for graft.

This individual impressed us most unfavorably. He was short and bow-legged with an oily gray complexion and muddy eyes. Immediately upon meeting us he started telling us old and pointless smutty stories and commonplace jokes. The other clerks surrounded him and applauded him with servile snickering.

We were offered some tea and taken upstairs to inspect the sleeping quarters. The bunks all stood quite close to each other, almost adjoining, with tiny passage-ways between. My bunk was in a little room and stood next to the bunk of the office cook, the Georgian Eradse, former proprietor of a Caucasian restaurant in Moscow.

I was lucky in my neighbor; he was a very likable chap, but unfortunately he had the bad professional habit of getting up at four in the morning and lighting the fire in the tremendous stove whose back wall adjoined my bunk. The wall would get so dreadfully hot that by six o'clock it became unbearable to remain in bed and I would jump out of it as out of a frying-pan. All my efforts to make the cook unlearn this habit proved unavailing.

The head-clerk Wahl evidently took a dislike to me, probably for my lack of enthusiasm over his smutty stories, for he immediately brought up a large bundle of papers and ordered me in the name of the boss to copy them. I started hammering on an old rickety Remington with my stiff fingers, which were badly coarsened by the hard labor in camp. It took me three hours to become accustomed again to this kind of work and by one o'clock in the morning half my assignment was completed. The work in the office continued, nobody going to bed, though most of the clerks spent more time in conversation than at office work.

The telephone rang constantly. Most of the calls came from the nearest camp division, the Uftug timber-works, and often they contained reports of the latest escapes.

The telephone operator repeated in a monotonous voice while another clerk wrote down the message: "Dark, medium height, thirty-five years old, dressed in black coat, no special marks. Take all steps necessary to catch the fugitive."

Usually we received some five to ten such messages a day. In the morning they would be transmitted to the secret intelligence department of the camp, which was in charge of escapes.

At one A. M. I was interrupted in my work by a young employee of the secret intelligence department. He gave me a special assignment, to type one hundred questionnaire blanks for prisoners to be employed by the intelligence service. Such prisoners had to fill in the questionnaires and accept all responsibilities arising out of their obligation to report on their fellow prisoners. This highly gratifying special work took me about two hours. Fighting off drowsiness during the next three hours, I finally completed my original assignment. The office was now empty except for the clerk on watch-duty. It was morning when I went up to my room in the hope of getting some sleep, but the little room was already so hot that I soon had to get out of my bunk and try to find a substitute for sleep in a refreshing wash with cold water.

At eight o'clock work was resumed at the office. As usual in all Soviet institutions, most of the work consisted of writing a multitude of documents which nobody needed or read. There was plenty of work for the typist. At noon I was so tired that I could hardly keep my eyes on the words I had to copy.

There was great activity all around me. Bukhaltzev's loud orders came from his private office, the clerks rushed from desk to desk in search of data he demanded, the telephone rang, my old typewriter generously contributed to the noise.

Peasants came in dressed in huge reindeer coats and dogskin mittens, fur outside, all covered with ice and snow and with icicles hanging down from their long beards. They were teamsters who came to the office to receive their allowance of food supplies in payment for delivery of goods.

The office furnished all the necessary goods and materials to the various camp divisions. Food supplies, clothing and tobacco for the prisoners, horse-fodder, tools and all other supplies were sent to Kotlas from the interior of the U.S.S.R. were stored in the huge warehouses, which dated from before the war, and were distributed from there by the EKO office.

In a very few days I realized the full extent of the confusion reigning in the office. The usual Soviet disorder was augmented by the furious tempo adopted and resulted in chaos. Telegrams came in from all sides:

"Send hay immediately," from one division.

"Send oats, the horses are starving," telephoned another.

"Interruption of your supplies endangers life of two hundred prisoners."

"Supplies left for three days only, catastrophe impending unless relieved."

"Bar iron imperatively needed at once, otherwise obliged stop construction work," telegraphed the railway construction division.

"Absence of medicine nullifies all our efforts to fight typhus epidemic," telegraphed the camp hospital, and so on, without end. Most urgent emergencies were reported from all sides.

The division nearest to Kotlas, preparing timber for export, was in worse shape than all the others as a result of some costly errors in planning.

The administration of the penal camps had made a contract with the State Trust "Severoles" (North-Timber) which was in charge of all forestry operations in the Northern territories. The camp administration was to supply the Uftug timber district with all its labor requirements consisting of eight thousand men and eight hundred horses. "Severoles" was to supply warm clothing for the men and tools to work with, was to organize the transport of supplies to the various outposts, and the baking of bread there.

As soon as this contract was concluded, Moscow started sending to Kotlas trainloads of prisoners from all parts of the U.S.S.R. After a short stay at the Transfer Station they were marched to their points of destination where their trials really began.

The State Trust "Severoles" had not made a careful calculation of its resources and had blundered into the contract with the blind optimism so common to Soviet institutions. It had not expected such a speedy delivery of the man-power contracted for. It could not supply warm clothing to the prisoners because of the general lack of warm clothing in the country, it could not organize the transport because of the unwillingness of peasants to place their horses at its disposal, and it could not bake enough bread for similar reasons. In spite of this disorganization, the camp administration continued to pour prisoners into the forests, and when we arrived at Kotlas the situation had assumed catastrophic proportions.

There were six thousand prisoners and seven hundred horses in the forests. They were scattered over the tremendous territory of the Uftug forest district, which consisted of eight bases subdivided into many outposts of two hundred to two hundred and fifty men each. The whole net of the Uftug timber-works was managed by Orlov, a typical shiftless OGPU official.

At the outposts there was a shortage of housing, axes, saws, clothing and footwear. The insufficient supplies of food which had been brought to the outposts by the seven hundred horses sent there, were all coming to an end. Horses died from lack of fodder. All available hay was requisitioned from the peasants of the adjoining districts. The District Soviet passed an urgent resolution mobilizing for work all the peasants within its territory.

Our office was instructed to pay the teamster-peasants a bonus of a certain amount of food supplies for each delivery. Moscow was sending us axes and saws by express. The communist director of "Severoles" who had signed the contract was discharged, his technical assistant, a bourgeois expert, was arrested on the charge of sabotage, the whole contract was somewhat altered. For an additional remuneration the camp administration undertook to fulfill the former obligations of "Severoles" which the latter had not been able to accomplish.

This was a typical instance of Soviet planning. The usual practise in the U.S.S.R. in such cases is that the two parties declare that the contract cannot be fulfilled for reasons beyond their control and therefore is canceled. They put a stop to the work started and the whole new undertaking dies a natural death. At the beginning of each such new enterprise the newspapers are full of descriptions of the "imposing new example of Socialist construction," but when the work is discontinued the papers do not mention a word about it, so that the reading public remains under the impression that it is prospering, while actually it no longer exists.

In this case things were different, because the OGPU itself had undertaken to aid Socialist construction by supplying certain needs in the execution of the Five-Year Plan. Relinquishment of the contract meant loss of prestige, acknowledgment of faulty calculations and of insurmountable obstacles the existence of which the OGPU had never been willing to acknowledge. It finally meant an interruption of work in the Five-Year Plan program, throwing a monkey-wrench into the machine of Socialist construction. Outrageous and quite impossible! Besides, the prisons throughout the land had already been emptied and the prisoners were already at their destinations. They would have to be brought back to the prisons and the OGPU would have to give up the profitable agreement under which it was paid for supplying the man-power necessary for the execution of the timber export provisions of the Five-Year Plan.

Therefore it was decided to continue the work in spite of all obstacles. Comrade Boksha, the chief commander of the Northern Penal Camps Administration, was expected any day to arrive from Ust-Sysolsk, the seat of the head-office. Special deputies were making the rounds of the surrounding villages to check up on the fulfilment by the peasants of their newly-imposed teamster duties and to arrest slackers.

The forest outposts were furnished small quantities of the goods most urgently required. The timber-works bases were advised that they would be required to fulfil their full assignments. Their remonstrating telegrams were either left unanswered or were countered by assuaging promises.

Even assuming that the peasants lent their willing co-operation, which they were not doing, it was evident that the number of teamsters available would be unable to cope with the transport of even the most urgent requirements for the timber outposts.

The prisoners' lot in the forests was becoming unbearable, escapes were more frequent, mortality grew, and typhus epidemics broke out at all the outposts.

At this critical moment Boksha arrived in Kotlas. He was the man on whom all Moscow hopes were centered, but of course he was quite powerless in this instance. During his visit I had my first opportunity to observe the working methods of one of the highest OGPU penal-camp officials.

Chief of the Administration Boksha was a Lett and a locksmith by trade. He was about forty-five, tall and haggard. He had established his reputation in the cheka by his brutality in the suppression of uprisings during the civil war. His low and narrow forehead, his extremely long arms with large hands which were covered with a blond fuzz, his little squinting eyes with yellow lashes, all made him look something like a blond orang-utan.

He arrived at six o'clock in the morning, accompanied by the penal camp's chief of sanitation Dr. Movsh, who was a former prisoner and had elected to remain in the camps' employ after the expiration of his term. They were both escorted by the chief of the camp's armed guards, Gashofsky, a typical army officer.

Boksha went to work at half past six, raising a tremendous racket in our office. He sat at the telephone and shouted a mass of threats, accusations and impossible instructions into the receiver. Our head-clerk Wahl stood at attention at his side and was scared stiff by the great man's repeated threats to have him shot. Every fifteen minutes Orlov, the manager of the Uftug timber-works, was called away from his work in order to listen to Boksha's promises to have him court-martialed. There was lots of noise but nothing useful was accomplished.

Bukhaltzev tried to compose the pale and frightened Wahl and assured him that after lunch the boss would calm down. After lunch the boss did not come at all. Later on we heard that during lunch five of them had consumed six liters of alcohol. All the next day Boksha spent drinking beer in Bukhaltzev's private office. At night he slept in the private office, on the floor, rolled up in his fur coat. In another day he left us and went to Archangel, where conditions were as alarming as at Uftug.

During his short stay at Kotlas he issued instructions that all prisoners trying to escape or refusing to work were to be shot. He sent orders to all district managers insisting on the fulfilment of their entire assignments without excuses of any kind and threatening the managers to have them put back into the ranks of common labor prisoners in case of failure. He also pointed out the necessity of preserving the lives of the horses and ordered that if there was not enough oats the horses should be fed bread at the expense of prisoners' rations.

"Better let ten prisoners die than one horse!" read his order.

Comrade Boksha's system of work astounded me then by its singularity. But during the next two years I frequently had an opportunity to see men, who considered themselves the cream of Soviet officialdom, at work. My observations convinced me that Boksha's behavior was not in the least singular, but was common practise from which there were but few exceptions. A lot of noise, shouting, peremptory commands, idiotic orders impossible to execute, innumerable long, complicated and contradictory telegrams, infuriated telephone conversations full of intimidation, useless summoning of department heads for personal interviews which only interrupted their fruitful work, constant travelling, artificial feverish activity — such were uniformly the working habits of the high officials with whom I came in contact.

Most of them were ignorant people who had no idea of productive work. The confusion they brought into their departments greatly retarded the efforts of their assistants who were technical experts and who had to execute their instructions. When any documents reached the bosses themselves, they considered it their duty to compose a long, high-sounding resolution and write it in red ink right across the document, invariably closing it with the showy display of a flowery signature. The resolution was usually the direct opposite of the logical measures which should have been adopted.

The prisoners who were employed as technical assistants to the communist bosses usually paid no attention to the fancy resolutions or prepared instructions counteracting the same, which were then accepted and signed by the bosses with the same display. Those assistants who did not know any better and who blindly followed the bosses' resolutions eventually found themselves caught in a trap. If the resolution brought gratifying results the bosses were given the credit, if they did harm the responsibility fell on the prisoner assistant who had acted as technical advisor.

Another characteristic common to Soviet officials was their youth. They were rarely over forty years old. The most responsible positions were frequently held by young men of twenty or twenty-five.

While Boksha was at our office I had to copy five or more times the altered contract with "Severoles." After each alteration the contract was reconsidered by Boksha and his board and had to be re-copied again. The final version was almost identical with the one which was prepared before the arrival of the "redoubtable chief."

Boksha's companion, Dr. Movsh, returned to our office ten days after Boksha's departure. He had been making an inspection of some of the Uftug timber-works outposts. His report to the chief, which was to follow the latter to Archangel, was given me to copy. The report was inscribed: "absolutely confidential." I was told to bring my typewriter into Bukhaltzev's office and to keep my mouth shut about the contents, for if they became known to anybody I would be prosecuted "to the full extent of the law."

The report disclosed that the mortality rate among the prisoners showed appalling growth and was due to undernourishment. In December alone six percent of all prisoners working in the forests had died. Typhus epidemics were assuming disastrous proportions at some of the outposts. Twenty percent of all prisoners had scurvy and dysentery. Medical assistance was not available, the whole tremendous district had only one doctor and two assistants. There were practically no medicines. The attitude of the commanders to the sick prisoners was disgraceful. In the absence of doctors and even of thermometers some commanders did not hesitate to drive the sick prisoners out to work together with all the rest. Cases were enumerated where prisoners sick with dysentery had been chased out of the barracks by soldiers armed with clubs and had died in the forest. The sick were housed in the same barracks with the others and slept all huddled together on the ground. The barracks were not heated as there were no stoves. There were absolutely no bathhouses at any of the outposts and the prisoners never washed at all. The report ended with a recommendation that drastic measures be resorted to at once.

Later rumors had it that the chief of the penal camp administration never sent this report to Moscow, that it was either forgotten or intentionally hidden. In any event it did not result in any instructions to change the existing conditions.

As a consequence it was later certified that by the spring of 1930, twenty-two percent of the prisoners at the timberworks had died and that up to sixty percent had become incapacitated to an average degree of forty percent, even according to the conservative figures of the camp administration. The Archangel district presented a similar picture.

After the departure of the high official, the life in the EKO office returned to normal. We got up at seven, started work at eight and worked late into the night, with one hour recess for dinner. After dinner, and sometimes at night, we took little walks, luckily without escort, as Bukhaltzev accepted full responsibility for his office workers and they were not guarded.

The walks over the frozen river at night were particularly pleasant. The constant disagreeable winds quieted down in the evening and the frosty air felt very refreshing. The snow was lighted by the soft glimmer of stars. Nerves calmed down and rejoiced in the absolute silence of the night, which was broken only by the occasional far-away barking of dogs or by a sudden snap of cracking ice.

We had no Sundays or holidays in our office. They differed from other days only by the noise which came from the streets when communist officials got drunk and wildly drove through, making good use of their government horses, scaring the population and the pasturing goats.

Bukhaltzev usually came to the office about ten o'clock and, in spite of a hangover from the night before, proceeded to sign papers, give instructions and hustle up things. At twelve o'clock he went out to lunch. Now and then he came back to the office after luncheon, sometimes accompanied by Monakhov. All clerks took advantage of his after-luncheon inebriated good humor to make, requests and ask special favors, which he invariably granted with mellow kindliness. Thanks to his intemperance, we always had a sufficient supply of cigarettes and those who had money were able to purchase second-rate fish preserves, sausages and other delicacies which the ordinary prisoner could not obtain.

Once a week the city bathhouse was placed at the disposal of our office force. This was done in exchange for certain rights to purchase edibles from the EKO stores. The office cook could draw from the store of edibles an amount greatly in excess of the established rations and for this reason we had nothing to complain of in the way of meals. Quite the contrary, in spite of the fact that we had very long working hours, we were the objects of envy to the clerks of other Soviet offices in town who sometimes called on us on business. They were not prisoners but they all looked undernourished, sickly and weak. Within a very short time I became an expert typist and a valued member of the staff.

About the middle of January a new official arrived at our office. It was the chekist Ulanovsky who had been sent from Moscow to act as Bukhaltzev's assistant. He gave himself airs, but was totally unfit for work. He first came to the office in Bukhaltzev's absence and tried to impress us with his importance by making us all get up and greet him by the familiar "zdrah." He did not get far with this innovation as we resented it and upset it by disappearing in a body at the moment he was expected to enter the room.

We had also arranged that Ulanovsky should be met in the entrance hall by our office-messenger, a giant Vilna Jew who possessed a quite extraordinary voice. He was to greet Ulanovsky with a thundering "zdrah." He overdid the trick and bawled "zdrah" at the moment when Ulanovsky had turned his back to him. The sound was so terrific and unexpected that poor elderly Ulanovsky almost got a stroke. He reached for his chest, fell into a chair and stammered for water. The messenger appeared greatly perturbed and dumbly repeated again and again the studied phrase: "Beg pardon, comrade commander, these were your orders, please forgive me."

Ulanovsky, afraid for his heart, drank a glass of water and left the office for the day. This incident put an end to his endeavour to bring camp discipline into our office.

Ulanovsky was formerly the warden of one of the OGPU prisons in the provinces. He had one weakness, he imagined himself to be an authority on the theory of communism. He decided to become a contributor to the local newspaper and soon after his arrival composed a thoroughly illiterate "Appeal to Peasant Comrades," which he gave me to copy.

He was probably aware of the degree of his illiteracy, for when he handed it to me, he bent down to my ear and whispered:

"You may correct it a bit where necessary, you know."

The document appealed to the peasants not to stint in giving all their strength and that of their horses to the job of transporting camp supplies. It was a good example of an asinine collection of typical Soviet exclamations and stupidities, not to mention the abominable grammar. At dinner the manuscript was handed around and caused much merriment. In the morning Ulanovsky received its corrected transcription and from that time on his attitude to me was one of esteem.

It was an expensive esteem, however. His compositions poured in upon me as from a horn of plenty. He would give me themes and request me to "elaborate on the subject a bit." It all grew very tiresome and finally I lost my patience and "elaborated" one of his platitudes in such a way that any reader would consider it sheer nonsense. As usual, the dullard read my composition, signed it boldly, and sent it on to its destination. Three weeks later Ulanovsky suddenly stopped heaping commissions upon me and his attitude towards me changed from near-familiarity to distant frigidity. Subsequently he revenged himself and my practical joke proved very expensive.

In spite of the order forbidding intercourse with free citizens, I met some of these within the first week or two and visited them sometimes at night, after office hours. They were what remained of the old merchants and government officials, who now had jobs as accountants and clerks in Soviet institutions. Their quarters were invariably a "hole-in-the-wall," they were underfed and led a pauper's life on their tiny salaries. The younger generation of communist origin overtook them and left them behind at their menial jobs.

They mused sadly on the former glory of Kotlas when it was a large commercial center with huge warehouses filled to capacity with Siberian grain bound for Archangel exports, when they had their own homes, which were all "nationalized" by the communists for the common weal, and which were now in a dilapidated state. They shook their heads dejectedly when they spoke of the destruction of the people's religious feeling, of the actual if not official interdiction of going to church, of their children whom Bolshevik teachings and associations turned into monstrosities, and generally of all those ills which form the open sore of all Russian people not in sympathy with the Bolsheviks.

Cautiously I approached these people with inquiries about the possibility of escape. By the end of January my plans were ready and all I needed was a substantial amount of money to be paid to a trusted peasant who guaranteed to get me to Viatka. It was imprudent to try the trains direct from Kotlas as the patrols were sure to detain any suspicious-looking individual, even if his passport was in order. It was proposed to drive about three hundred kilometers in a sleigh, to pass the barriers of armed guards patrolling the exits from the penal camp territory, and to board a train at Viatka, in an attempt to reach the border and freedom.

CHAPTER TEN: INSPECTORS OF DEATH

A long sequence of events blasted all my preparations to escape. It all started with the old Remington getting out of order.

Bukhaltzev took the typewriter in order to write personally a message of a very confidential nature. His fat fingers broke several levers, which the local watchmaker promised to repair in four days. I was left without work.

At that very time the camp administration decided to make an inspection of the Pitsky timber-works base, where conditions were very unsatisfactory. Production was retarded, escapes had increased, the percentage of sickness and mortality was greatly in excess of normal, and besides, there were persistent rumors of brutality by Aaronovich, chief of the base, in his treatment of the prisoners.

The inspection was to be made by a physician, Dr. S., and by the chief of the secret intelligence department, Zakhariantz. Bukhaltzev was requested to furnish one of his office workers for the inspection of the business end and of accounts.

Bukhaltzev was annoyed, as he disapproved of all "investigations." "What do they want with an inspecting committee? It is only a loss of time. Everybody is busy whom could we send? Ah, I have it, let us send the idle typist."

That same day found us on our way to Solvychegodsh. Dressed in new warm sheepskin coats and felt boots provided by the state, we sat in our sleighs and drove at a fast pace over the ice-covered surface of the Vychegda river. The hard snow crackled and squeaked under the runners. The bright sun, reflected in the snowy surface, blinded our eyes. It was four below zero, and the frost bit our faces and stuck in our eye-lashes. After sitting in the office all those days, it was a great pleasure to be out in the open and to breathe the clear, cold, invigorating air. There was not a cloud in the sky.

Zakhariantz was driving the first sleigh himself and was going very fast. Our driver had a hard time keeping up with him. We made a stop at the half-way village Yakovlevskaya. Zakhariantz stopped his horse in front of a pretty, well-built cottage, jumped out of the sleigh, and beckoned us to stop there for a bite.

Inside the cottage its bearded owner welcomed us. The cottage consisted of one large room, which was divided by hangings. Pretty soon the peasant's wife appeared from behind the hangings and brought a boiling samovar, a little black bread, and some cakes with potato stuffing.

"Please excuse us, but we have no tea," said our hostess. "We cannot get it in the cooperative store."

Zakhariantz opened his bag and produced some tea, sugar, two tins of preserves and a piece of butter; the peasant got a bottle of vodka out of his little chest. The Russian village has changed little in this respect. In each cottage you could be sure of finding a bottle of the national invigorator hidden away for "emergencies."

Ikons were hanging in the main corner of the room, as of old, but under them were hung pictures of the Red leaders, Marx, Lenin, Stalin and Voroshilov. Next to them were prints of the Russo-Japanese War showing little yellow Japs running away from the Cossacks. Then came an old photograph of our host in a soldier's uniform and some more faded color prints of the World War. Brighter prints portrayed the more recent events of the revolution and civil war. In a central position hung the familiar reproduction of the painting showing Emperor Alexander II, liberator of the serfs, surrounded by his grateful people.

Our host sat on a bench near the table and took part in the conversation. His wife stood at the center curtain in a typical peasant posture with chin in hand and stomach sticking out. Her five-year-old boy, pale and sickly, in tremendous felt boots, clung to her skirts. The elder children had climbed onto the sleeping-shelves and were examining us with curiosity.

In another half-hour we were again under way. The horses were rested and easily climbed up the steep bank of the river. We continued through the forest at the same fast pace as before. All around us were dark fir trees covered with dazzling white snow. The pines lifted their graceful heads high above the firs. In the snow were some impressions made by skis, and rabbit tracks.

We passed an old cemetery and a remarkable view opened up before us. In definite relief the outlines of the cupolas and steeples of the famous Solvychegodsk churches stood out against the bright sky. Especially beautiful were the Stroganov cathedrals built in the sixteenth and seventeenth centuries.

As we drove through the city streets I admired the fine old residences of former merchants, built of stone and well preserved. In comparison with the little gray wooden buildings of Kotlas, this town looked like a real metropolis.

One of the old residences housed the executive offices of the Uftug timber-works. We were met by the assistant to the manager, prisoner Zvegintsev, a tall, good-looking man with well-bred manners and a pleasant voice.

In the office I found several of my old Moscow prison companions, who were employed there and had a tolerable existence.

"We are all right," they said, "life is quite bearable. But wait till you see the conditions in the forest!"

I asked about Timofeyich, my old cell-mate from the Lefortovsky prison, but there were no records of him.

"He must be somewhere in the forest," I was told by the clerk in charge of assignments. "You know, everything is in great disorder here. They keep transferring prisoners from one outpost to another at random. How can we keep records of them all?"

He had a somewhat original system of keeping records and did not believe in overburdening himself with work.

The man in charge of supplies immediately jumped on me: "It is a shame the way you treat us! I am torn to pieces by all our outposts needing supplies and all you do is write us pretty letters and promise to do something tomorrow!"

I advised him to make his complaints to Bukhaltzev, as my being on the commission was purely accidental and I could not help him in any way.

"Complain to Bukhaltzev!" he exclaimed with a despairing gesture. "But it is absolutely useless. Our men are actually starving and Bukhaltzev stays in Kotlas and gets drunk every day."

In another hour we were again on our way. It was getting dark. After sunset it had grown colder and we felt the frost sharply on our faces. That night we had to make another fifty kilometers over a forest road. The doctor and I were not armed; an armed guard accompanied Zakhariantz in his sleigh. Our coachman was a little scared. "There are wolves around here," he said. "I hope they leave us alone."

The doctor and I entrusted our fate to the will of the Lord, wrapped ourselves up in our high collars, and dozed off, lulled by the even pull of the sled and the monotonous swish of crumpling snow beneath the runners. It was comfortable. The high back of the sleigh held us up in position and we awoke only from sudden bumps or on sharp turns. It was curious how circumstances shaped themselves. Quite recently I was marking time and jumping about in the snow to the humiliating orders of Grigoriantz at the Kotlas Transfer Station. Now, a few weeks later, I was a member of an inspection committee of the penal servitude system!

About two o'clock we reached a little village, aroused the owners of a cottage, and had tea there. We gave the horses a rest of two hours and then proceeded onward, without sleep.

Again sitting in the sleigh, the doctor related to me the hushed-up affair of Labsdin, former commander of the Novikov timber-base.

This Labsdin was convicted of the rape of a thirteen-year-old girl and was sent to the penal camps. As he had had some experience in forestry, he soon made a way for himself and was appointed commander of a base, where he was in charge of a thousand men and forty women prisoners. All the women who were half-way good-looking passed through his hands before getting their jobs assigned to them. It was a sort of a quarantine station. But there was one girl, a young country school-teacher from the Ukraine, who resisted him. Neither promises nor threats had any effect. She continued rebuffing all his advances in spite of the fact that all the hardest and dirtiest work was heaped upon her.

Once when he was under the influence of liquor, Labsdin, exasperated by his failure and sensuously inflamed, ordered her to make up his rooms. There he seized her and, with the assistance of two convict murderers, who were devoted to him, subjected her to the "torture with a rat in the pot and a red-hot poker," which is described in Mirbeau's "Garden of Tortures." As there was no rat available, a mouse was used, but due to carelessness it burnt to death in the pot and could not fulfill its mission. The torture was therefore continued with the red-hot poker. The school-teacher died in agony.

In spite of Labsdin's efforts to conceal his crime, it was all brought to light and both he and his two helpers were arrested and sent to Solvychegodsk. Orlov, the commander of the Uftug district, wished to avoid a sensational trial and personally shot all three of them. He then advised the higher authorities that they were killed while attempting to escape. The case was hushed up but not entirely and now the camp administration was in the predicament of having to decide whether it should arrest Orlov for illegal action or forget the whole matter. The doctor thought that the latter solution was much more probable.

"Of course, it is an exceptional, pathological case," said the doctor, "but just try to imagine the position of prisoners at these bases. Any Orlov can dispatch you to your forefathers, any Labsdin may subject you to his most fantastic whims, and still, if desired by the authorities, the matter will be hushed up and allowed to die. The OGPU camps are a state within a state, with little Czars at their head. The local district attorney may not interfere even if he wishes to, because the camps are under martial law. The commanders of the remote outposts are real Czars. But who are they, let me ask you? Former chekists, caught by the OGPU in some villainy and sentenced to a term in the camps, where they are appointed commanders. And the prisoners? They are entirely defenseless, handed over into the unbounded power of chekists of the very worst category. They have to obey every order, comply with every whim. They are underfed and work at hard and unaccustomed labor for twelve or fourteen hours a day. If they protest or refuse to work they are 'sent west' or 'liquidated' as they call it, in other words, they are shot. The same report is always sent to the higher authorities, stating that the prisoner attempted escape or resisted arrest. Men are literally worked to death, women are debauched, and it is all done with absolute impunity. Just try to reflect on it a moment and it will drive you to despair."

I thought to myself that the doctor was probably exaggerating a bit, but the fact remained that we were on an inspection trip caused by just such stories.

It was getting a little lighter. The tired horses slowly climbed a hill and from the top of it a fine view opened before our eyes. The wide river looked like a white ribbon against the dark grayish-purple forest background. Lights glimmered in the far distance. The armed guard in the sleigh ahead of us pointed towards them. It was evidently our destination. The horses, sensing the nearness of rest, increased their pace. The sleigh followed easily, gliding down the hill over the crunching snow. Down in the valley it was noticeably colder, the sharp wind stung our cheeks and we had to hide them in our high collars.

Going a little further we saw a dark spot on the road ahead of us. It was a party of some fifty men carrying axes and saws. They were surrounded on all sides by armed guards, holding their rifles ready for action.

We stopped when we came alongside the party. It was a detachment of prisoners from the Pitsky base who were going out to their work in the forest. They got off the road and let us pass and were now standing knee-deep in the snow. Exhausted, dirty, bearded faces with dark frost-bitten spots on noses and ears; torn, inadequate clothing, no gloves or mittens — no wonder there was undisguised hatred in the prisoners' eyes. Several young fellows who looked like petty thieves caught my eye. They had no overcoats and were trying to keep their footing at the edge of the road. One of them wore torn low shoes held together by a string. Naked dirty toes were sticking out of them, blue with cold. The man seemed in dreadful pain and his slanty eyes looked at us with venom.

A red-bearded prisoner, a typical peasant, stepped out of the group and slowly came up to Zakhariantz, blowing on his red, frozen hands, coughing and mumbling.

"What is it? Why can't you work?" asked Zakhariantz.

"I am sick, comrade commander, for Christ's sake let me go, please be charitable. I am all in a fever, I can't work."

A coughing attack interrupted him and he could not continue.

"Get back, get back," shouted the armed guard at him menacingly.

The doctor jumped out of his sleigh, stuck his hand under the man's collar and said something to Zakhariantz.

"Take him along in your sleigh. Let's go!" ordered the head of our commission.

Hurriedly the red-bearded fellow climbed in next to our driver. He was crossing himself and muttering: "Oh, my Lord, oh, my dear Lord!" We started quickly in pursuit of Zakhariantz' sleigh. It was dawning. Feverish eyes looked at us from the sick man's red face.

"Give me your hand," said the doctor. He pulled out his watch and felt his pulse. He shook his head as he let go of the hand. "Pulse 115, temperature not less than 102, evidently a bad case of influenza or pneumonia." He turned to the peasant, "Say, is there any medical attendant at the outpost?"

"Nobody at all, citizen doctor," answered the sick man impetuously. "No doctor, not even a doctor's helper! It is dreadful how many men have died. And still they drive us out. 'Go ahead and work,' they say. Only if you are so ill that you start raving, do they leave you in the barracks. All the others are driven out. But, God forgive, how can I work in the state I'm in? I have no strength and am about to drop." He was very excited and was wiping the perspiration from his forehead with his hand, leaving a dirty mark.

We turned left and came alongside the Pitsky base.

The gates were opened and we drove into the yard. It was surrounded by a high barbed-wire fence and had two watch-turrets. A sentry-box with a soldier on duty stood at the gate. At the right side of the yard were two large barracks, at the left, several detached buildings; in the center, between them, two small one-story houses. All the buildings were newly-built of green timber. Next to the sentry-box was a shed for horses with walls made of firtree branches.

Suddenly the yard became animated. Men were emerging from all the doors, running past us and looking us over. A stout man of medium height, dressed in a short coat, came out of one of the center buildings and walked toward us. He was accompanied by a man in a military great-coat.

Zakhariantz bulged his thick lips and looked at them without budging from his place. His lobster eyes peered from behind his thick glasses with an unfriendly expression. The man in the short coat was not in the least abashed by this attitude and welcomed him in the most cheerful manner. The doctor and I took off our sheepskin coats and joined the group. We introduced ourselves and met Aaronovich, commander of the base, and his assistant Sergeyev, chief of the guards.

Aaronovich was the very embodiment of friendliness. His fat cheeks constantly spread in an artificial smile, his thick lips baring a row of strong yellow teeth.

"Please step in and have a bit of tea, it will warm you up after this long trip. You are welcome to all we have to offer," he invited Zakhariantz obsequiously.

The chief of the guards was not as hard-boiled and could not quite hide his embarrassment.

Zakhariantz remained morose all during tea and questioned Aaronovich as to the conditions at his base. The latter remained unabashed.

"Everything is in excellent order, comrade commander, as I shall presently have the pleasure to report to you. But do have some jam, or would you like to have something more substantial for breakfast? You must be hungry after the long trip."

The tea was served by a pretty young woman prisoner dressed in a padded short jacket, a dark woolen skirt, and new felt boots. She wore a kerchief around her head and several little ringlets of curly blond hair hung over her forehead. Her attractive, full lips were opened in a perky smile. Her manner was rather free and familiar and her eyes revealed a certain masked insolence.

"What are you convicted of?" Zakhariantz asked her.

"I am from Rostov, and they got me in the regular clean-up," she boldly replied. This meant that she was either a prostitute or a thief.

"What do you do now?" continued Zakhariantz.

"Oh, I am now the comrade commander's maid," she replied saucily.

So it appeared that the commander of the base had his own personal pretty maid, who was dressed in new felt boots while the prisoners were driven into the forest with hardly any shoes at all. This was odd. Zakhariantz sipped his tea and scrutinized Aaronovich through his thick glasses.

"Oh, not exactly a maid, but she helps out here now and then," quickly interposed Aaronovich. "Do have some more tea!"

There was an awkward pause.

"I'll tell you what we'll do, comrade Aaronovich," said Zakhariantz, rising from the table. "Let us go right into the office and discuss things. We'll also talk about your personal maid."

Zakhariantz beckoned to Aaronovich and Sergeyev to follow him and we all went to the adjoining building, the office of the base.

The base held over a thousand prisoners. Five hundred of them lived there and the others stayed at the little outposts about five kilometers away. We started our inspection. The local chiefs took the chairman of our commission into Aaronovich's private office. The doctor went to the barracks. I asked for the books.

Due to lack of supplies the prisoners received only half the usual inadequate rations. There was no bathhouse for want of a boiler. The workhorses were fed only hay; there were no oats. There was no warm clothing or underwear in the store-room. There was a shortage of tools. The barracks were not lighted because there was no kerosene. There were no stoves, as the iron had not been sent. The natural conclusion was that the commanders of the base should be making an investigation at our EKO office rather than that we should inquire into their deficiencies. The accounting appeared to be in good order.

The bookkeeper was at first non-communicative but after an hour or so he became more friendly and confiding. He told me that conditions at the base were appalling. In spite of their half-rations men were required to do their full assignments of work and were not allowed to return from the forest until they had finished them. Men were beaten and were thrown into the dungeon at the slightest provocation. The unheated barracks were damp, cold and dirty. The sick slept together with the rest and the mortality was frightful. Several men died daily and were buried naked in a hole in the ground within a hundred yards of the base.

"So it is really all quite true, what we hear about the Pitsky base," I said.

The truth was really much worse than the rumors. In despair the prisoners chopped off their fingers in order to be excused from work. Scurvy was common among the underfed prisoners and still they were driven out to work in spite of their swollen bodies and loose teeth. Another unknown disease was rampant. Prisoners got large black spots on their hands and feet, which would then fester and rot. Work was continued in the coldest weather and many of the prisoners had frostbitten hands and feet, let alone their faces. The prisoners were all filthy and full of vermin. They were in such a state of fatigue that they often dropped and died from exhaustion. Quite a number "folded up" from cold in the forest.

"The worst off are the men in the disciplinary squad," continued the bookkeeper. "Forty of the original two hundred have already died and the rest will follow them soon if no change is made. Yes, we are fulfiling our part of the plan, but at what a cost! At the end of the season we shall figure out the number of logs produced per capita of the dead; then we shall know."

Loud shouting came from the private office. "I'll have you arrested for that!" thundered Zakhariantz. The bookkeeper's face brightened. "Will they really send him away?" he murmured.

From time to time the loud voice of Zakhariantz resounded from the private office followed by the steady low murmur of Aaronovich's replies. Three hours passed.

The doctor returned from his inspection, took off his smock outside the door, and hung it out in the yard to air. He then came into the office.

"Yes, indeed, there is something to report all right," he said, and turning to the bookkeeper, added: "You will all die out here before spring; you have a typhus epidemic in full swing, and you let the healthy, the sick and the dying all sleep together. How can you do that? I am not even mentioning those sick with the flu; they were all driven out to work this morning and I shall inspect them tonight. But my hair stands on end from the horrors I've seen so far. Where is Aaronovich? He should order the sick transferred to another building at once."

The commander acceded to the doctor's demands and decided to clear one of the warehouses and to have the sick taken there. All the prisoners left at the base were mobilized for this work.

Towards evening squads of prisoners began arriving at the base from their work in the forest. Their miserable appearance defied description. They had not eaten all day and were hungry as wolves. The familiar washbasins filled with thin fish soup and porridge were brought into the barracks. One washbasin had to do for ten prisoners.

My work at the base was finished. I had made my "investigation" and had nothing more to do. Therefore I decided to inspect the barracks. But the doctor, whom I met in the yard, stopped me and advised against it.

"Why take an unnecessary risk?" he said. "The lice in the barracks will immediately creep upon you, one bite and you are done for, and typhus is no joke. I simply cannot understand how it is that all of them are not sick yet. Most of the prisoners are barely keeping body and soul together. They sleep beside the sick without undressing, don't wash at all, are underfed and overworked, and still they do not catch it. It is an astounding example of vitality. But I'll guarantee that when spring comes the epidemic will spare no one."

Another squad entered the gates and came toward us. The doctor's white smock attracted attention and we were immediately surrounded. Three young men with pale, haggard faces begged the doctor to do something to help their sick friends in the barracks.

They were young Ukrainians, students of Kiev University, who were accused of being politically unsafe and socially dangerous and had been sentenced to the penal camps. Seven of them had come to the Pitsky base. Two had died, two were sick with typhus and the remaining three were sent out to the forest every day.

The doctor went into the barracks. Just at this time a sleigh drove up to the gates and several half-frozen prisoners literally fell out of it. They were dressed in rags, quite inadequate for work in the bitter cold. Shivering and half congealed, they made their way towards the barracks with difficulty. Especially pathetic was the last prisoner, a little Turcoman with a black beard. Pie crawled on all fours, yelping like a pup. I tried to lift him but he could not stand and continued on his way, weeping and emitting some piteous, unintelligible guttural sounds. The watchman looked at him indifferently and continued to smoke.

I went into the office and, spreading my sheepskin coat on the floor, lay down. The doctor had not come back. About an hour earlier the commander of the base had taken Zakhariantz to his house for dinner. Our meal was brought to us at the office.

"It will end up in a general drinking bout," said the bookkeeper. "They will all get tight, make friends, and everything will be settled. Don't forget that Aaronovich, Sergeyev and your Zakhariantz are all chekists, birds of a feather. They will have a little chat and a good drink, your commission will go back to Kotlas, and we shall all remain here exactly as before. Men will get half-rations, will continue chopping off their fingers, will die, will be beaten and thrown into the dungeon, and finally Aaronovich will receive official thanks for his efficiency and for completing his share of the plan."

The cook came in and whispered something to him.

"There, you see, it is just as I predicted! They are calling for Lizzie. They say the cook does not know how to serve at table."

We waited till the doctor came and then started to eat the fried salt fish and the millet gruel. We heard singing coming from the yard.

"As I told you," said the bookkeeper. "They are already singing. Remember this morning's loud threats of arrest?"

The doctor was silently chewing his food and at the same time writing and rapidly filling in page after page of the pad before him. Though it was late in the day, not more than half of the prisoners had returned from their work in the forest. The doctor wanted to inspect them all that night. The next day he planned to supervise the installation of the sick prisoners in their new quarters and after that he wanted to proceed in the evening to the timber-works division nearest to the base to inspect the seventy prisoners working there. During the week he hoped to inspect all divisions, to transfer the sick prisoners to the base, to turn over the work to the assistant doctor who was to be sent over from Solvychegodsk, and only after that to return to Kotlas.

"Tomorrow I shall not permit half the men to be ordered out to work," the doctor exclaimed. "None of those half-dressed unfortunates will be driven out to work until they get some warm clothes, if I can help it. Today twenty-two of them returned frostbitten. One man in particular is in a dreadful condition — the soles of both his feet are frostbitten, he cannot walk. I am sure that tomorrow I shall have quite a clash with Aaronovich."

The doctor continued to write. His fine, high-strung features were clouded and serious. I stretched out and tried to sleep. The clock on the wall resolutely beat out the seconds, the bookkeeper clattered away on the bones of his abacus, the doctor's pen scratched on. Outside the night was perfectly still. The window-panes were covered with frost in pretty and delicate designs, and inside the room it was warm and cozy. Sleep gradually overcame me.

CHAPTER ELEVEN: THE MANURE OF COMMUNISM

I was awakened by the deep bass voice of Aaronovich. He was talking to the doctor.

"But, doctor," he said, "be reasonable and do not exaggerate. You cannot call these men sick; the majority of them are just slackers, trying to be let off from work. You simply cannot treat them humanely. If you pay attention to every complaint you will find that pretty soon none of them will work at all. And I am required to fulfill a definite program. Judge for yourself, what else can I do? Come, let us better drown our sorrows and have a drink."

The doctor refused.

"As you like, doctor," Aaronovich continued. "But you are making a mistake by even giving them hope. Tomorrow I shall send them all out to work again, just the same. I am looking after number one first."

The tone of his voice was sharp and confident. There was no trace of the affable geniality he had shown that morning.

The doctor lost his temper. "Look here, Aaronovich," he said, "you are the commander of the base and you are responsible for the condition of the prisoners. One does not have to be a doctor in order to see that the majority of your prisoners are sick. The thing you are doing here is a crime. The penal camp regulations do not allow you to send sick men to work. I shall not permit it. Perhaps you do not understand the situation. Please realize that you are now in the very thick of a typhus epidemic. If you do not take precautionary measures at once, all the prisoners will be sick by next spring. Can you understand it now?"

"This is all quite clear, my dear doctor," answered Aaronovich with a growing insolence in his voice, "but you forget the instructions of Commander Boksha: 'to fulfil the plan, no matter at what cost.' And I shall fulfil it. Tomorrow all those will go out to work whom I shall order to do so, and we are not going to consult you about it at all."

He slammed the door and left the room.

The doctor jumped up excitedly and started pacing the room and heaping abuse on Aaronovich. I was sleepy, but he sought my advice and could not calm down. Our conversation was interrupted by Zakhariantz, who came in from the outside, rubbing the frost from his glasses and squinting in the bright light of the room. He stepped up to the table.

"What is this I hear, doctor, about your little tiff with Aaronovich. This isn't right. He is a very valuable worker, strict but efficient. His work is progressing in very good shape..."

"At the expense of the dead," interjected the doctor.

"Oh, you see, that is not so important," continued Zakhariantz in the kindly tone of a man who has had too much to drink. "We do not build the revolution with kid gloves. There must be sacrifices and if so, rather let the enemies of the revolution be sacrificed. The export plan must be completed and it will be completed even if it costs the lives of thousands. Have you really not yet come to understand that we are not afraid of the dead? For us the herd of humanity is but the manure for fertilizing the fields of socialism."

Like all chekists, Zakhariantz liked to use high-sounding phrases. He started his speech in a kindly tone of voice but ended it with loud gusto.

"You had better not quarrel with us, doctor," he resumed. "You know our slogan — 'he who is not with us is against us.' What is your term, for instance? Three years? There, you see how it is. A three years' sentence should be understood as a sort of admonition. If you do not reform, we shall add another five, and after that we might give you some three years of exile. Be level-headed and consider whether it pays to quarrel with us."

Snickering and rubbing his hands, he looked at the doctor and then at me. His manner of thinking and his cynicism were exactly the same as that of all his counterparts in the OGPU. He meaningly pulled in his lips, got up and walked out of the room with an unsteady gait. The doctor remained quiet for a while, thinking and holding his head in his hands.

"No, I shall not be a party to such baseness," he said at last. "What a scoundrel! You don't know this man. Have you ever heard the story of the prisoner Tretiskova? This Zakhariantz forced her to sleep with him and she was infected by him. I am now giving her treatment in Kotlas. It is such a pity. She is quite young and an irresponsible sort. She told me all about it and he probably suspects it. Well, there was a certain engineer N. at the Transfer Station, a very decent young man who had known her in Moscow before her arrest. She told him the whole story and he persuaded her to come to me for treatment. Then he wrote to Monakhov, the commander of the Transfer Station and sent him a complaint against Zakhariantz. Now the unfortunate N. is kept under lock and key on a charge of 'wrecking,' and a new sentence awaits him. That's what comes from interfering with the cheka. All for one and one for all. And still, in spite of it all, I shall have to quarrel with them."

The bookkeeper came in. "Another squad has just returned," he said to the doctor. "If you want to inspect them, go right now, before they go to sleep."

It was half past twelve. The bookkeeper lowered the light of the kerosene lamp and stretched out on his bunk near the stove without undressing. Then, in a low and pleasant tenor voice, he started to hum the aria of Lensky from the opera Evgeniy Onegin. When he came to the phrase "I learned that life is not a romance" he stopped, repeated it once again and then remained silent. Curses and angry ejaculations came from outside. Gradually the noise calmed down. The indefinite outline of the moon could be dimly seen on the frosted window-pane. I finished my last cigarette, rolled my coat close around me, and fell asleep.

The annoying monotonous tolling of a bell aroused me early the next morning. The doctor got up from the floor with an effort. He was tired and his eyes were swollen.

We went out into the dark yard and rubbed our hands and faces with snow. Even the office staff had no place to wash. The protracted ringing of a bell signaled the prisoners to come out into the yard after their tea.

The doctor put on his smock with a resolute air. He had evidently decided to give battle to the enemy, though he fully realized the risk.

It was just beginning to dawn. The prisoners were already forming in squares. The disciplinary squad stood in full formation, surrounded by armed guards. Prisoners came from all sides and joined the other square. Young fellows in rags were being thrown out of the barracks nearest to us; they were yelling and cursing. From the open door of the barracks came bawling and weeping. Somebody was begging to be left behind just for one single day and crying for the doctor. Nearby was a heap of saws and axes. The women stood in a separate group. Everybody waited for the commanders.

Aaronovich appeared at his door-step, buttoning his fur jacket. He was followed by the chief of the guards Sergeyev and by the timekeeper of the base. Aaronovich walked to the center of the yard and cried: "Prisoners of the Pitsky Base, greetings!"

"Zdrah," came the reply.

The doctor stepped up to Aaronovich and handed him a list of names of the sick. He demanded in a firm voice that the men included in his list should not be sent out to work.

Aaronovich waved him aside. "What are you talking about, doctor? They are not sick, they are slackers. The timekeeper inspected all those who reported that they are ill. I shall leave behind five of them, but all the rest must go."

He took the lists of prisoners from the timekeeper and commanded:

"Prisoners of the disciplinary squad, march to the seventh kilometer. Attention. Go!"

The head of the column started to go.

"Stop!" cried the doctor. "In accordance with the penal camp regulations I demand that the following prisoners be excused from duty," and he started calling out the names from his list.

Sergeyev stepped in. "Disciplinary squad, go!" he shouted. There was hesitancy in the ranks. "Squad commander, what's the delay?" he continued.

The squad commander pulled out his gun: "Column, attention, go!" he commanded.

Followed by the murmuring of the prisoners of the other square the disciplinary squad marched past us in double file. At the head of the column marched a monk in his long cassock with a rope around the waist. There were many faces of educated men among these unfortunates. Some of the prisoners greeted the doctor as they passed by and exclaimed "Bravo, doctor." Others just shrugged their shoulders as they looked at him, as much as to say that one good man cannot conquer an army of bandits. Two priests walked at the end of the column. Some of the prisoners had swollen faces, others looked gray and haggard with hollow eyes and sharpened features. They wore every kind of clothing, but very few of them had warm overcoats or felt boots. Most of them were dressed in light overcoats and low shoes, and the feet of some were wrapped with rags held together by strings. Almost none of them had mittens. They walked by us in gruesome procession, their axes and saws glimmering in the semi-darkness of the early winter morning.

Aaronovich began calling out names of the next list. Men stepped out of the square and formed in double file. Among those called was a pitiable-looking peasant in his middle fifties who could hardly stand up, and two young half-dressed petty gangsters shivering in the cold.

"Comrade Aaronovich," said the doctor, pointing them out, "I cannot permit that these three prisoners go out."

"It cannot be done, doctor, they are just soldiering. I know them. They will get well in the forest. Go, hurry up, you three," Aaronovich bawled at the prisoners, handing the list to the foreman. Twenty men with a foreman and two armed guards marched out of the gates.

The call of names continued. Before the departure of each detachment the doctor vainly protested, but nobody paid any attention to him. Finally only some forty men and women were left.

"The rest of you," commanded Aaronovich, "go to the third kilometer. All women are to do housework, you divide the jobs yourself," he directed the timekeeper.

There was a commotion in the remaining group. The prisoners were all huddled together and were bending over someone. We came up to them. Lying on the snow in an unnatural position was a man of about forty dressed in a short jacket. His dirty knee stuck out sharply through a big hole in his trousers. The unhealthy skin of his worn face contrasted unpleasantly with the pure, white snow. Saliva trickled down his thin whiskers. His lips were blue, his eyeballs were rolled back in agony.

"What's the matter here, another fit?" asked Aaronovich, stepping up closer.

The doctor got down on his knee, lifted the man's eyelid, quickly bared his chest and listened to the heartbeat. We waited in tense silence.

"It is all over, he is dead," said the doctor. "This is the kind of people you send to the forest!"

"This is not the first time a man died," frantically exclaimed one of the Kiev students, shaking his fists. "Scoundrels, cads, bandits that they are, they will kill us all! We are all doomed to die here, all of us..."

"Into the dungeon with him," roared Aaronovich, shouting him down. "I'll show you what it means to start a riot."

Several guards rushed for the student. Zakhariantz came running up to our group. "What's going on here?" he exclaimed.

"Comrade Zakhariantz," the doctor appealed, "I insist that all the prisoners mentioned in this list be returned from work at once. They are sick and were sent into the forest in spite of it. Here's an example for you, a man just died here, at the base, during the roll-call..."

"Don't butt into other people's business, doctor," cried Zakhariantz. "You were sent here to inspect and not to give orders. In the name of the commander of the camps, I order you to go to the office at once. Another word and I'll arrest you."

In exasperation the doctor pulled off his smock and quickly walked towards the office. Several guards lifted the dead body. The last column of prisoners left the yard. The women scattered to their various jobs.

"Let us go in and sign the report," Zakhariantz said to me. We went into the office. The doctor sat at the window, leaning against a desk. His face had a petrified expression and he was gazing into space, not noticing anybody.

"If you please, doctor," said Zakhariantz, pulling out a sheet of paper and starting to read it. The drunken orgy of the night before had left its mark. His voice was hoarse, his eyes dull and his skin flabby: they all testified to the amount of alcohol consumed. The report described the excellent fulfillment of the plan by the Pitsky base, the satisfactory condition of the prisoners, gave reasons for the temporary increase of illness, reported a normal percentage of mortality, praised the condition of the horses, and gave credit for all this excellent record to the commander of the base, Aaronovich, and to his faithful assistant Sergeyev, commander of the armed guards.

"Sign this, doctor," said Zakhariantz.

"No, I shall not sign this report," calmly replied the doctor. "I shall write myself to the head of the sanitation department of the camp administration, and describe the deplorable condition of the prisoners at the base. I am entrusted with an inspection of the base and of the outposts, and I shall finish my job. Good-bye."

Not waiting for any reply the doctor went out of the office. Zakhariantz looked after him and frowned, then shrugged his shoulders, smiled and, mumbling something to himself, turned to me.

"You will sign here," he said.

I refused. No; I would not sign this report, I said. I did not examine the sick, I did not take part in the investigation of the fulfillment of the plan, all of this is outside of my jurisdiction, therefore I could not sign the report. I had no right to do it. I have made a report on the condition of accounts, here it is, and here is the copy of it. It can be attached to the general report.

My refusal was unexpected. Not one of the members of our commission wished to sign the report. It was an unpleasant situation, to say the least.

"Look here," said Zakhariantz pointedly. "I advise you to sign the report. You were present last night when I talked with the doctor. Well then, please note that all I said then also refers to you. You may sign with reservations, but sign you must."

I knew their methods of coercion and thought of all the cross-examinations I had gone through at the Shpalernaya prison. He was not a bit different from those other inquisitors. They had probably all been taught at the same OGPU school. I reiterated my refusal to sign.

"Very well, then. We shall leave here in fifteen minutes. Please get ready," said Zakhariantz sourly.

In half an hour our horse was ready for us. Aaronovich saw us off to the sleigh and was telling Zakhariantz a funny story and slapping him on the back. They both laughed and looked at each other with cordial understanding. They had already become bosom friends. Sergeyev saluted us, the sentry covered up our feet, and we started off.

Two hours passed in silence, interrupted only by our driver's outcries and yapping, and now and then by the clang of horseshoes. The sleigh glided along lightly over the crunching snow. The dark snow-covered firs and graceful pines reminded me of our jolly picnics in Finland, with a gay crowd, tasty luncheon, and lively little Swedish horses. How long ago it all seemed! And what a contrast now, returning to the penal camp, a prisoner convicted of violating the fifty-ninth regulation of the criminal code, travelling in the company of a vulgar blackguard who was gradually sobering up and whose long, red nose was sticking out of the high overcoat collar and emitting a hissing noise.

I could not understand the purpose of our investigation. If it was intended to obtain the signatures of two prisoners to a mock report, they had made a bad choice. It was easy to find any number of accommodating prisoners without leaving the Transfer Station. The administration was well informed through the report of Dr. Movsh of the actual state of affairs at the Pitsky base. So what was the need of an "investigation"? I pondered on this problem without finding an answer. At that time I did not know that Dr. Movsh's report had never reached the administration and that the commission was appointed in compliance with a demand from Moscow where a few finicky communists had shown an undue interest in conditions prevailing at the penal camps of the OGPU.

"You are sentenced to four years, are you not?" suddenly inquired Zakhariantz. I confirmed this.

"There, you see how imprudent you are. You are barely through with half your term and already you do not hesitate to make enemies. Your affair with Ulanovsky, for instance, what good did it do you? You should make every effort to finish your term as soon as possible, even to have it shortened, and get back home. Instead of throwing monkey-wrenches into our machinery, you ought to cultivate friendship with us chekists. Otherwise you will gain nothing except a longer term. Take the doctor, for example. After today's incident we shall surely send him somewhere to the farthest corners of the North, to Ukhta, or still farther, and let him play cricket there with the polar bears. But why should you do such a thing? Why play with fire? Haven't you enough of four years? Why don't you wish to sign the report?"

I understood what he was driving at. He continued after a short pause:

"Isn't it immaterial to you how many people fold up as long as you remain well yourself? There is no room for sentimentality here. This is no democracy. It is the OGPU penal camp. If you do not sit on others, you will be sat on and crushed, and will fold up like a worm. Does it pay? Consider it a bit: is it better to work in the EKO office or in the forest? And you are exposing yourself to the risk of being transferred to the Pitsky base or to another camp fully as vile as that. Will you never understand that we are not to be trifled with? Use your brains a little before it is too late. You seem to have a good head on your shoulders; it was surely not put there merely to wear a hat."

After this long oration, he pulled out a bottle of diluted alcohol from his brief-case, took a gulp and followed it up with a handful of snow. Evidently the hangover from last night was still with him. Like a true drunkard, he tried to get rid of it in suitable company.

"Here, take it," he said, passing the bottle. "Have a drink with me."

"With pleasure," I said, surreptitiously rinsing the throat of the bottle with alcohol and taking a couple of swallows. The solution was very strong and burned the palate.

"Don't be backward, we'll get some more of it," said Zakhariantz, happy to have found a boon companion.

He was content, the ice was broken and opened the way to closer relationship. He lifted the bottle to his mouth again and again and followed it up with chunks of snow which he picked up from the road. A typical drunkard. Soon he was thoroughly intoxicated and his manner became familiar.

"It is too bad that you did not have supper with us last night," he said. "This Aaronovich is a capital fellow and his Lizzie is a ducky. You could have had a bit of it too. Jealousy is a silly bourgeois fad. We communists have no such prejudices. Take Aaronovich, for instance: He shared with me what he had like a good comrade. One of your kind would have made a terrible row about a woman. And what is there to a woman? Is she worth fighting about? There is no difference between them, whether they are bourgeois or communist, they have just one thing to offer. Say, are you married?" he asked the coachman, nudging him in the back.

"Yes, citizen commander," answered the driver.

"Well, I suppose that your wife has another fellow around when you're away, hasn't she?" The cad winked at me as he spoke, for now he thought that I was in full sympathy with him.

"I don't know, citizen commander," said the driver with a slight tremor in his voice. He raised his whip and hit the horse with all his might. "Get up, you lazy hag!" he muttered.

"It hit the mark all right," whispered Zakhariantz into my ear and roared with laughter.

We again stopped at our mid-way peasant cottage. Zakhariantz had finished his alcohol and asked for vodka, but neither our host nor the neighbors had any. Perhaps they were afraid of being framed by the OGPU official and did not dare produce it from their hiding-places. His desires thwarted, my drunken companion angrily laid himself down on a bench and in another minute was snoring lustily.

Zakhariantz was a chekist of the standard type. He was half-educated, having gathered most of his knowledge from practical experience in the employ of the OGPU. His reasoning ran strictly along Bolshevist lines. He was cynical but stupid, and was dangerous chiefly because of his unprincipled villainy and his utter lack of moral restraint. He was probably about thirty-five years old. His coarse features indicated a low origin. A drunkard and a libertine, he was cunningly making his career along the line of least resistance, in the service of the OGPU. There are hundreds of OGPU henchmen just like him. They are all made of the same material, speak the same stupidly stereotyped language, and their souls are as dirty as their unwashed hands.

Two hours later our coachman came in to report that the horse had rested sufficiently and that we could continue our journey. The alcohol still affected my companion; he was morose and uncommunicative. We did not talk any more and he slept most of the way to Solvychegodsk.

This time we were met by Orlov himself, the commander of the Uftug timber-works. He was a stocky man about forty years old with a hard, pale face and a black Charlie Chaplin moustache. He was great friends with Zakhariantz, treated him with coarse familiarity, and immediately took him into his house to have dinner. On parting with me, Zakhariantz said that we would have another little talk later on and that in the morning we would start back for Kotlas.

Early next morning I went out to take a look at the historic churches, which were really of rare beauty. When I came back I was told that Zakhariantz and Orlov were having breakfast and did not wish to be disturbed. This suited me splendidly. I telephoned to Kotlas and was instructed to return at once. My typewriter had been repaired and was waiting for me.

Upon arrival I handed my report to Bukhaltzev, who shoved it into his desk without reading, and said:

"Thanks. I know all about it. And now will you please get back to work and do something useful."

And in a few minutes I was again drumming on my typewriter.

Life went on as before. The prisoner-clerks worked from morning till night; the bosses got drunk; the local peasants were intimidated into teamster duty; the prisoner forest-workers suffered terrible privations, fell sick and died. Upon my return, I learned of the death of the seminarist Seryozha, whom Monakhov had ordered to stand naked in the cold.

The Transfer Station also remained unchanged. New arrivals came in, were drilled, taught submission, and sent to the forest to take the place of those who had "gone west."

The warehouses were busy with the delivery of garlic to the various districts. It had been sent from Moscow on the theory that it would quickly stop the ravages of scurvy and would bring back to the ranks the many incapacitated forest-workers. My friend Dr. S., who had returned to the Transfer Station, made fun of this panacea and was in disfavor with Monakhov, his former protector. He was now expecting from day to day to be deported in accordance with the vengeful threats of Zakhariantz.

About two weeks after my return from the inspection trip the storm broke over my head. It was not quite unexpected, for I remembered Zakhariantz' hints and threats with reference to my not signing the report. Still I had hoped that he might have forgotten about it under the influence of liquor. Unfortunately this was not the case.

The first stroke was an order from the secret intelligence department forbidding me to correspond with my wife, who was living abroad.

This did not particularly affect me, as I was already sending and receiving letters with the aid of my town friends, thus avoiding the censor. Then came a special order, forbidding me alone of all the clerks ever to leave the office or to walk about the town. In another week this order was followed by another, instructing that I be transferred to the barracks from where I should daily walk to the office under guard. It was quite evident now that Zakhariantz had not forgotten me. Bukhaltzev refused to comply with the last request and in another week it was followed by a specific secret command for me to report at the Transfer Station in twenty-four hours.

All my plans for escape crumbled. I was faced with entirely different prospects: the horrible food of the Transfer Station, sleep on the barrack floor, hard labor in the forest. It all came when my arrangements for escape had been completed, and I was only waiting for the necessary money. But I had no choice.

There were few changes at the Transfer Station. The barracks and tents were as overcrowded as before, only instead of gangsters they housed Turcoman and Usbek beys deported from Turkestan and Bokhara.

These Mohammedans were mostly dignified, bearded men, with calm proud faces, dressed in long padded robes of bright striped silk. They suffered dreadfully from the unaccustomed climate. At that particular time it had grown especially cold. The temperature varied between thirty-one and fifty-seven below zero.

They were pitiful to look at when they ran across the yard holding their little flasks with cleansing liquid ordained by the Koran, or to see them in the evening when they came back from work, blue and congealed. Every day some of the "Turks," as they were called, were taken to the hospital. They could not stand the cold and came down with pleurisy and pneumonia. Those few who recovered at the hospital were sent back to work in the forest and sooner or later "folded up." Later, when I was working in the central office of the camp administration, I saw the statistics of the sanitation department. They showed that seventy-six percent of the "Turks" had perished. This figure was reported to Moscow and after 1930 no more Turcomans were sent to the North; this had proved inexpedient.

The "Turks" did not understand Russian and were utterly bewildered by the shouting of the raging squad commanders. They did not implicitly obey the hateful outcries of the guards such as "Get going!" or "Like a flash!" and the guards then used their clubs.

Some of them took the beating with philosophic submission, others roared like lions and attacked the guards with clenched fists. The latter were undressed and drenched with water, and then forced to stand out in the cold, as decreed by Monakhov.

Several days after my return to the Transfer Station the life of the "Turks" changed for the better, thanks to Prince Karamanov from the Crimea, a fresh arrival in their midst. He was tall and handsome, with a huge aquiline nose and a pointed grayish beard. He possessed great suavity of manner and, speaking both languages, arranged to have all orders to the "Turks" given through him. Thus he became their leader and saved them many painful misunderstandings with the Russian commanders.

The last case of "torture by freezing" which I witnessed had for its victim a young gangster, Borisov, who was caught exacting bribes of ten kopecks for each tea-pot of boiling water which he was entrusted to dispense. The cunning lad stood there several minutes and then fell down in a faked swoon. He was kicked and hit with butts of rifles, but was consistent and showed no signs of life. They picked him up and carried him to the doctor, who poured some alcohol down his throat.

He survived and a week later was up and about. He became my "caddy" and carried my belongings during our march to Ust-Sysolsk, where I was next ordered to proceed.

One of my friends from the Lefortovsky prison had become head-accountant at the Transfer Station. Thanks to his intervention I was spared hard labor and was transferred to his office. In order to accomplish this he had devised a very urgent job which had to be completed and sent to Moscow without delay, and I was the only prisoner who could be entrusted with it. Like a clever fellow, he had this job all completed and in readiness for some time, but was holding it for emergencies. Under this pretext he and I spent two weeks in comparative idleness. My friend also procured for me a place on the sleeping-shelves in the office workers' barracks, by declaring that my work was so difficult that it required a well-rested mental condition and therefore a chance to sleep well at night. In this manner I was protected by Monakhov's special orders from the persecutions of Zakhariantz.

Poor Dr. S. fared differently. As soon as Zakhariantz heard that there was another physician among the newly-arrived prisoners, he had Dr. S.

relieved from duty, in spite of the acute need of medical help at the camps. Dr. S. was placed among the common prisoners in the awful third squadron and was included in the list of those to be deported to Ukhta. This meant a march of about six hundred and fifty kilometers in February, when it is particularly cold in the North country. The doctor had no warm overcoat, but Prince Karamanov, who was devoted to him, procured for him a padded silk robe from one of his countrymen. The stripes in the silk were particularly bright and the doctor looked magnificent as he started out on his march dressed in the long exotic robe, high boots and a felt hat.

A year later I met the doctor again at Ukhta and he told me how all during the march he was the object of curiosity and admiration in all the villages they passed. The peasant women ran out to see the "Turk," pitied him and shoved potato-cakes into his hands.

I remained at the Transfer Station for two weeks. Then I was included in the list of prisoners detached for railway construction duty at a distant point. Our detachment contained two hundred and ninety-five prisoners and we were to march to our destination escorted by fifteen armed guards.

CHAPTER TWELVE : THE MARCH OF THE DAMNED

We were driven out into the yard in the early morning and kept there in formation until two P. M., in preparation for a march to Work Post No. 6. We were chilled to the bone. The criminals cursed and ran into the barracks to get warm whenever the guards relaxed their vigilance. About eight roll-calls were made. Each time one or more were missing and the camp militia had to go and find them. In warmer climes the disorderliness of the procedure might have been quite amusing, but here the cold and wind killed the last remnants of our sense of humor. The fine falling snow was slowly covering us.

Dr. I., a Leningrad dentist, who had just arrived at the Transfer Station and did not know its methods, stood there in his fur coat and kangaroo cap, and gazed in amazement at the jumble before him.

More than half the departing prisoners had no winter clothes. Lyskin, the manager of the commissariat department, came up to us on several occasions and was each time besieged by requests for warm clothing. He pacified us with the promise that "everything will be given you at Penug. Calm down, you will not freeze in the car."

Fortunately more teamsters were driving their empty sleighs back to town and we were allowed to put our belongings in them. But even here the lack of confidence in the OGPU showed itself. Many of the prisoners preferred to carry their belongings themselves.

We quickly covered the five kilometers to town. The freezing prisoners walked at a brisk pace in order to warm up. At the station a special train with regular third-class carriages was already waiting for us. The train was to bring us to the Penug station, where the new railway line began. We were to stop over there for the night and then start out on our march the next morning, walking partly on the track and partly across country, a total of three hundred and fifty kilometers. Our destination was the newly-opened sixth penal camp district, the so-called "thirty-fifth kilometer."

It was close in the train, but not excessively so. My "caddy" brought in my baggage and helped the panting dentist with his too numerous things. Then he miraculously procured a tea-kettle of boiling water, prepared tea, and made ready to share our supper.

During the next twelve days I continually marveled at his extraordinary appetite, but this time I was perfectly stunned by his capacity. Bread, cheese, sausage and preserves, all disappeared with incredible speed. The inexperienced dentist had hospitably emptied his food basket on our improvised table and was viewing his melting supplies first with alarm and then with horror. I had to step in and put an end to the gluttony.

In the penal camps men become avaricious not because they are unwilling to share their food with their hungry companions, but for the simple reason that supplies cannot be replenished at any cost.

It got dark toward the end of our supper. The little bit of the monotonous Northern landscape which could be seen through our dirty window, now disappeared. The train proceeded slowly, making some fifteen kilometers per hour and stopping occasionally. It was dark in our carriage: the candles, which were supposed to be included in the equipment, had been duly stolen either by the conductor or by one of our light-fingered gentry. The doctor had a remnant of a candle and it shed a flickering dim light over our corner, once more bearing testimony to the poor quality of Soviet state products. On the wall was the grotesque dancing shadow of air-pilot Simanko's long nose. The stuffy air was filled with smoke and made us sleepy.

At midnight we arrived at Penug. Numerous guards, armed with rifles and lanterns, immediately conducted us to the barracks which had formerly served as a locomotive-shed. As we filed across the track we resembled a fancy torch-pageant. At the barracks we were installed on three-tier sleeping-shelves. The manager of supplies, who was supposed to have received instructions from Kotlas to furnish us warm clothing, was nowhere to be found. His benevolent assistant assured us with perfect composure that warm clothing would be distributed in the morning.

At seven A. M. we stood on the track, ready to start. The benevolent assistant of the night before cursed and fulminated:

"Warm clothing? For what unearthly use? You are going to walk and not ride."

He was partly right. Before starting from Kotlas I had declined the kind offer of my friend the bookkeeper, who wanted to give me some felt boots and a padded jacket. I decided that it was better to march dressed in light clothes, so I wore my light overcoat, golf knickers, warm Scotch stockings, and comfortable low brown shoes with rubber soles. My face and head, which were the most vulnerable spot, were protected by my warm beaver cap.

The majority of the prisoners, however, thought differently, and demanded warm clothing, saying that they had been promised some by Lyskin. The criminal convicts were especially boisterous, as they wanted some surplus clothes with which they could gamble at cards. Incongruous as it seemed in the penal camp atmosphere, some of them actually shouted defiantly that they would not go. Finally, in order to mollify the ringleaders, six pairs of worn felt boots and two jackets were given to the whole crowd. The local commander of the guards, a sturdy blond fellow, stopped the rioting convicts by a loud command in the style so well remembered by all of us from Kotlas:

"Silence! You will get nothing more! Understand?"

This familiar outcry had the desired effect. The noise quieted down. The dentist was no longer in our midst. He had been held for professional work at Penug. The poor man had told me that he could not forgive himself for his frankness at the cross-examination, which eventually led to a ten-year sentence. He artlessly told the examining chekist that he corresponded with his son who lived in Poland, and that the Polish consul, who was his patient, forwarded the letters. This artless avowal was the only reason for his conviction. He had not thought that he was doing anything wrong in corresponding through channels other than the mail, but to the OGPU it was a grave crime. A kindly simpleton, this dentist. Twelve years surrounded by evidences of the chekist regime had not taught him anything.

It was nearly ten o'clock, but we were still standing there, waiting for we knew not what. That day we were supposed to march fifty kilometers, twenty of which were on the railroad track and the other thirty by forest trails in the direction of the nearest village. The weather was favorable; it was a bright, sunny day without wind.

The chief of convoy was a little red-faced man who walked around our column with a worried look on his face. He told us that we would get nothing to eat until we arrived at the village at the end of our day's march. This was not very encouraging, but on the other hand it was pleasant to be out in the open instead of being confined at the Transfer Station. Orlov, a giant cossack who was to act as medical attendant to our column, wore his white smock. It was said that during the civil war he killed his own son who was fighting on the side of the Reds. He was an indefatigable counter-revolutionary and as such had been convicted to ten years in the penal camps. There were not over thirty educated men in our column. Half of the rest were peasants, and half criminals. The big thugs and gangster leaders kept in a group by themselves; their leader was a good-looking, light-haired, dandyish young man. Particularly picturesque was the group of some twenty Turcomans, whose bright-striped silk robes contrasted gaily with the gray clothing of the others.

Among the educated group were the Red Army flyer Simanko, two young officers of the Denikin army, the railroad engineer Chernayev, the Moscow broker Orlov, a Soviet district attorney, the cashier of a bank, three bookkeepers, a monk, an agricultural expert, a communist embezzler, the former landowner Vadim Korolkov, a custom-house official, the electrical engineer Tselikov, the professor of railroad engineering Yanushevsky, the Estonian sea captain Brandt, the Moscow business-man Blumberg, the travelling salesman Levin, the young draughtsman Petrov, who had strangled his bride, the Sebastopol artist Ertel, and an Ukrainian nationalist, who oddly enough bore the typical Russian name of Ivan Ivanovich.

Behind the column marched the medical attendant Orlov, the convoy-chief and his five soldiers who guarded the sleigh containing a ten-day supply of food for the column. My omniscient caddy informed me that it contained sugar, tea, frozen meat, salt fish and buckwheat. Bread and potatoes we were expected to obtain en route from the local cooperative stores. The convoy-soldiers were well armed. They carried heavy, clubs in addition to their rifles. Our belongings had been sent on by sleds on a roundabout route. We carried our own hand baggage.

All went well for the first twenty kilometers of march along the railroad track. It was in the process of construction and contained a surprisingly large number of trestles. We passed several posts of penal camps with their barbed-wire enclosures and watch-turrets manned by sentries. All posts were built on the same lines and were identical with the Pitsky base which I had recently inspected.

We made good headway and reached the last camp on the railroad track at two in the afternoon. We still had thirty kilometers ahead of us. The weather remained favorable, the sun was shining, and we did not feel the cold. The last post furnished us a guide who was supposed to lead us along the forest trails for the first ten kilometers and give us our general direction from that point on. We took advantage of the stop at the last post to have a bite to eat of whatever food we carried with us, and, after a little rest, we started again on our march. We now had to walk along a trail in single file and our line stretched out in a long ribbon. It was much more difficult to walk along the snow-covered path and our pace slackened perceptibly. Those at the head of the line had a hard task trampling down the loose snow. It was not so bad walking in the middle of the line, after the snow had been packed by the many pairs of feet ahead. Nevertheless in places the snow was still soft and one's feet sank into it ankle-deep. The fat Korolkov, who walked ahead of me and who had been keeping us in good humor all the morning, was now quiet, breathing hard and wiping the perspiration from his brow. He had a hard time of it carrying his weight of a hundred kilograms. Besides, he wore large felt boots and two warm hunting jackets under a waterproof coat.

The column began stopping for rest at more frequent intervals. In the first part of our march we had been stopping every five kilometers, but now every kilometer brought the sound of "sto-o-op," echoed back to us from the leaders. This signal halted our march. Some of us immediately sat down in the snow and lit cigarettes, only to feel our fatigue more keenly when we started up again in another two minutes. At four o'clock we emerged from the forest. It was getting dark.

Our guide passed us on his way back to the last camp post. So far we had made thirty kilometers and had twenty still to go. We were told that the trail led through open country along a small river and we could easily find our way. This would have been true enough if any one of us knew the territory, but no one did.

"We shall surely lose our way," prophesied Professor Yanushevsky, a slender white-haired old man with a fine profile and sarcastic eyes. "Have you ever heard of such stupidity, exposing all of us to this risk."

However, we were not consulted. The head of the column started and behind crept the long line of the rest of us. The trail wound in zigzags more or less parallel to the river-bed and the country was far from answering to the optimistic description of "flat and open." When we climbed a hill I was panting and felt my knees trembling — the result of my long stay in prison. I felt that I had lost weight and grown thinner in a day. The old pain in my knee recurred and added to my discomfort. Now the rest periods were even more frequent. After every half-kilometer we would hear the welcome "sto-o-op," repeated by voices all down the line. Sometimes the stop signal came from the rear. At the sound of it men now simply fell down on the snow. I took my rests standing up, knowing well how difficult it is to get up again from a lying or sitting position. Men were stumbling in their march and walked slowly, breathing hard. It was getting much colder and had grown quite dark. The convoy soldiers now carried little lanterns, which accentuated the darkness. We moved on at a pitiful pace; there were more stops than marches. I felt a severe pain in the back, my feet burned when walking and froze under their cover of icy crust when we stopped. My muscles almost refused to obey. Somebody advised eating sugar. It did help a little.

Another prolonged "sto-o-op" came from afar. A rest period. Everybody was down in the snow in a moment, nobody talked, prostration was universal. Five, ten minutes passed, the rest continued. Some inarticulate shouts came from behind. At first nobody paid attention to them, but then they became louder and we heard curses and imprecations such as "get up, you son of a bitch" and the like, accompanied by dull thuds and cries of pain. They had begun to beat the exhausted criminals.

The convoy-chief was as tired as we. With difficulty he made his way over the prostrate bodies, giving each soldier he passed the same order: "If anybody refuses to go, beat the son of a bitch until he gets up."

A signal shot was heard in front and we started up again.

Having heard the chief's orders, the mortally tired men mustered their last bit of strength and walked a little faster. I figured that we had made about forty kilometers and had ten yet to go. Shall we make it? I was eating sugar, munching bread and swallowing chunks of snow. It refreshed me, but not for long. My mouth was dry, breathing came hard, efforts to breathe through the nose were useless. My eyelids kept closing and I moved with the crowd in a semi-swoon, urged on by the sole thought of "when do we rest again?"

"Sto-o-op," came the outcry at last. I remained true to my system and did not sit down, for I felt that I would not get up again. In a few minutes we were marching. The army flyer Simanko, marching near me, suddenly fell down. We came up to him and tried to lift him, but did not succeed. "Sto-o-op."

Simanko was unconscious and lay face down in the snow. He was done for. A soldier came up, grabbed him under the arms and lifted him to his feet. When he let him go, poor Simanko collapsed again. The soldier got angry.

"Get up, you lout!" He kicked him in the side and, suddenly getting furious, gave him a heavy blow on the back with the butt of his rifle.

"Enough!" shouted young Tselikov, an engineer and football player who had been brought to Penug direct from Moscow and had had no experience in camp discipline. He interposed his heavy bulk between the soldier and Simanko.

"Can't you see, you bloke, that he is unconscious? Why do you beat him? Get the chief of the convoy!" he cried.

"What do you mean — unconscious! Get away, citizen, don't interfere or I'll shoot," said the soldier, raising his rifle.

"Silence!" thundered Tselikov. "Do what you are told, get the chief!"

The commanding tone had a magical effect. The soldier mumbled something in confusion, stepped back and disappeared in the darkness.

"No revolution will ever change our muzhik," said Korolkov. "Just shout at him properly and he'll get scared and obey. Here's an example. The fellow is carrying a rifle and has the right to shoot. But stun him with a real command and he immediately runs to do your bidding."

We surrounded Simanko and tried to revive him, but nothing worked, neither shaking, nor shoving snow under his collar, nor the well-tried method of rubbing ears with snow. He lay there, a lifeless bundle.

"What is the matter here?" said the convoy-chief, coming up.

He threw the light of his lantern on Simanko's lifeless features. The medical attendant stuck a vial under his nose. Next to Simanko, Professor Yanushevsky was lying stretched out in the snow. The medical attendant bent down to him as well.

"They cannot go any farther," he reported as he got up. "Let us load them up on the sleigh. We'll get them there somehow."

The convoy-chief seemed perturbed. He was in a difficult position. He was entrusted with three hundred men. Two of them were already lying in the snow and could not go on. They were the first. What next? He covered his eyes with a tired gesture, thinking over the situation.

Without waiting for his answer, the medical attendant lifted Simanko on his Herculean back and disappeared with him in the dark. Two soldiers grabbed the professor under the arms and dragged him away. In another ten minutes we resumed our march.

After that, events followed each other as in a fog. Men walked as if they were drunk, wabbling and stumbling, falling down and getting up again, helping each other, all tired and hungry. From the rear came uninterruptedly the cries of beaten men. All soldiers except the leader had concentrated in the rear and helped arouse the convicts with their clubs and rifle-butts after each stop. By the flickering light of the lanterns we could observe the punishment administered. The rest periods were quite frequent now — about every two hundred meters we flopped. I was so tired that my eyelids closed, my ankles, knees, hips and back ached frightfully. My head felt quite empty, and fell forward lifelessly. My arms hung down like ropes. Where was my former strength and endurance?

We emerged into an open stretch. The river was somewhere to the right. There was deep snow on either side of us and our path resembled a trench.

Two more rest periods went by. The last was so long that many of us fell asleep. Our leader walked past us on his way to the rear. He seemed disturbed.

In another ten minutes, as he passed us again, he reassured us with: "We're on the right track all right." So there had been some doubt. This was a pleasant surprise! We went on again. Low bushes appeared, then some lone trees, and finally we went right into a dark and dense forest. Muffled cries came from the front, followed by the familiar "sto-o-op," and we dropped into the snow. The leader passed us again and this time he was cursing.

"Well, where are we going now? Are we headed right?"

"You go to hell, all of you. Thanks to one fool's advice we have now lost our way. We should have borne more to the left."

So we were lost. It was midnight, we had marched about fifty kilometers without eating, were as tired as dogs, and now, instead of a rest and a meal, we had to try to find our way in the dark or spend the night in the forest. Truly, an efficient system!

The chiefs were in conference. Almost all of us were already asleep when two soldiers hurried by us on their way to the head of the column. They called out to everybody as they passed: "Turn back, we're marching back."

"Back. But back to where?" we asked ourselves.

"Back to the devil's own den. We'll keep fumbling about until morning," was the consolation we got from Tselikov who apparently possessed extraordinary endurance.

There was nothing else to do. We retraced our steps along the same path, now well beaten, at a snail-like pace. Never before in my life had I felt such utter exhaustion. My system was weakened by the long confinement in prison and not yet able to stand the strain of such a nocturnal walk on an empty stomach. Sometimes I felt myself losing consciousness. Only with the greatest effort of will-power could I resist the desire to fling myself down in the snow.

Only one prisoner, the engineer Chernayev, seemed in a worse state than I. Originally he had been sentenced to five years in prison for a train wreck on his line. He finished his term, returned home, and two weeks later was again arrested on a charge of "wrecking" and sentenced by the OGPU to ten years in the penal camps. It was difficult to understand how he could have done so much harm to the Socialist Republic in a fortnight. The five years of imprisonment had already affected his health and then they were followed by five months at the Shpalernaya prison in Leningrad while he was awaiting his second sentence. He was in very poor condition when sent out to the penal camps. That very morning he had drawn my compassion by the expression of hopelessness in his eyes and by his gray-green complexion. He walked like an old man, hardly able to drag one foot after another, leaning on his cane and stumbling and falling repeatedly.

After many more stops we came back to the river. Following another protracted argument of our convoy, who were as tired as we were, we headed in a direction still further to the left, made a few more kilometers, and having spent whatever strength still remained in us, found ourselves again in the forest.

This time there was no doubt that we had lost our way. Only one alternative was left, to spend the night in the forest, for the utter exhaustion was now quite general. But our leader was unwilling to give up and went out to reconnoiter the surrounding country, while we got busy lighting fires. When he came back our fires were blazing and men were sleeping all around them. I stretched out my feet towards the fire, wedged myself between the fat warm Korolkov and my faithful "caddy" Borisov and immediately fell fast asleep.

At early dawn our indefatigable leader went out again to reconnoiter and discovered the large village we were seeking some five kilometers from our bivouac. Judging by the tracks we had left in the snow, we should have borne a little further right and would have easily reached the edge of the forest from where the village lights would have been visible.

Spending a winter night in the forest is only relatively amusing, but our early awakening was positively hateful. Every bone in my body ached and I wanted terribly to sleep. We were filled with new energy, however, by the news that the village was quite near and the very thought of an early meal made us march briskly. The professor and the flyer, refreshed by the sleep, joined our group again. We soon came out of the forest and at some distance saw the first rays of the sun fall on the steeples of a large sky-blue church surrounded by many snow-covered roofs.

Columns of whitish-gray smoke were coming out of the chimneys and rising high to the clear blue sky. The cottagers' stoves were heated early in the morning in order to radiate heat throughout the day. The welcoming smoke-streams, absolute silence and a beautiful church warmed our hearts. Soon we hit upon the regular road which brought us to the village. We entered it preceded by a crowd of village boys.

In the center of the village stood the boarded-up church. It was later explained that the local priest had been arrested and deported to Siberia a year before. Opposite the church was a well-built house occupied by the local soviet. Next to it was the post-office and a little farther the cooperative store. At the door of the local soviet stood several sleighs of teamsters who were waiting for their assignments.

We stood in formation in the village square. The convoy-chief came up to us accompanied by the head of the local soviet, who did not bother to hide his displeasure. They were having an argument and all the emphatic reasoning of our drab-looking convoy-chief did not seem to impress the head of the soviet at all.

"Where shall I put them? Let them take care of themselves, there is plenty of room. Why was I not told that a column was on its way?"

They argued for a long time and finally reached some conclusion. Detachments started to leave the left wing of our column one after another, escorted by soldiers. In a half-hour or so the square was emptied.

Our group of "intelligentsia" was escorted by a young convoy-soldier who was instructed to find us quarters and to keep watch over us. He made several unsuccessful attempts. We were not admitted into one of the cottages because the head of the house was absent and his wife was afraid of such a number of questionable-looking guests. We were rebuffed in the next by the host himself, a communist who did not wish to extend hospitality to "convicts," as he contemptuously called us. The third cottage had children sick with diphtheria, the fourth was not large enough. Finally we found two cottages, side by side, which took us in.

Our hostess was a kind woman about forty years old who served a samovar, some boiled potatoes, millet cakes, and even a jar of sour milk.

The indefatigable engineer Tselikov went to fetch our allotment of food from the convoy sleigh and in another hour we were sitting around the sizzling samovar and eating a delicious but quite original puree of potatoes "Polonaise" which he had concocted for us.

With royal generosity we gave our hostess the allotment of fish and groats we had received. Several days later we had occasion to remember our generosity and to regret it.

My wet shoes and stockings were drying on top of the stove; my coat folded into a bundle under my head seemed softer than down; the floor felt like a hair mattress. In another hour we were all sound asleep, some of us on the floor, some on the benches, and some even on top of the stove.

At noon, after a roll-call, we resumed our march. The next village was twenty kilometers away and our convoy determined to get us there the same evening without fail. The whole village came out to see us off: old men, women and girls stood around us in groups. Children played and jumped around us like puppies.

The weather remained beautiful. The bright sun, reflected in the snowy blanket, made us blink. The pure cold air was invigorating and after the first hour my tired legs stopped aching. Our path lay through open country with snow-covered fields on either side of us. Soon the village disappeared behind the horizon. By three o'clock we had gone half way. We all walked along merrily and from the ranks of the gangsters came one of their favorite songs ending in the refrain:

"I hold up the state official,
"Make him raise his hands to heaven,
"And escape with all his cash."

Refreshed after the rest, Korolkov was again dishing out his funny stories and time passed quickly. We made few stops. As it grew dark we saw lights in the distance and at half past six we reached a village which was to shelter us overnight.

We stopped at the cottage of a shrewd little drunkard who tried his best to trade a bottle of vodka for the meat which we were to receive from the convoy. However, there was a hitch in getting the meat. First we were told to come and fetch it; then it was to be distributed in the morning. A little later that evening all the members of the convoy assembled at their chief's cottage for a drinking bout.

The village proved to be well stocked with vodka. The convoy first spent on vodka all the money entrusted to them for feeding the prisoners en route and then bartered away all our supplies. All the meat, fish, groats and sugar disappeared. At three in the morning our convoy-chief, dead-drunk and accompanied by his soldiers, who could hardly stand up, made the rounds of the cottages to check up on the number of prisoners.

We were all sound asleep when the bunch of drunkards broke into our cottage with a roar and a bang. They sat around the table, stared at us with unseeing eyes, and began making the roll-call.

"Where is Saveliev? Let me see him. Where is he hiding?" cried the convoy-chief, waving his revolver.

Saveliev was one of the six thieves lodged at our neighbor's cottage. He had spent the whole evening with our host drinking and mysteriously discussing something.

"Come on! Produce Saveliev!" continued our little convoy-chief poking his revolver right into our host's face.

"Please don't scare me," calmly replied the latter. "How on earth can I get this Saveliev for you? Better let us have a drink and we'll find Saveliev tomorrow." With a cunning smirk he took a bottle out of his pocket, uncorked it by a blow against his knee, lifted it to his mouth, took a few gulps, smacked his lips contentedly, wiped off the neck of the bottle with his sleeve and placed it on the table before our convoy-chief.

The latter was somewhat embarrassed. He had never yet taken a drink in our presence. But the temptation was too great. No money was demanded, it was hard to resist. The first bottle was followed by another, then a third. They drank without eating. When the supply gave out, our host took the entire drunken crowd to the neighbor's house. The bout continued until morning.

CHAPTER THIRTEEN: THE HUNGER MARCH CONTINUES

We were scheduled to resume our march at eight A. M. Our convoy-soldiers were thoroughly drunk when they awakened us. At ten o'clock we were finally all assembled and the roll-call started. It revealed that two Cossacks and the whole group of thieves were missing. They had taken advantage of the drinking orgy to make their getaway.

Our host, still somewhat tipsy, stood a little way off with a knowing smile on his face. His long discussion with Saveliev would indicate that he had had his hand in the preparation of the escape, but he was not afraid of being accused, as the convoy had partaken of his free liquor and had thus become his accomplices. He was quite sure of himself and counseled the convoy contemptuously to "try to find the wind in the open field."

The chairman of the local soviet did not show up at all. He and his associates, together with the head of the village militia, continued their carousal at the soviet hall, whence came curses, shouts and abuse.

There was nothing to be done. The convoy-chief angrily gave orders to start. It was cold and a disagreeable wind blew in our faces. The sky was covered with threatening clouds. The sobering soldiers marched dismally alongside of us and gave vent to their anger by abusing the petty criminals. Certainly they were not in an enviable situation. On the third day of the march eight prisoners were missing, all the money spent, and all the food gone.

They were responsible to the camp administration and would be taken to task. How they intended to feed themselves and the three hundred prisoners during the rest of the march was a mystery.

As usual, the first half of the way was rapidly traversed. Our road lay through several small villages. At the entrance of each one of these we were met by pale village children dressed in rags and wearing huge felt boots discarded by their elders. No peasants were about; they had all been mobilized for the transportation of timber. The peasants' wives and mothers stood on their porches, looked at us compassionately, shook their heads and threw bread to us.

The convoy, fearing further escapes, would not allow us to stop at the villages or to drink water from the village wells. They told us to eat snow instead. We were to march thirty-five kilometers that day. About mid-way we stopped for a long rest. The convoy-chief suggested that I, as a prisoner with penal camp experience, take entire charge, assume responsibility for fifteen members of the "intelligentsia," and arrange for their food and lodgings. I promptly accepted his proposal on condition that we would not be bothered with escorts and that we be given free choice in the selection of our quarters.

We marched less briskly the second half of the way. After thirty kilometers I was again overcome by the familiar feeling of fatigue, pain in the knees, and a peculiar lightness. I tried to replenish my energy by munching bits of bread and sugar. At nine in the evening we reached our village. It was the last settlement in the Northern area. The next day we were to enter the territory occupied by the Komi people.

The vast Komi territory is but very sparsely populated by the Zyryan race. The Zyryans are descendants of Finnish tribes which were pushed north by the Slavs. They settled in the impenetrable forests and swamps, forcing the Slavs to leave them alone. The very name of the people, "Komi," means "the pursued."

The Komi people had been Christianized by Greek-Orthodox missionaries and monks. Then came Russian traders who gave them manufactured goods, especially alcohol, in exchange for furs. Alcohol brought the usual dread results; the people were dying out, and at the time of the Bolshevik revolution they numbered only some three hundred and fifty thousand.

Our last stop on Russian territory was marked by the escape of ten city bums who managed to make their getaway in spite of the renewed vigilance of the guards. Our total number now was reduced by eighteen.

In the morning, it was found that the village cooperative store had no supplies to give us in exchange for the note which our convoy-chief had procured with great difficulty from the village soviet. The convoy was panic-stricken. What could they do? We were far from telephone or telegraph lines. They decided to go on. The hungry criminal gang loudly protested during the roll-call and threats were made to report the convoy for spending the money and food on drink.

My group was in a gloomy mood. We had almost no supplies. Having shared all our food the night before, we had nothing except a little sugar, lard and garlic. I had recourse to the monk who persuaded the recalcitrants that the dear Lord would not leave us alone or let us famish. We put our faith in his promises and started off. We had only eighteen kilometers to go that day.

The Zyryan people proved very kind-hearted. As we passed through villages the criminal group loudly shouted "bread, give us some bread," and stretched out their hands to the Zyryan women. The women rushed back into their houses, brought out some barley-cakes and buns in their aprons and threw them into our midst. The criminals pounced on the bread-cakes like wild animals.

One old woman ran for a long way alongside of our group. She mumbled something in her native tongue, pointed to my feet, lamented and wept.

This Northern woman, who was used to warm clothing, was apparently shaken to the core at the sight of my stockings and low shoes. Finally she rushed up to me, took off her thick, embroidered, woolen mittens and handed them to me with a sob. I was deeply touched by this manifestation of motherly affection. Later on these mittens rendered me faithful service and I still have one of them, violet-colored with a primitive design in bright yellow and green.

The monk immediately took advantage of the situation to reassure the doubters of Heavenly Providence by citing the mitten incident as an example.

"He had no gloves and the Lord sent him mittens," he said with conviction. "God is with us and will not abandon us."

We wondered at the large size of the Zyryan cottages as contrasted with the small Russian peasant cabins. The Zyryans did not believe in sparing timber. The corners of the cottages were all painted dark red and some were decorated with fancy balconies. The windows were disproportionately small. The logs in the walls were well cut and accurately fitted. We noticed that many cottages had brooms standing outside their doors. The Zyryans had remained true to the Finnish traditions of honesty; they had no locks on their doors and a broom left on the doorstep indicated that the owners of the cottage were out. This was a quite effective guarantee that nobody would enter the house. Even the influence of fifteen years of Soviet rule had not displaced the traditional broom.

Time flew; we left behind one kilometer after another. Our group marched on boldly and was kept in good humor by Korolkov, our invaluable wit. We soon reached our destination, a large village with a beautiful boarded-up church. We had no difficulty finding quarters for the night. The monk, the priest and the Pole immediately went to look for food. Our hostess gave us a pot of boiled potatoes, the only food she could scrape together. We paid for it with a pair of trousers. After an hour and a half the Pole came back with an empty sack. Our countenances fell, we had only one hope left — in the Lord. We began making bets. As the daylight dwindled and the clergy did not come back, the odds were five to two in favor of divine intercession, and when it had grown quite dark they were ten to one.

About eight o'clock we heard the monk's voice on the porch and in another minute he was with us. He placed a jug of milk on the table and pulled some treasures out of his sack consisting of freshly baked cakes with salt fish stuffing, millet bread, potatoes, cottage cheese, two partridges and some dried mushrooms.

We lifted the hero in our arms and tossed him up to the ceiling again and again in grateful triumph. He humbly accepted our exultation. It appeared that he owed his success to the fact that the local priest had been deported and the village was left without a spiritual head. The peasant women prevailed on our clergy to read the evening service in church, to christen two babies and to wed a young couple whose parents had forbidden any but a church wedding. The newlyweds, overjoyed at the unexpected stroke of luck, were the principal donors to our fund of supplies.

During the feast that followed the convoy-soldiers came to our cottage to ask our advice about finding food. Their situation was worse than that of the others. The criminals had not eaten for forty-eight hours and demanded food. There was even a real riot in one of the cottages. The convoy-soldiers realized their guilt and tried to meet the situation by persuasion rather than by force. They told the prisoners that the chairman of the local soviet had left the village in search of supplies and that bread would be distributed in the morning.

There was no truth in this promise. The prisoners were doomed to bitter disappointment. In order to get the convicts to come out of their cottages in the morning, the convoy told them that the bread would be handed out after the roll-call.

At seven A. M. we were already standing in formation in the village square. The roll-call was made and to the convoy's great relief we were all there. Then came the command to start. Rioting began at once.

"Where is our bread? We can't start without bread. We won't go!" came from the ranks.

The hungry convicts did not budge. The quiet peasant group did not move either. The convoy tried persuasion, telling the prisoners that there were only twenty-five kilometers left to the next stop where bread was prepared for us, that nothing could be obtained in this village, and that therefore the only thing to do was to march to the next one. The peasants hesitated, but the criminals would not listen. They were promised their bread in the morning and bread they must have. No bread — no march.

Our little convoy-chief became furious.

"What do you mean you won't march," he cried, pulling out his gun. "Remember this," and he shot into the air. "And now: attention! Go!"

The shot made no impression whatever. A young convict with a long nose jumped forward and yelled at the top of his voice:

"You drank it all up, you scoundrels, and we have to go hungry. We won't go, that's all. Don't budge, anybody!"

A terrible racket followed. Some shouted, "Let us go, there's nothing to be had here anyway!" Others bellowed, "Don't budge; if we don't get bread, we'll sack the village." Curses and abuse fell on the convoy from all sides.

The convoy-chief got his men in line and commanded them to aim their rifles at the rioters. A tense pause followed.

"I'm telling you for the last time," shouted the flushed commander as loudly as he could. "Start immediately when you hear the command. Anybody who stays behind will be shot. Understand? Attention! Go!"

This decisive command was effective. The criminal gang gave in and slowly started forward. The column left the village. The peasant women whom the shooting had scared away, now came back and saw us off with loud vociferations in their native tongue. They threw breadcakes into our ranks and the prisoners fought for them like dogs.

The hungry men resumed their march. It was difficult to walk in the deep snow and the weaker ones in the criminal gang soon showed signs of exhaustion and fell in their tracks. They were mercilessly beaten with clubs and rifle-butts. At three o'clock we entered a dense forest, it grew easier to walk, but there was no sign of the promised village. The rests became more frequent, men stumbled and fell again and again.

"We have lost our way again," said Korolkov, taking me by the arm and breathing heavily.

I was surprised at his endurance. He was about fifty and, judging by his face and by the size of his waistline, he must have been fond of good food and drink. Still he marched on indefatigably and did not miss a chance for a pun, a funny story or a laugh. His supply of humor was inexhaustible. The strength of his determination was partly responsible for his long sentence. After serving a three-year term of exile, he had gone to the local OGPU to obtain his release documents. He was asked to step in "for a moment" to see the head of the department in his private office. The latter asked him whether the three years of exile had made him change his former convictions as to the incapacity of communists for fruitful work. Just this conviction, expressed at the wrong moment, had led to his arrest and exile.

Anybody else would have decided on a slight compromise with his conscience, and answered in the negative. Korolkov, however, immediately told the fable of the gypsy who tried to teach his horse to do without food by reducing the measure of oats from day to day. The horse died in spite of all his efforts at the very time when he thought he had accomplished the desired result. Korolkov then explained the parable and stated that he was too old to change his convictions.

The head of the local OGPU listened to him attentively, laughed at his story and finally expressed his regret at being unable to release him at once. The fable was written into the report and sent to Moscow and Korolkov was temporarily detained pending receipt of instructions from headquarters. Thus his fate was decided. The answer came in three months and read: "Ten years imprisonment in the penal labor camps."

Full liberty is never really restored to those unfortunates who receive a five or ten-year sentence in the U.S.S.R. for their political convictions. When they finish their term, they are exiled for five years and after this they have to spend three more years in so-called partial exile. Then they acquire the right of residence in any part of the country except Moscow and Leningrad. Therefore as a rule it takes eighteen years before a man imprisoned for his political convictions is again able to return to the centers of population. Of late this rule has been rigidly adhered to and many tens of thousands of people at the present time continue to live in exile in Siberia and other remote districts of Russia even after having completed their original term of penal labor.

The procedure is even simpler in the case of socialists other than communists, i. e., of social democrats or social revolutionaries as well as of anarchists: they are told at the time of their arrest that nothing can save them from exile save a written declaration that they renounce their former convictions and if they are not willing to do this, their exile will be for life. Though a sentence for life is theoretically unlawful, as the maximum term of "measures for social protection" in the U.S.S.R. does not exceed ten years, still, in actual practise these limitations are freely circumvented by the imposition of various additional terms and similar tricks of which the OGPU are past masters.

Korolkov clearly understood that he was in for life, now that his name was added to the category of "enemies of the working class." In spite of this, he bore his misfortune heroically and never lost courage. During the year in which I saw him almost every day I never noticed even momentary despair in the expression of his eyes.

In spite of Korolkov's sense of humor our predicament was deplorable. It was now quite dark and the air had grown colder. We had covered about thirty kilometers, but there was no indication of a village anywhere. It became more and more difficult to walk, the beating of the exhausted criminals became more frequent, and the resting intervals were longer and longer. All of us had clearly come to the end of our endurance.

Professor Yanushevsky, a handsome and likable old man, walked bravely on though he was visibly fatigued.

He was a railroad engineer, an outstanding expert who had represented his country on many occasions at various international conventions. The OGPU had sentenced him to be shot because he insisted that in order to make the U.S.S.R. railroads capable of bearing the burden imposed upon them by the Five-Year Plan, they would have to adopt automatic coupling, more powerful locomotives, reinforced track and other basic improvements.

This opinion of an outstanding expert who defended it to the end as a conviction derived from his long practical experience, served only to cause his arrest on the accusation of "wrecking." He was sentenced to the "highest measure for social protection."

In wording the sentence the board of the OGPU called attention to the fact that the professor had made his recommendations in order to bring the railroads of the U.S.S.R. into a chaotic state and at the same time to destroy the financial strength of the country by the imposition of the large expenditures necessitated by his innovations. He was saved from execution only by the efforts of influential friends and the sentence was commuted to a ten-year term in the penal labor camps.

Two years later the Soviet Government invited the American expert on railroad engineering, Mr. Budd, to make an investigation of the Soviet railroads. Mr. Budd submitted his report, which contained exactly the same recommendations as those proposed by Yanushevsky. The American expert received a high fee and was honored for his work whereas Mr. Yanushevsky was made a prisoner and barely escaped execution.

To free Yanushevsky would be tantamount to acknowledging that a mistake had been made by the OGPU. No this would mean that a doubt would be cast on the infallibility of the OGPU judgments in general, and all the sentences of engineers accused of "wrecking" would have had to be revised. Only the cases of those already shot could be left undisturbed. What was to be done? The OGPU considered it for a long time, during which Yanushevsky continued serving his term. Having completed his job, Mr. Budd returned to America in comfort and esteem, but Mr. Yanushevsky, after much travelling from one prison to another without any comfort whatsoever and always escorted by armed guards, was subsequently brought to Moscow in a prison railway-carriage and there was graciously re-employed by the railroad administration.

Every kilometer made our progress more difficult. We now stopped and rested after every half-kilometer. After ten of such rests, we finally saw the twinkling of lights through the trees. We made a last effort and, crawling rather than walking, we reached the edge of the forest. The moon was shining and it was quite light. The convoy put out its lanterns and slowly we dragged ourselves to the village.

In the village we went into the first available huts, dropped on the floor and almost instantly fell asleep, happy that our leaden feet were finally at rest. In the morning we were pleasantly surprised by the news that we were to rest all day and that the march would not be resumed until the following morning.

It was a prosperous village. We procured a goodly number of quail and bartered a shirt for a half a sack of potatoes and a jug of milk. Our appointed caterer, the Pole, stewed the quail with the potatoes in a large casserole. It was placed in the middle of the table and after gulping down a drink of vodka which Korolkov had mysteriously procured, we went to it tooth and nail, muzhik-fashion, dipping our wooden spoons into the delicious pot and feasting like kings.

We had been en route for six days and had made one hundred and fifty kilometers. Soon we were to reach Palaus, a large village. We had all lost weight, but the enforced march in the open air had done us good in spite of our fatigue. We looked healthier; Korolkov's ruddy complexion gave evidence of this; even the professor's thin cheeks were brighter and the priests' faces seemed freshened.

We quickly covered twenty-four kilometers, made thirty more to Palaus on the next day and were ready for another day's march, when we noticed by our convoy's gloomy faces that something unforeseen had happened. By this time we had stopped quarreling with our convoy. By hook or crook they were procuring bread for us and this was more important than anything else. The prisoners managed to get additional supplies by barter, as the natives were unwilling to sell anything for money.

We questioned our convoy and were told that a messenger had arrived from the penal camp administration instructing us to wait at the next village for Mosagin, commander of the guards.

We made the thirteen kilometers to the next village in three hours. At noon we had already formed a square, waiting for the high commander. The convoy-chief was fidgety, calling out prisoners from the various groups and asking them to forget the few misunderstandings we had had en route. In spite of these little talks, the expression on the faces of the convicts was not reassuring.

After two hours of waiting, we saw several sleighs in the distance coming towards us at a brisk pace. In the first sleigh sat a man in a lounging position dressed in a military great-coat and a Samoyed reindeer cap with ear-flaps. His young insolent red face was clean-shaven and stood out in marked contrast to the full week's growth on ours. The sleigh behind him held two passengers, one of them a huge fellow with a protruding jaw, and the second a little red-haired man with foxy eyes and a trimmed moustache. Two more sleighs followed.

"Prisoners of the first winter marching party, greetings!" yelled the chief the minute he jumped out of the sleigh. The Kotlas atmosphere suddenly came back to us strongly, for during the march our convoy-chief had not bothered us with greetings.

"Zdrah," answered our square.

The convoy-chief stepped up to report. He spoke in a low voice and we could see from the expression on the face of the commander that it would go hard with him. The further he went the more his listener frowned.

"Is that all?" he suddenly exclaimed.

"That's all, comrade commander."

"You'll be court-martialed for such laxity," ferociously shouted the man in the reindeer cap, grabbing the little fellow by the collar and shaking him viciously. "Hand over your gun and into the ranks with you. You are under arrest and you'll march with the convicts."

The little rosy face of our convoy-chief turned ashen gray. With trembling hands he unloosened his holster, handed it over, and stepped into the ranks.

"Fifteen soldiers of convoy were not enough to watch a column of prisoners! Eighteen escaped! I'll give you what is coming to you, too!" continued the commander walking in front of the line of soldiers, shouting and poking his revolver in their faces.

Our criminal gang was encouraged by such an exhibition of temper on the part of the higher authorities. They raised their voices in a clamor:

"We want to eat, citizen commander. We were left without food all this time and were beaten while they spent all our supplies on vodka. Please order some bread to be distributed."

"Silence," bawled the commander. "We'll get to the bottom of it. You'll get your bread. From now on I'll feed you myself and I'll house you myself so that you can't get away. I appoint comrade Khmyra your new chief of convoy. Obey his orders implicitly. He's not to be trifled with."

Khmyra was a stocky man with a tremendous spread of shoulders and a round face, which was a curious mixture of cherub and bandit. He had small cunning blue eyes and rosy cheeks. His pouted lips were twisted in a suggestive smile. His thick short neck added to the depressing effect of his appearance. In another day we learned that he had been convicted of banditry and sentenced to ten years in the penal camps; that he had served half his term at the Solovetsky camp, and had in some way achieved dismissal from there and a promotion to a good position in the new penal camps, where he was rapidly making his career.

The commander inspected our square, and then gave the order to start. We were to march twenty more kilometers. The high commander got into his sleigh and drove away, but Khmyra stayed with us and marched at the head of our column. He had examined us thoroughly and had placed a freezing criminal lad and two coughing "Turks" in the trailing sleigh. At every stop he inspected our lines minutely and maintained order with unfailing energy. The sturdy fellow apparently did not know fatigue.

We arrived at nine o'clock. Khmyra made us stand in formation in the village square and went to fetch the high commander who returned with him in a little while. We inferred from commander Mosagin's appearance that he had already managed to consume a goodly amount of alcohol. Mosagin incoherently told us that there would be no meals that night and that we were to sleep in the village church. The prospect of spending the night without dinner in an unheated church was not alluring, but nothing could be done about it.

The church had remained unheated during the winter and was even colder than we had expected. The stone floor was as cold as ice and we were not tempted to lie down. We walked around for a long time, trying to devise ways for spending the night. My shoes, which were wet from the march, had frozen stiff and my stockings were covered with a thin icy crust.

As Khmyra entered the church the long-nosed ring-leader of the criminal gang stepped up to him and declared in an insolent tone that it was impossible to sleep there.

"Oh, you can't sleep? Is that so?" retorted Khmyra. "Take this!" and the sound of a frightful blow echoed back from the church walls. The long-nosed leader covered his face with his hands, tottered and howled.

"That'll warm you up," cried Khmyra. "Is anyone else dissatisfied? Come out here, if you are."

Dead silence followed. Yes, it really seemed as if Khmyra was not given to trifling. Alas, it was the repetition of Kotlas and an end had come to our freedom and stop-overs at night at the peasant cottages with their warm stoves, samovars and other delights of cozy home-life. Those of my companions who had not seen Kotlas were staggered, but after my experience there, this was child's play.

Khmyra made the rounds of the prisoners asking if there were any further complaints, but there were none, and the criminal convicts shrank from him in fear. His reputation was established.

"And now, to sleep," he ordered loudly. "Tomorrow at six we start again. No noise during the night. Understand?"

A sentry stood inside the door. The gold of the ikons on the walls glimmered in the dark. On the floor lay men closely bunched together, reminding me of scenes at the railroad stations during the revolution. With my light overcoat, I did not dare lie down on the floor, so I spent the greater part of the night walking about the spacious church. Finally I made a high bid for a place on the window-sill. The morning signal found me crumpled up on it, with my wet feet shoved into the beaver cap turned inside out. Next to me were my shoes, frozen to the window-sill and I had to work for a good fifteen minutes to get them on. I felt awful. There was an intolerable soreness in my back, legs and feet, a buzzing in my ears, and I had a frightful headache.

I drank a cup of cold water and ate a crust of black bread with salt and garlic. I was one of the last to leave the church and must have looked very funny, for as I came out, a roar of laughter from the commanding authorities greeted me. They were well fed and well rested and could appreciate the drollery of my appearance. My beaver cap was pushed deep over my forehead, my light overcoat was belted with a rope, I wore greenish-gray stockings, and my low shoes were reinforced with string as the soles were beginning to come loose. All of this must have made me look rather ridiculous.

After the roll-call we started on our march. The pain in my legs subsided, my feet began to get warm and I boldly kept step with my companions. The temperature was about four below zero. By ten o'clock we were overtaken by a snowstorm. Snowflakes stuck to the face, got into the eyes and inside the collar. It seemed to blow from all sides at once. It penetrated to the bone and made one's skin burn. My poor nose was saved only by the mittens which the good old Zyryan woman had given me.

Our road led through barren open land which gave full sway to the wind. Walking was very difficult. Khmyra was like a shepherd dog, running ahead or walking back of his herd, inspiring the tired ones with his energy. He did not have to resort to beating. After the twentieth kilometer, men began to stumble and fall, but his urging always gave them enough strength to get up and resume the march. Finally we saw the steeple of a church in the distance. Straining our energy to the utmost we climbed the last hill and marched into the village, where we were welcomed by the chief village executive and conducted directly to the church.

The commander and his retinue met us on the church steps. Our exhausted appearance probably made an impression, for they did not honor us with their greeting and we quickly went into the church. This time there was a pleasant surprise awaiting us. Our hearts were gladdened by the sight of a large boiling kettle with the steam rising from it. We were given half a kilogram of bread each and were told to prepare for dinner. Another source of comfort was a large antique tile stove which had been heated. The church was not exactly warm, but one could take off his cap without danger of freezing his ears.

It was a day and a half since we last had tea, and two full days since we had had a meal. During these two days we had made sixty-three kilometers and were dreadfully tired. All our thoughts were bent on getting something into our stomachs. The very first gulps of tea diffused the hatred in our hearts into a feeling of blessed drowsiness. In this we were a good example of the actual condition of the great mass of the population in the U.S.S.R. They are being starved and held in submission by terror. Like throwing a bone to a famished dog, their overlords give them breathing spells and relief only at critical moments.

We had a long wait for dinner and when it came, we were sorely disappointed. Some defect in the cooking utensils had given a vile flavor to the cabbage soup and it was unfit for consumption. The porridge was burnt and dry. However, I managed to concoct a stew made of porridge moistened with a bit of soup and flavored with sugar and garlic. I took the risk and swallowed it without undue annoyance.

"Eat well," Khmyra was saying as he walked among the prisoners sitting on the floor. "Tomorrow we'll have to march forty-five kilometers. It is a long stretch and your legs will have to be in good working order."

After dinner we all fell asleep. I hastened to secure a place on the window-sill, which was hardly the most comfortable of beds. After squirming about for a while I relapsed into a half-dead, half-drowsy state which could hardly be called sleep. At times I was aroused by cramps in the calf of my leg and had to do a jig on the window-sill, probably looking like a clown. Directly below my group of companions slept all scrambled together. A little further on was a fantastic blotch of color made by the bright silk robes of the Turcomans. The even snoring of the sleepers was interrupted by the continual coughing of the unfortunate "Turks." They could not stand the cold and most of them were obviously destined to perish in the Komi territory.

The next day's march was one continuous nightmare. The temperature had dropped to twenty-two below zero. It was difficult to breathe; the air felt like a knife entering the lungs. We walked fast to keep warm, but still we felt the cold getting the best of us and benumbing our muscles. After the first hour or so all the "Turks" were coughing hard. One of them, a dignified old man of about sixty, started stumbling and falling down after the first ten kilometers. Finally he stayed behind his group and remained sitting there in his yellow silk robe with red stripes, blowing on his blue fingers, coughing and spitting clots of blood into the snow. He wailed and uttered lamentations, as if forecasting his approaching end. His eyes were filled with abject terror.

We lifted him, wound a woolen scarf around his head, stuck a pipe in his mouth and led him forward. After another couple of kilometers he broke down altogether and Khmyra had him put in the sleigh.

After we had gone half our distance, men began to fall. Khmyra changed his tactics and gave drastic instructions to the soldiers to employ any means in order to make us march. Again rifle-butts went into action and men were kicked and beaten over the head. Khmyra himself was as brutal as a wild beast.

The thirtieth kilometer had us crawling instead of marching. On the thirty-fifth we passed a village where we left forty of our number, who were totally unable to go on and who had been driven forward with clubs during the last few kilometers.

Only ten kilometers were left. I clenched my teeth in blind determination to last to the end and marched on in a daze. I only remember the increasing pain in my knees, the swinging backs of the men, the innumerable stops, the cold, the difficult breathing, and the repeated attacks of dizziness.

On reaching the village we were given shelter in the schoolhouse, which was warm and clean and had a good wooden floor. We were given porridge and boiling water, accompanied, to our regret, by conversation with the commanders who were anxious to learn of our experiences during the march.

Ten minutes after the meal was over, we were all sound asleep on the floor.

For eleven days we had marched, had not undressed, had eaten very poorly and had covered three hundred and twenty-five kilometers. Only one more march of forty kilometers separated us from our final destination, where we would have a chance to wash up. Since the high commander had taken charge of us, we had had no opportunity to wash in the peasants' cottages and had to resort to rubbing our faces with snow.

At dawn we heard the signal for the resumption of our march. A roll-call and walking again. After the first half-hour, it seemed as if we had not slept at all but were continuing the march of the day before. The scenery changed and the monotonous plains gave way to sparse forest. The wind had subsided and it was warmer. My hardened leg muscles had no great difficulty in carrying my emaciated body and my feet automatically kept step with those ahead. Conversation and witticisms ceased — we were all too tired. Only one thought prevailed — to reach our destination.

At one of the stops Korolkov laughingly gave me a fragment of mirror which he had found somewhere. "Can this really be I," I wondered, gazing at my sunken eyes surrounded by black rings, my cracked lips, my red nose and the long stubble of a reddish-gray beard.

Korolkov could not hold back any longer. "Wouldn't be bad for you and me to go and have dinner at Contant's, just as we are," he ventured gaily.

Instead of dinner at Contant's, we shared the small supply of garlic which I still had with me and reinforced ourselves with it during the rest of the march.

At five o'clock we struck the railroad-track and slowly continued our trek over it, our feet sinking to the ankles in the loose snow. Gradually we approached our coveted destination, the Sixth Work Post of the new railroad under construction. In twelve days we had made three hundred and sixty-five kilometers, an average of thirty kilometers a day. Little lights appeared in the distance, the track widened, and then some buildings loomed up before us in the darkness.

CHAPTER FOURTEEN: WORK POST NO. 6

At the work post we were immediately installed in the barracks. The roll-call was dispensed with, the men climbed onto the double sleeping-shelves and instantly fell asleep. We were told that we would be given one day of rest and that after that we would start in on the jobs awaiting us.

In the morning I was one of the first to arise, prompted by the hope of finding a place to wash. Our barracks resembled all the others which I had seen. They were meant for two hundred people, but now held three hundred. It was pretty crowded, but we were used to that. There were double sleeping-shelves, little windows and a single entrance, adjoining which was the tiny room of the squad commander.

I did not find any wash-stand in the barracks and went out into the yard.

"A wash-stand? You're asking too much! Nobody washes in this place. There is a small bathhouse for the commanding officers, but the prisoners are not allowed there."

This encouraging information was given me by a sturdy little dark-eyed Ukrainian, a former sailor of the Black Sea Fleet, an old revolutionary and a member of the Socialist Revolutionary Party. He had taken part in the pre-war rebellion on the dreadnought "Potemkin" and had seen the inside of many Czarist prisons. Unluckily for him in 1918 he was elected member of the All-Russian Constituent Assembly and later on was chosen a member of the Ukrainian Rada. These two circumstances proved quite sufficient grounds to keep him in prison ever since the Bolsheviks came into power.

This sailor also gave me general information about conditions at the work post. He told me that the commander of this newly-opened post was the drunkard Shapovalov, a former bandit who knew nothing about railroad construction, but who had made a hit with the chief of the administration by his energy. He had been appointed during the winter when the preparation of timber was in progress and it was expected that he would be displaced in the spring when the earthwork construction began, since he was utterly ignorant of such work.

Assisting the chief was Zurin, a former Moscow commander of an OGPU squadron, who had been convicted of embezzlement. He drank like a horse and was not at all interested in his work. The head of the commissariat department was another drunkard and the young medical attendant completed the alcoholic foursome and supplied all the necessary alcohol from his stores.

Every evening these four bosom friends had supper together and did not separate until late at night. The next day they recuperated and attended to their respective duties.

I thanked the sailor for the information and walked on to inspect the work post. Two barracks were ready and the third still needed a roof. The buildings seemed in good order, but the chinks between the logs indicated hasty construction.

The barracks we were in had recently been completed. The chinks between the logs were stuffed with moss. There was no stove. The small windows let in but little light.

After dinner, which was not much better than at the Kotlas Transfer Station, we were suddenly subjected to a search. We had to undress, we were felt all over, our bundles were ransacked in search for money, valuable articles and watches. Letters were left untouched. As usual my money was in the double shirt-cuff and I got by with it, but my watch, which I had regained with difficulty in Kotlas, was taken away and a receipt for it given. Ten days later I saw my watch on the wrist of our commander, who claimed that he needed it to check up on the prisoners' work according to the Taylor system, though he had not the slightest inkling of what that system was. Only three months later when I felt myself firmly established at the office of the camp administration did I succeed in getting it back.

After the search, all the commanding officers came to our barracks. Mosagin, who had met us on our way, declared that as far as the penal camp administration was concerned, his mission was finished and the prisoners were transferred to the local authorities.

"From now on everything will depend on you," he concluded. "If you work well, you will be treated well."

Our new chief Shapovalov, commander of the Sixth Work Post, voiced the same sentiment.

"From now on," he said, "you will work for me. It is easy forest work and you will like it. You 'intelligentsia,' for instance, are used to work hard with your pens and pencils. Now you'll have to exchange these for axes and saws. Today you may have a good rest, but tomorrow — out you go to your jobs."

His retinue smiled, they enjoyed the joke. It is quite possible that Shapovalov would have continued in the same humorous strain, but a guard came in just then and reported that "a woman from Ust-Sysolsk" had just arrived.

We followed our commanders out of the barracks and saw a sleigh entering the gates. The woman wore an Astrakhan coat and too much rouge. She looked like a pretty chambermaid.

"Olga," cried Mosagin, running up to her. "This is a delightful surprise. I'm glad to see you. We have such a jolly crowd here. Come on up, boys, and meet my wife." Golubatnikov, the big fellow of Mosagin's staff, quickly ran up to the sleigh and helped the lady to alight. Surrounded by admirers, she sauntered coquettishly up to the house and all the men followed her in. We went to the store to investigate "the main problem."

"Without the commander's orders I cannot sell anything except on ration-cards. I have to keep an accurate record, so please don't even ask me." The prisoner storekeeper was adamant.

Dejectedly we went back to the barracks. Our supplies had come to an end. But our bodies urgently demanded food to replenish their spent energy. However, there was nothing we could do about it, so some of us lay down on the sleeping-shelves and some played dominoes. Conversation was devoted to the crucial question of how to procure food.

In the evening, we decided to try our luck with the commanders themselves. Korolkov and I went up to the lighted house of our local commander and knocked at the door. Inside we heard the clamor of many male voices and some chirping in a higher pitch. Nobody responded to our knock, so we opened the door and entered the little entry hall. From the next room came the sound of a falling chair and a loud cry:

"Don't you dare kiss her, you son of a bitch."

A shot resounded, followed by a shout from everybody. Then all was still. The door opened and the head of the commissariat department rushed out, pale and frightened. After him came the flushed commander of the work post, who pulled open the outer door and shouted at the top of his voice:

"Horses! Horses at once!"

It was good policy for us to sneak out. People were rushing up to the house from all sides. The head of the commissariat had fetched the medical attendant and they both ran in.

We waited. In a few minutes a horse and sleigh drove up to the porch and Golubatnikov's large hulk was carried out of the house and placed in it. His head was bandaged and covered with blood, his face was livid. Mosagin jumped into the sleigh, braced the wounded man against his shoulder, and held him around the waist.

"Full speed to Ust-Sysolsk," he shouted.

The next day the whole work post knew that Mosagin had shot Golubatnikov in a fit of jealousy, when the latter took advantage of his standing as an old friend to kiss his wife in front of the others. Our medical attendant said that the wound was mortal.

It was a ticklish situation. According to penal camp regulations, it was the duty of the local commander to arrest the murderer. But the local commander was a prisoner and the transgressor a free official of the administration who could not be arrested by a prisoner, no matter what his position. Therefore Mosagin left on his own accord, carrying with him the victim of his unbridled jealousy.

This incident caused but little commotion at the work post. Life went on as usual. But the mercury went down to thirty below.

It was cold and damp in our barracks in spite of the heat exuded by the bodies of three hundred inmates. Our little group was still together and we took possession of the lower tier of shelves from the door to the window. There was not quite enough room, but the cold made a certain degree of closeness even desirable. Of course, we could not think of undressing, first because there were no mattresses, blankets or pillows, but chiefly because of the temperature.

The ordinary prisoners in the camps of the OGPU are not furnished bedding. Those who have their own may use it, but the state supplies only the wooden sleeping-shelves. The space on the shelves is determined by the number of prisoners to be housed rather than by the needs of each prisoner. Exceptions are rare and are limited to office workers, members of the sanitary corps and those prisoners who have a "pull." These latter categories have usually more or less tolerable living conditions, though this is by no means always the case.

I was cold in spite of the fact that my place on the shelves was next to my constant companion, the fat Korolkov. There was a crevice between the logs near my head through which I could see the stars. Our shelf adjoined the entrance-door, which was constantly opened by groups of prisoners going in and out with the lantern. The lantern was the official pass.

Every time a group left the barracks, a stream of icy-cold air hit me, made me shiver, and increased the pain in my sore legs. I tried to shove my feet under Korolkov, but he pushed them back in his sleep. All my efforts to stop up the hole in the wall with a handkerchief or with my precious mittens proved futile. My head was thoroughly chilled and I was getting despondent. Still after several hours I fell sound asleep.

At five A. M. the loud signal bell put an end to my dreams and at half past five we were already standing in the yard waiting for our commanders. Shapovalov gave instructions that the "intelligentsia" was to have an easy assignment for the first day in order to get used to manual labor. We were to carry the boards which had been sawed in the forest to the work post, a distance of one to two kilometers.

When we came to the forest the foreman appointed the army flyer Simanko to take charge of our group and left us. We distributed the work and started on our task. I was among the group who had to carry the boards out of the forest, the weaker ones carried them along the road, and the rest, among whom were Professor Yanushevsky, engineer Chernayev, Korolkov and the acting foreman Simanko, stayed in the forest, kept warm around the fire and helped load the boards on our backs. The help in loading did not amount to much and our aged companions really spent most of their time in conversation. There were no soldiers to guard us.

At three o'clock the work was finished. We were all pretty cold and were hoping for a good meal. Upon our return to the work post we tried to find our foreman, but did not succeed and went into the barracks to wait for our dinner. Shapovalov came in, saw us sitting around, and got furious. In spite of our explanations he said that we had no right to leave the forest without orders and as a punishment he gave us an additional assignment to bring the unsawed logs out of the forest and to place them on the road. Our foreman was found and threatened with confinement to the dungeon. In the meantime, he was to see to it that we completed the additional assignment.

The foreman led us back to the forest, swearing like a trooper. The new work was much more difficult. The snow was deep, the little crooked paths wound their way among the trees and the logs were very heavy. Several of the largest logs got the best of us. We thought we could never carry them to the road, a distance of some five hundred yards. When we finally got them there we were all in. The largest log was abandoned in the forest as we simply could not move it. We finished our additional assignment at eight o'clock and waited for our foreman. He did not come and we sent one of our old men to fetch him. In the meantime we sat around the fire and tried to keep warm. It was dark and the moonlight shone but dimly through the snow-covered trees.

The foreman brought us grief instead of joy. The large log had to be brought out and we could not go back until it was done. The log was long and difficult to handle. It seemed weighted with lead. Inexperienced as we were, we lifted it several times and dropped it again. Finally we succeeded in heaving it up on our shoulders and carried it forward. The heavy load pressed unmercifully on our shoulders. The foreman walked ahead and yelled at us.

We were within twenty feet of the road when the agriculturist, who was at the head of the line, uttered a loud scream and fell down in the snow. He was the strongest of our group and had selected the most responsible position and the big end of the log. The man next to him gave in under the added strain, and the others followed suit. The foreman pounced on us with a torrent of licentious cursing.

"You weak sons of bitches, damn your tra-ta-ta-ta-ta," he shouted. "Lift that log or I'll make you stay here all night."

He stepped up to the agriculturist, who was still lying in the snow, and kicked him in the ribs. He cursed at him and ordered him to get up. Dull moaning came in reply.

The foreman lowered his lantern to the man's face. It was pale and covered with perspiration. A dark stream of blood trickled down to the snow. Everybody got excited. Some ran to the work post looking for the medical attendant, others improvised a stretcher and carried the moaning agriculturist towards the work post, stepping carefully. The warm blood ran down our hands and dropped to the road, marking our trail in the snow.

When we brought our load in, Orlov, our medical attendant, quickly undressed the agriculturist and diagnosed the casualty as a burst intestine. It was a serious case and the loss of blood was considerable. It should have been operated on immediately. But there was no doctor at the work post and Orlov hoped to save the victim with household remedies and ice. Until morning he tried to stop the flow of blood. All requests to provide a horse to take the sick man to Ust-Sysolsk met with refusal. The commander said horses were more urgently needed in the forest, and that the medical attendant was talking nonsense.

"He won't die," he stubbornly retorted to all arguments. "No, he'll come through well enough, don't worry. You may carry him there if you like, but I won't give you a horse."

Two days later the agriculturist died. We had been fond of this jovial, kindly man and mourned his loss. "Who will come next?" we thought. The agriculturist was buried the same day. Two prisoners dug the hole into which his body was lowered.

Our next assignment was to cut timber. Shapovalov remained faithful to the belief he had expressed on the first day, namely, that it would do the "intelligentsia" good to work a little with an axe instead of a pen. He divided our group and added two of our number to each detachment going into the forest.

"We'll see now how you work," was his jeering farewell to us.

Only Professor Yanushevsky escaped our fate, as he had been urgently ordered to proceed to Ust-Sysolsk where his services were required. It was my good luck to be attached to a group of peasants, who were used to hard work of this kind. By seven P. M. we finished our assignment. The first day I had worked sixteen hours; the second brought only thirteen. I had done the same kind of work at Kotlas and it came easier now.

The next day, our commander decided that we worked very well and sent a group composed of the "intelligentsia" alone to a remote section of the forest. We went there with our saws and axes and were followed by the colorful Turcomans whose assignment was located next to ours. This time things did not go so well. By noon we were all pretty tired and only one third of the assignment was finished. At nightfall there was no doubt that we could not complete the job. Then recourse was taken to a bribe, which settled matters to everybody's satisfaction. It cost us fifty kopecks apiece but we were allowed to go back to our barracks; the foreman gave a false report to Shapovalov, who in turn was pleased to forward it on to the administration by telephone.

I then received an assignment of household work and became expert in cleaning dried fish. This work also made me understand why there were so many fish-scales in the soup which was served to the prisoners every other day.

At that time our clever army flyer Simanko succeeded in a little trick, thanks to which our whole group of "intelligentsia" was assigned to the easy task of preparing firewood for the work post.

For some reason Simanko was once urgently called out of the barracks by Shapovalov. By mistake he had on the uniform cap of engineer Chernayev when he ran out. As he reported to the commander, he noticed that the latter was covetously looking at the uniform emblem on the cap. Simanko immediately suggested that the commander try on the cap and made some flattering remarks to the effect that it was particularly becoming. The commander was as pleased as a child with a toy, stepped up to the mirror, saluted, took the cap off and put it on again. Impressed by this interest, Simanko immediately made him a present of the cap. They started talking and, taking advantage of the good humor of the commander, Simanko persuaded him to organize a special detachment of "intelligentsia," to put him at the head of it, and to give it assignments of an easier nature.

The sacrifice was fully rewarded. Simanko was invited to have supper with the commander and returned to the barracks drunk as a lord. He was not quite sober in the morning and took extraordinary pains to explain to engineer Chernayev what benefits he expected to obtain from the simple present.

At roll-call we saw our commander wearing his new cap. He was as proud of it as a little boy and ordered with a broad grin:

"Detachment of intelligentsia, to the cutting of firewood!"

Having arrived at their destination in the forest, the cutters of firewood immediately built a large fire and relaxed around it, telling stories and making merry. Several days were spent in this manner. The supply of firewood at the work post increased somewhat, but none too much.

However, Simanko 's star was not destined to shine for long and he was replaced in the affections of the boss by a new favorite, the artist Ertel who made a good portrait of the commander in his new cap. The detachment of "intelligentsia" was disbanded and again we were allotted one job or another, as luck determined. Some of us went back to the forest, some to the kitchen, some to other tasks. Ertel used his popularity with the boss to advantage and procured us a supply of spoilt herring which the store had not been allowed to sell.

The storekeeper called these herring "anchovy-flavored," but as a matter of fact they were so far gone that one could not look at them without holding one's nose. But "hunger will break stone walls." We accepted the Pole's advice, washed the herring thoroughly and placed them outside in the cold. We then chopped off pieces of this frozen fish and ate it with our bread. It was quite a delectable dish. Nobody even thought of the danger, we were too hungry for that.

After we had been at the work post ten days, a commission from the central office of the administration suddenly arrived; this brought about a change in our fate. The regulations of the penal camp code expressly provided that all prisoners sentenced on counter-revolutionary charges were to spend their first six months at the penal camps in special disciplinary squads doing hard labor. However, the need for trained workers was so great that it was decided to make an exception and to use the "intelligentsia" prisoners at the work for which they were best fitted.

In this manner the evil plan of Zakhariantz to have me sent to the Sixth Work Post, in the hope that I would there get my full share of brutality and physical labor, was thwarted. Together with my other companions I was projected right into the very center of the penal camps, the offices of the administration at Ust-Sysolsk.

It all came about quite accidentally, without my trying for it in any way. Just as at Kotlas, my guardian angel took charge of my fate at the critical moment.

This time my guardian angel attained his ends through the medium of the assistant to the chairman of the commission, prisoner Petkin from Moscow. The chairman himself was the bonehead Fedakov, a typical chekist with an infamous reputation at the Solovetsky camp. He was only the loud-speaker; the real guiding power was Petkin. My questionnaire showed that I knew several foreign languages. Petkin called Fedakov's attention to it and asked to make a test of my knowledge. A remarkable scene followed.

I stood facing the long table at which the important commission was in session. In the center sat Fedakov, flaxen-haired with a puffy face and light blue eyes, faded from alcoholic excesses. To the right and to the left of him were officials in uniform, trying to show off their importance. At the end of the table stood Petkin.

Petkin addressed me in French and delivered the following tirade without batting an eyelash:

"Regardez ces idiots. Ils forment la commission qui doit etablir votre specialite. Observez leus figures: le president a l'air d'un vrai cochon, son compagnon de droite est un salaud, celui de gauche — un imbecile. Ces messieurs decideront tout de suite de votre sort. Mais n'ayez aucune crainte, nous vous tirerons d'affaire et vous caserons a une bonne place."

["Look at these idiots. They form a commission whose business it is to determine your specialty. Look at their faces. The president has the appearance of a pig, his companion on the right is a bum and the one on the left — an imbecile. These gentlemen will presently decide your fate, but have no fear, for we will pull you through and get you a good job."]

I was petrified. This was so unexpected, so bold and impudent, that for a moment I thought that I was dreaming. But Petkin's laughing eyes, contrasting with his otherwise perfectly unperturbed expression, reassured me. He stroked his short moustache and waited for my answer.

Trying my best to hold back a smile I told him a short French anecdote.

"He knows the French language well," declared Petkin in a firm tone. "Now we shall try English. At Archangel they need a man for loading ships who knows languages." The high officials nodded assent, yes, yes, they need one, indeed.

"Look here," Petkin continued in English. "Don't mind these scoundrels, they don't understand a single word. Say something in English. Fire away."

He made a serious face and comically inclined his head as if waiting for my reply. This was getting too ridiculous. I felt that in another moment I would burst out laughing and convulsions were gripping my throat. I cannot remember what my answer was, but Petkin was satisfied and informed the commission that I was a most suitable person for the position they had in mind. He proposed that I should be temporarily transferred to the offices of the administration and then sent to Archangel.

Fedakov thought well of the proposal and my fate was decided.

Next morning at daybreak eleven members of the "intelligentsia," escorted by three soldiers, left Work Post No. 6, never to return. We easily walked the thirty-five kilometers and at five o'clock entered Ust-Sysolsk, the capital of the Komi territory.

CHAPTER FIFTEEN: "AT MIDNIGHT I SHALL HANG MYSELF"

On March 16, 1930, I entered Ust-Sysolsk, the capital of the Zyryan Autonomous Komi Territory. Soon after my arrival the name was changed to the Zyryan "Syktyvkar."

The change of name was the result of the local Zyryan communists' nationalistic tendencies directed toward the suppression of everything Russian in their territory. This was not difficult to achieve with respect to language, as the peasantry had never spoken Russian anyway and the urban population eagerly accepted the Zyryan. They even went so far as to invent a Zyryan alphabet by adding some hooks and twists to the Russian letters, and, thanks to this invention, it became difficult to decipher the new signboards and posters.

A year later, when the foreign press started its campaign against the use of penal labor in the U.S.S.R., the Moscow papers took advantage of the change of name of Ust-Sysolsk to make a clever reply to the attacks. They denied the existence of penal camps and stated that there was even no such town as Ust-Sysolsk in the U.S.S.R. Since there was no such town, and it had been mentioned by the foreign press as the seat of the penal camp administration, it was evident that the camps did not exist and that such reports were nothing but base calumny.

Ust-Sysolsk, or Syktyvkar, is located on the picturesque high bank of Sysola River where it joins the Vychegda. Two churches and a cathedral, substantially built of stone, had remained untouched by the communist authorities, who were wary of butting their heads against the Zyryans' religious convictions.

One of the churches stood on a high hill. It commanded a beautiful view, especially in summer, when the Sysola River meandered through thick verdure. In the evening the Northern sun slowly set behind the horizon, coloring it with delicate hues.

On the river one could see the little side-wheel steamers which formed the principal means of communication between the capital and the rest of the territory. The other bank of the river presented an amusing spectacle when herds of cows returned to town every evening. They pastured without cowherds. Just before sunset they assembled at the river, mooed in concert and waited until the last cow had joined their ranks. Then the whole herd quickly went into the water and swam across the river. They did this with great ease though the current was strong.

The population of the capital did not exceed four thousand. The streets were unpaved, but the ditches running on either side were covered with wooden sidewalks, which were kept in fair condition. The churches were the only stone buildings. The ancient custom of placing a broom at the entrance of the dwelling when the owners were out was also observed at the capital. The population consisted of twenty-five hundred natives, dumb-looking, flaxen-haired Zyryans; five hundred exiles from Russia; and a thousand prisoners of the Northern penal camps. About two hundred and fifty of the prisoners worked in the administration offices; the rest, on the railroad line under construction.

The administration offices occupied five buildings. I was attached to the supply department and our offices were in an old wooden church from which the cross had been removed, leaving a large hole in the cupola. The other departments occupied the adjoining two-story buildings. Prisoners assigned to the railroad construction lived in regular barracks within a barbed-wire enclosure at the First Work Post, which was an exact reproduction of other camp posts.

We were first placed in the local prison. It was an old prison which the city had transferred to the camp administration. It was surrounded by high paling. A good-sized chapel was attached to it and the camp administration had transformed this into barracks by installing a double tier of sleeping-shelves around the walls. The chapel formed a little transfer station for newly arriving prisoners and our group was assigned to it. The lower tier of sleeping-shelves was occupied by prisoner students of the school for railroad foremen. During the day they were out at their field jobs and in the evening they studied at the barracks. We had to occupy the upper tier of shelves.

In the middle of the chapel stood a small portable iron stove which was heated from morning to night. The stove got red hot; all the heat rose to the ceiling and to our upper tier, making it quite impossible to stay there any length of time. We had to come down, but down below the temperature was kept near the freezing point by the large crevices between the floor boards. On the shelves one had to sit half-naked, down below an overcoat was needed. Some prisoners were frying bits of salt fish in rancid oil on the little stove and the smells of the cooking were suffocating.

To add to our discomfort, the place was alive with vermin. Wherever one looked, one saw naked men crushing lice with their fingers or burning them with matches. But there were untold millions of lice and fighting them was a losing struggle. Clean linen was immediately infested by these nauseating insects. Bedbugs were also abundant.

On the first day we were taken to our work under escort, but thereafter went unaccompanied. Camp discipline was not very severe. We were told that at most of the other camps even the office workers were daily taken to and from their work under escort.

Several of my former companions were also assigned to the supply department. Among these was Korolkov, who soon rose to the position of chief agriculturist of the camp. Ertel, the artist, had by some dark magic qualified as an expert on horses and hauling, though he confessed that his experience with horses was limited to having been a passenger in hired droshkies. Engineer Blumberg was made manager of the technical department and I was temporarily appointed his assistant.

The usual chaos reigned in the supply department. It was not a whit different from any other Soviet supply department or from the other departments of our administration. The young communist, Volkov, who was in charge of hauling teams, had not the faintest idea of the number of horses employed at the camp and answered my request for information with: "I guess there should be about fifteen hundred horses, but who knows, perhaps there are more, perhaps less. How can I keep track of the bastards, foaling and dying all the time?" He knew even less about the available quantity of oats and hay and was in this respect no different from the manager of the commissariat department, who could furnish no information as to the quantity of food on hand.

Two young murderers had installed a card system for keeping records, but it was always in such confusion that they were the only ones who could make head or tail of it. But whenever they were asked for information, they invariably gave incorrect figures.

The manager of the supply department was Alexander Grinstein, a railroad construction engineer who had spent two years in Berlin in connection with a government project and on his return was arrested and sentenced to ten years. Grinstein was orderly and punctilious; he understood supply problems. He had been appointed recently and made every effort to bring order into his department. He was happy that engineer Blumberg, his former college friend, was appointed to his department. We worked hard for a week, putting in fourteen hours a day, and at the end of that time we had everything in complete order. The administration took notice of our effort and sent us a letter of thanks, which served me to good purpose later on.

Just at that time my resistance finally failed and I succumbed to an attack of flu. My temperature quickly rose to one hundred and four, and for a week the medical attendant did not believe that I would live. He offered to have me transferred to the hospital, but warned me of conditions there. I declined the kind offer and relied on my own powers of resistance. I lay in high fever on my upper shelf, suffocating from the stench, fighting the insects and scratching myself. It was so unbearably hot that I broke the window next to my head and, sticking my mouth close to the opening, inhaled the cold outside air. The medical attendant assured me that this method of easing my suffering would surely result in pneumonia and an untimely death. Still I persisted. There were no medicines to be had and I substituted the cold fresh air and fasting. In ten days I went back to work. The sickness and the ten-day fast left their mark; I looked like a corpse. I was offered a seven day vacation, but refused it as I did not fancy staying a whole week confined in our stinking domicile.

I soon got to know the most important officials of the administration. It was a most original collection. During the absence of Boksha, whom I had had the pleasure of meeting at Kotlas, the whole complicated machinery of the administration was manipulated by his secretary Vaskov, who had been transferred to Ust-Sysolsk from the Solovetsky camp.

Vaskov, pudgy-faced, round-shouldered and fat, was a short individual with a dirty, oily complexion and a drunkard's bulbous nose. By trade he was a shoemaker. Before noon he managed the administration by shouting, but after lunch he could not speak coherently and expressed himself by grunting. He consumed a liter of alcohol daily, which was the basic minimum. Quite often the minimum was considerably exceeded and on those days he stayed home, a doctor was called in, and diagnosed a heart attack. He was vulgarly familiar with the chekists who were his associates or employees and with the common prisoners. He reserved a more polite form of address for the "intelligentsia," whom he hated and respected at the same time.

He tried to keep track of all the details and every letter addressed to the administration first came to his desk. He read it and adorned it with his comment which was oftentimes so absurd as to be a source of amusement for the prisoners on the office staff.

Every morning at ten o'clock all commanders of the penal camp came to report to Vaskov, like ministers of state to their chief. Vaskov's shouting was invariably heard and after a while the reporting chekist bounced out of the door followed by a volley of Vaskov's obscene cursing.

Ter-Stepanov, who was appointed chief clerk and who had been called simply "Ter" ever since the Kotlas incident, sat at the entrance to Vaskov's private office. It was his duty to admit the reporting chekists and to announce the next in line after the preceding one had been dismissed by the chief.

The reports of the engineers in charge of construction were received in a totally different manner. Vaskov held them in awe "for their learning," treated them politely and always concurred with their views and sanctioned their recommendations.

His treatment of the prisoners was generally fair, "for lack of time," some of us thought; but he did not concern himself with their needs. He enjoyed a happy family life, was a loving father and was henpecked by his wife, who beat him from time to time. He never punished drunken prisoners and generally was not offensive. He never visited the work posts except the one at Ust-Sysolsk, and had no idea what happened in them. All his time was spent either at his office or at the dinner table, where he consumed his allotment of moderately diluted alcohol. He had no use for vodka.

Sometimes Vaskov invited all the high executives of the administration to his house, for a "conference." On those occasions the camp druggist, Kalvarsky, received special orders for the delivery of several liters of state alcohol. The conferences lasted far into the night and the executives' coachmen waited for them outside and drove them home. In the morning the conferees were favored with an excessive dose of curses. He swore like a truck-driver, but with gusto and art, enjoying the sound and the effect of it.

In Vaskov's absence, the Lett, Shkele, took charge. He was the head of the secret intelligence, the most important of all the departments, which was manned by a veritable army of convicted chekists. Shkele had a gray-green complexion and looked like a mummy. He was tall and haggard, with a square head balanced on a long thin neck. He had close-cropped hair and his flattened skull indicated dullness of imagination. He was a painstaking official, a heartless OGPU worker, but was fair to the prisoners. He was said to be a tender husband and had been seen holding hands with his wife under the table, during meals.

Quite separate from the administration, were the construction and engineering offices of the new Ust-Sysolsk-Penug railroad line. I was very happy to find Professor Yanushevsky there, and my old friends from the Butirsky prison, the engineers Mamontov, Alpers and Khomiakov. There I met the engineer Bakhtiarov, who had received world-wide publicity in 1928 when he was convicted as a "wrecker" during the notorious "Shakhta" trial. At the head of the construction work were the engineers Mamontov, Himmelfarb and Alpers, who were held in great esteem as its "directors."

The "directors" enjoyed exceptional privileges in spite of the fact that there was really no essential difference of status between them and the other engineers working on the construction project. The administration made every concession to their comfort, gave them the right to rent apartments in town, paid them a salary of one hundred roubles a month, and even allowed Mamontov's wife to live with him. Before they reached this privileged position, however, they had all undergone the regular routine of privation, and done such manual labor as unloading barges, carrying sacks of flour on their backs, etc.

The standing of prisoners at the penal camps depended on their profession. At the beginning, the engineers were the most privileged, then came the architects, and after them the doctors, and so down the line. Then came a new order from Moscow and we were all classified in definite groups. The engineers were again placed in the first group, and, strange as it may seem from the Soviet point of view, this also included business men. The second category comprised physicians, economists and technical experts. Lawyers were at the very end, in the twelfth group.

A month after my arrival at Ust-Sysolsk the engineer Khomiakov died of consumption and two weeks later the engineer Bakhtiarov hanged himself.

Bakhtiarov lived in private quarters and I often dropped in there for a chat. On my way home from work I passed the house where he rented a room and was always glad to see a light in his window and to stop for an hour for an unreserved talk with this charming man. Nobody checked up on our time and after work we were free to go about as we pleased. A little later, this freedom was restricted by Moscow.

Bakhtiarov's little room was poorly furnished, but warm, clean and orderly. A kerosene lamp hung on a large hook above the table. It was this hook that Bakhtiarov made use of in settling his accounts with life.

Bakhtiarov was an engineer of renown and had held a high position in the Soviet coal-mining industry. Several months before the "Shakhta" trial he had been sent abroad on a government mission. Passing through Berlin on his way home, he received a letter from some of his close friends imploring him not to return to the U.S.S.R. The letter stated that upon his return he would be arrested and charged, together with his associates, with premeditated "wrecking," for the ultimate purpose of overthrowing the Soviet regime.

Bakhtiarov knew he was perfectly innocent and took the next train to Moscow. A day after his arrival he was arrested. He was tried together with other engineers charged with complicity in the "plot," and was sentenced to be shot for his "wrecking" activities. The sentence was commuted to a term of ten years in the penal camps.

During his confinement, he had come to the conclusion that the work he had done in the last ten years was harmful rather than useful to Russia and the Russian people; and that as long as he continued to work for the Bolsheviks at the penal camps and to add his mite to the realization of their plans, he was harming his country. The only logical thing to do was to put an end to this work.

He talked to me for two hours before committing suicide: "Thanks to my work and the work of other engineers and experts," he said, "the Bolsheviks are enabled to continue the achievement of their plans and wage their war against the people, the majority of whom are against them. Why should I help them? I have already committed an unpardonable sin by indirectly helping to support the Bolsheviks during all the years I have worked for them. Have I the moral right to continue? No. Therefore I should refuse to work, shouldn't I? If I decline to perform tasks given me in my professional capacity, I shall be sent back to the forest, or thrown into the dungeon, or shall be tried again and shot. To escape these eventualities, I prefer to put an end to it myself. I have thought about it for a long time and it is the only way out. Besides, I am old, I have lived my life, and it is time to quit."

I tried to reason with him as one normally does in such cases. He looked at me sadly.

"No, my friend, I am resolved. I am talking to you in all earnestness. At midnight I shall hang myself. Goodbye." He shook hands with me and led me to the door.

I could not take his gloomy words literally. Again asking him to dismiss the thought of suicide from his mind, I left his doorstep and stepped out into the dark.

I remember stopping twice on my way home, in obedience to a vague impulse bidding me to return. The second time I even turned back and took several steps, but overcame my feeling of uneasiness and went back to our little chapel.

The first thing I heard the next morning was the news of Bakhtiarov's suicide. He left no note.

Bakhtiarov's death left a deep impression on me and often made me think of his views as to where the responsibility for the Russian tragedy rested. He thought the Russian intelligentsia was chiefly to blame for it. He was quite adamant on the theory that the intelligentsia had done more than anybody else to bring the country under the Bolsheviks' domination and to enable them to conduct their experiment in it.

Bakhtiarov thought that the former established classes of society, such as the landed nobility, peasants, laboring classes, merchants, manufacturers and petty bourgeois, were responsible only in a minor way for the Bolshevik revolution and, except for the industrial workers, had taken no active part in it. His indictment, however, was directed at the intelligentsia of Russia.

"The intelligentsia was the brains of the people. It had innumerable points of contact through which it reached and influenced all classes. During several decades preceding the revolution it sought passionately to overthrow the Czarist tyranny. It conducted a subversive propaganda by means of the press, literature, schools, public and private discussions. It never gave a thought to what was going to follow the Czar's regime. It did not understand the basic character of the Russian people. It had no notion how to govern them. It idealized the people and lived in a stratosphere of dreams from which it could not see the disintegrating effects of its own activity.

"Part of the intelligentsia was devoted to revolutionary and Marxist theories, and actively fought the existing authorities by seditious propaganda among the workers and peasants, and by acts of terrorism against the Czar, his ministers and governors. Another part, the more numerous groups of parlor radicals, juggled with liberal and democratic ideas, criticized and poked fun at the authorities, and in the final analysis did as much harm as the first. The intelligentsia was composed of men of all classes and each one devitalized his associates in his own sphere of life.

"It maintained a sceptical attitude toward religion, but offered nothing in its place. Religion was the chief source of moral restraint for the Russian people who were generally deficient in a feeling for legal justice and equity. Therefore, by taking away the people's religion, ignoring their inborn peculiarities and the nation's historical traditions, it led the people to an abyss, seducing them by Utopian dreams and hopes.

"What did the members of the intelligentsia do when the storm broke, destroying everything in its path? They went to work for the new rulers of Russia. They forgot their democratic ideals and placed themselves entirely at the disposal of the communists. They did not rise in arms against the tyrants, but entered their service. They offered their knowledge and their skill to the debauchers, they prostituted themselves. They even stopped criticizing the dictatorship; criticism was punished by execution or exile. Some of them went abroad and even there continued to spread discord in the ranks of the emigres. But the majority remaining in Russia, teachers, doctors, engineers, leaders of the cooperative movement, some few of the military class, lawyers and professors, are like dogs catching the bones thrown to them by the communists and licking the hands of their new masters, who in turn despise them for their complete renunciation of democratic ideals.

"Could the communists conduct their experiment without the aid of the intelligentsia? Could they have launched the Five-Year Plan and similar schemes without its active cooperation? Could they possibly survive without its assistance? Never!"

Having come to this conclusion, and feeling in a way responsible for the sins of the intelligentsia, Bakhtiarov took his own life.

CHAPTER SIXTEEN: REFORMS

Bakhtiarov's suicide occupied the minds of the prisoners for a short time only. It soon gave way to news of the escape of a group of prisoners who were all caught and shot.

Fourteen men, headed by a bandit with a ten-year sentence, had disarmed the camp guards, pillaged the camp store, seized arms and a large amount of ammunition, sleighs and government horses, and tried to escape from the forests of Uftug. They were pursued and overtaken near Kotlas, on the banks of the Vychegda River, and took refuge on a little island. They were besieged for two days. Detachments of the local OGPU and of the military forces took part in the siege. A regular battle ensued, ending with the storming of the island over the ice. All the fugitives were killed. Eyewitnesses related that just before the fall of their stronghold, the bandit leader shot two of his companions who had wanted to surrender and then shot himself.

This news was published for the purpose of impressing the prisoners with the hopelessness of escape and the unfailing vigilance of the guards. It put an end to my plans for flight from this distant place. I would have to make seven hundred kilometers on foot!

Loud and bitter arguments interrupted my sad meditations. They came from the desk of the engineer Grinstein, manager of the supply department, who was arguing with the engineer Verkhovsky, superintendent of construction in the Ust-Sysolsk district.

Verkhovsky demanded a thousand barrels of pitch for trestle construction. After an animated controversy, which lasted over half an hour, he compromised on one barrel and, utterly discouraged, left the office, slamming the door. The plan provided for four thousand barrels of pitch, but there were only two barrels available. The same was true of iron, tools, nails — none of the required materials was at hand. Nevertheless Moscow demanded that all construction be finished within the stipulated time and in case of failure threatened to bring the heads of departments to trial for sabotage.

The railroad line under construction by our penal camp was one of the objectives of the Five-Year Plan. We were urged to make every possible effort and were told to buy all supplies locally when we could not obtain them in time from Moscow. It was good advice, but it was impossible. No supplies except timber could be bought locally.

The engineers were in a quandary. "How can we build a railroad under these conditions?" They sent requisitions to our department, came personally, remonstrated, begged — all in vain. Our warehouses were empty.

Time passed and warm weather was on its way. With the coming of spring earthwork construction was started. Prisoners were escorted to their tasks, received assignments they could not fulfill and were poorly fed because of insufficient supplies. There was a great shortage of tools; Soviet shovels were of poor quality, broke, were repaired, broke again and were thrown away. There were no picks or crow-bars at all. No machinery was dreamed of. All work was done by hand, as in primitive times. The earth was carted in wheelbarrows, it was often shoveled into them with bare hands. All work was rushed at a furious pace.

The ice was melting and breaking up in the rivers. Huge cakes, whole fields of rushing ice, were carried down in the swift current of the Sysola River. Several floats of timber which had been stuck in the ice since autumn went out into the Arctic Ocean together with the ice that had engulfed them. The speed of the current prevented the ice-blocks from jamming. As soon as one of them stopped, another got on top of it; for a minute or two a pile of them would collect at one spot, and then all of it would break away with a roar.

With the resumption of navigation barges loaded with hay, food, iron and other supplies began arriving at Ust-Sysolsk. Hard days commenced for the prisoners. Every day after finishing their office work, the clerks, as we were called by the other prisoners, were ordered out to the barges to do their share of unloading. The work was very fatiguing to the office force, but there were no exceptions made and every one of us had to complete his daily assignment before quitting. The assignment consisted of thirty hundred-kilogram bags of flour to be unloaded by each prisoner. The warehouses were located at the top of a very steep bank. The heavy bags had to be lifted from the barge, carried across a narrow wooden gang-plank, then up twenty-five steps and into the warehouse. The most unpleasant part of the work was crossing to the pier, over the narrow plank, with cold black water splashing below. The bag seemed incredibly heavy, one felt dizzy; great will-power was required to save one from falling.

Some prisoners fell into the water, but were not allowed to leave until they completed their assignments, wet as they were.

I remember what tremendous exertion it took to carry my first few bags. Later I adapted myself to the task and, following the advice of others, started loading the bags directly on my shoulders and head instead of on my back. It was easier this way.

It took six hours to unload thirty bags. We worked at the office until ten o'clock in the evening or even later; on unloading days we returned to our little chapel toward daybreak. At nine A. M. we had to be at our office jobs again.

The timekeeping book was handled by Berman, secretary of the administration, a former OGPU official sentenced to the camps for graft. For being late on the job the second time, the offender was required to spend twenty-four hours at the office, taking telephone messages, guarding the place and putting things in order. After the third offense, the prisoner was demoted from office work to earthwork construction for a week; and on the fourth occasion of tardiness, he was permanently removed from the office staff and transferred to hard labor. At first this book worried us. Later on we learned that there was a trick to it and that the book simply served Berman as a good paying proposition. For a package of cigarettes he inserted the desired time of arrival and for five roubles cash in advance he kindly took it upon himself to insert regularly the prisoner's name in his book instead of making him sign it. He was not afraid of being denounced because he rightly felt that the prisoners themselves were interested in the unmolested continuance of his good offices. As soon as I learned of this insurance, I immediately paid my premium for a month in advance and continued renewing my policy right up to the time that Berman was caught and sentenced to an additional term of three years.

The work of unloading barges continued during the entire period of open navigation. One instance I well remember: I had been on watch-duty at the office for twenty-four hours, then at regular work there for another twelve hours. In the evening I was ordered to assist in some urgent unloading of oats, carried heavy bags all night long, went back to the office directly from the pier, and at five o'clock of the same afternoon was again directed to the barge. We finished unloading it at three A. M. At nine I was back at the office.

Thanks to the influence of my engineer friends from the Butirsky prison I was saved the necessity of completing the full "disciplinary period" and was transferred to the ranks of "responsible workers of the administration" before the statutory six months were up. As a business man I was classed in the first category of specialists, was given cleaner living quarters together with the other workers of the administration, was allowed to get my meals from the administration's kitchen and, finally, was placed in charge of a section of work, making me department-head.

Never in my life had I been ambitious to become a Soviet department-head, but now I was genuinely glad. Formerly I had been more or less indifferent to my immediate future, as I had expected a transfer to Archangel from where I hoped to flee. But unloading barges quickly taught me not to neglect immediate benefits, and I was very happy when my position of department-head gave me certain privileges. Department-heads and all other prisoners in head-positions were ordered to the barges only in cases of great urgency.

In this manner day after day went by. The monotony was broken only by an occasional row, or by some particularly nonsensical resolution of Vaskov which caused general merriment, or by the arrival of the mail. Unfortunately I was still forbidden to correspond with my wife. I had not yet succeeded in finding other channels for the forwarding of correspondence.

With the coming of summer, prisoners' wives began arriving at the camp to see their husbands. Not all of them had obtained permission in Moscow and the others had to spend hours and hours trying to procure the necessary permit locally. They went from one department to the other, begging and imploring. In the end they usually succeeded if they came to Vaskov's office after lunch when he was in a kindly frame of mind and willing to grant a favor.

There were some exceptions, however, especially in cases of prisoners who worked on railroad construction. The wives came from afar, sometimes making a thousand kilometers or more in the hope of seeing their husbands. They made quite an uproar, weeping, shouting and abusing the OGPU authorities. A gipsy woman who had come from the center of Russia failed to procure permission to see her husband. For several hours she rolled in the dust in front of the administration offices, yelling and tearing her clothes in a fit of mad despair. She saw Vaskov leaving the building and jumped at him with a knife. They arrested her and sentenced her to three years in the penal camps. Later she and her husband escaped.

Of the prisoners, not one in a hundred was granted the privilege of receiving visitors. There were two kinds of permits. Some few wives were permitted to live with their husbands at private quarters for a period of two weeks, others were granted only the ordinary permit to talk across the barbed wire in the presence of a guard.

The construction of the railroad and of the highway to Ukhta was not proceeding according to schedule. Other divisions of work were also behind and the planned speed could not be maintained. The most dreadful reports continued to come from the timber regions where work had been carried on in the winter. At the end of the winter working season all prisoners who were still in fair condition were sent to Archangel to load ships, but there were not many of these. Of the total number of prisoners of the Uftug group two thousand men, or about twenty-two percent, died during the one winter. More than half of the remaining men were totally disabled. The same picture confronted the administration at the Kuloy group of timber-works.

After the winter work was over, the Uftug group was liquidated, discipline slackened, and crowds of left-over invalids wandered about Soloychegodsk dressed in pitiable rags, begging alms and occasionally pilfering small food supplies. The Solvychegodsk camp hospital daily buried over twenty prisoners in common graves. The scandal finally reached such proportions that the local committee of the Communist Party reported to Moscow and insisted on immediate relief. But the camp administration paid no attention whatever to complaints. It argued that the planned objective had been accomplished, even if a certain number of prisoners had perished. "Of what other use are criminals to the state?" asked Boksha. They should be pleased to expiate their guilt toward the proletariat by giving their lives and fertilizing the fields where the seeds of socialism are being sown.

But Moscow looked at things differently. There the gains and losses were computed and the results condemned. It was a losing enterprise. Who was to blame? A special investigating commission was appointed for the inspection of our camp district and of the Solovetsky camp.

The investigating commission started with the Solovetsky camp, both on the islands and in the Kem area, where over fifty thousand prisoners were employed in the preparation of timber for export. Crimes, corruption and deficiencies were brought to light. The prisoners were questioned, the accounts examined, and the arrests started. The entire commanding personnel of the Solovetsky camps was arrested and thrown into jail. Shortly afterwards the board of the OGPU sentenced thirty of the chief malefactors to be shot.

Monakhov, commander of the Kotlas Transfer Station, put a bullet through his head without waiting for the commission's arrival. Bukhaltzev met the commission, was arrested and came to Ust-Sysolsk a prisoner. The commission did not stay long at our camp. Within three days it hurriedly took its departure, without making the inspection. After it left, Vaskov, who had received it, suffered the usual heart attack which lasted three days and diminished the store of government alcohol on hand by ten liters.

After the commission's departure, an atmosphere of suspense descended on the administration. A threatening uncertainty hung in the air. Was the commission satisfied or was it not? Vaskov's nerves were ragged, his consumption of alcohol was doubled, his heart attacks became more frequent. The semi-inebriated officials of the secret intelligence department made sudden searches of the prisoners and some inexplicable arrests followed.

Just at this time a letter came from Archangel, containing the long-awaited request to send a prisoner who knew English. At last! I was asked to Vaskov's private office and went there with Petkin with whom I had remained friends ever since the memorable examination. Vaskov wanted to make the appointment himself. Two other prisoners were also ordered in, because their recent questionnaires showed they knew several languages.

The omnipotent man who held my fate in his hands sat at a desk covered with papers. He was dressed in a shabby dark suit; with his dirty nails he scratched his large head covered with black greasy hair which fell on his forehead in affected disorder. As usual, he was very drunk. His small, inflamed, bright, cunning gray eyes peeped at me from under his frowning brow.

"Gn." He emitted a strange unintelligible sound. It was after dinner.

"I bring you some prisoners who know the language, citizen commander, for appointment by you to the position at Archangel," said Petkin in a loud and clear voice.

"Gn," came in reply.

"This is prisoner L. who knows German and English," continued Petkin.

"Gn," grunted Vaskov again and held up a paper to Petkin in his dirty hand. "Let-tr-s-l-t."

"Let him translate it?" ventured Petkin.

"Gn," nodded Vaskov and pointed to an adjoining desk.

"Sit down and translate," said Petkin to prisoner L. The latter sat down, shrank a bit and looked at the paper.

"Gn, n-k-s," said Vaskov.

"The next is engineer B., who knows French," answered Petkin.

"Gn, no, gn, out, out." Vaskov waved him aside and pointed to me with another "Gn."

"Knows English, German, Swedish, French," rapidly reeled off Petkin. "A very suitable man, knows timber and loading operations." He was carried away by his enthusiasm and started fibbing.

"Gn," interjected Vaskov. He looked at me with his reddish bright eyes and at that moment he was the very image of a pig, especially when he emitted grunting sounds. I could not suppress a smile. Petkin stood behind his boss and twisted his body to a comical posture, but indicated with his eyes that laughing or smiling was not in order.

"Permit me to make an examination," proposed Petkin, who evidently wanted to repeat the old joke.

"Gn," uttered Vaskov, shaking his head negatively. He continued looking at me, puffed, snorted, and at times grunted his own peculiar "Gn." A minute went by.

Then he suddenly turned to the prisoner L., who was examining the paper given him. "Ts-av-it," he said.

Prisoner L. got up red in the face and began explaining that he did not know English well enough to translate a technical description without a dictionary, but if the commander wished, he would translate something from the German, or ..."

"Enough, away, three days dungeon for you," suddenly cried Vaskov, losing his temper and instantly sobering in both manner and speech. "How dare you cheat in the questionnaire? Don't know anything," he said to Petkin, crumpled the paper and impassionately crossed out something in the questionnaire before him with his red pencil. Then he wrote across the whole sheet: "Liar. Three days dungeon," signed and dated it, and handed the paper to the secretary Ter, who had entered to receive his orders. Angrily pointing at the door and at the abashed and frightened L., he snorted again: "Out, gn."

The excitement sobered Vaskov but for a moment. After that the alcoholic fumes again regained full possession of his tongue and I heard him say nothing more except his repeated "Gn." But Petkin seemed to understand him just the same. He handed me the same paper which proved to be an English bill of lading, and gave way to his playful inclinations, whispering to me in English:

"The boss does not know a word of English, so anything you care to put down will do."

I thanked him with a smile, and, standing right there in front of the desk began to translate the bill of lading rapidly into Russian, one word after the other: "I, the undersigned, captain of the good ship, etc." The speed of the translation astounded Vaskov. For a minute he stared at my hand with bulging eyes, then his dirty paw snatched the paper away from me and his gaze glued itself on it. He continued puffing in silence for a minute. I tried to urge him on mentally: "Go ahead, write your resolution," I mentally willed. The big paw reached for the pencil and traced with large red letters: "Telegraph Archangel advise when wanted." Finished. At last. New horizons opened before me. I did not doubt that escape could be arranged with the help of some English captain.

I left the room and profusely thanked Petkin for the good appointment to a large city. Of course I did not mention a word about my hopes for escape. That same evening we followed Vaskov's example and consumed a goodly quantity of alcohol. Two days passed in painful waiting, but there was no reply from Archangel. On the third day Petkin made Vaskov sign a telegram asking for a reply and Archangel immediately answered that there was no further need of a man, as the position was already filled by attorney A., who had been deported there directly from Leningrad. My plans collapsed. The chance of escape again eluded me.

The visit of the investigating commission and the purge at the Solovetsky camp were not in vain. About the end of July vague rumors began to reach the prisoners that great changes were impending, that martial law at the camps would be abolished and the entire commanding personnel changed. All of this information came to us chiefly through prisoner Yosilevich, who arrived at the camp in May and immediately was promoted to a high position.

Alexander Solomonovich Yosilevich was about thirty years old, slight and handsome. He arrived at the camp without convoy. His nervous features and waxen complexion testified to a long confinement in prison. He was a communist of the Troitsky faction and started his career by showing great efficiency in the Leningrad cheka. He was one of the first victims of the democratic wing within the party, and had been exiled to

Siberia. He stayed there three years, then ostensibly repented his delusions and was again appointed to a high position in the OGPU in the Caucasus. Six months later he was again arrested on a charge of having divulged the OGPU plans against the Troitsky faction to his friends and of operating a printing press at his house where the Troitskyists printed their proclamations and seditious literature. He was sentenced to be shot, but, thanks to the efforts of his influential friends, the sentence was commuted to a term of ten years in the penal camps. The same pull helped him to an immediate promotion. He deserved it, too, for he was actually the only intelligent man among the obtuse personnel of our OGPU commanders.

Two weeks after his arrival he became chief of the production department and a fast friend of Vaskov's. Soon he had the latter thoroughly in hand. He was energetic, clever, intelligent and sensible, scrupulously guarded the interests of his employees, released them from excessive manual labor, improved their living conditions, facilitated visits by their wives and generally was invaluable as a chief.

The expected changes came quite suddenly by telegraph from Moscow. The orders were: to abolish martial law, to improve the prisoners' living conditions, to lower the assignments of work, to increase food rations and to introduce days of rest. The commander of the administration was instructed to work out the details and was to be responsible for carrying out the orders.

Vaskov, who was used to the Solovetsky discipline, became confused, drank more than ever and entrusted all the detail of the new regime to Yosilevich, signing all the decrees which the latter put before him. First of all the name of the penal camps was changed from "Sevlon," which was synthetically composed from "Northern Camps of Special Designation" to "Sevitlag," meaning "Northern Corrective Penitentiary Camps."

Within a week the external aspect of the camps changed materially and the prisoners breathed more freely. The communist five-day week was introduced, prisoners were allowed the regular rest on the fifth day and more normal living conditions. There were even some instances where prisoners refused to do the work assigned them and the administration did not know how to handle such cases under the new regulations.

The efficiency of production, however, was badly lowered by these innovations and Moscow followed them up with indignant telegrams demanding that the former rate of production be maintained at all costs. The commanders were in distress. As usual in the U.S.S.R. one extreme had been substituted for another, while the solution lay in a happy medium. But something had to be done. Innumerable conferences followed, new plans were made, reams of paper were used up and drinking parties at Vaskov's were more frequent. In the meantime, the prisoners used the interim to rest up a bit and slackened considerably in their work.

The new rules made it much easier for wives to obtain permission to visit their husbands. The prisoners felt that the new order of things was too good to last. Many took advantage of it to telegraph their wives to come and soon all the rooms in town were rented and women's gay colored hats and kerchiefs were to be seen on the streets in numbers.

Camp discipline was relaxed. Prisoners went to the city beer garden in groups, drank vodka and had brawls with the town people. Some of them even went to church, which before was strictly forbidden. Two enterprising young men managed to get married to native women. Vaskov was no longer saluted by the prisoners in the street when he passed them in his elegant carriage. A month earlier such incivility would have been punished by the dungeon. Now it passed unnoticed.

Some prisoners of the criminal group stole axes, saws and nails from the camp's supplies and bartered them to the peasants at the market-place for milk and other farm products. Escapes became more frequent.

The barracks for women housed prostitutes together with prisoners of the peasant and the educated classes. The prostitutes freely received men in the general barracks. The latter brought vodka and regular orgies ensued, to the dismay of the other women. It was clear that a general disintegration was setting in which would bring its own reaction. It was not long in coming.

Early in August a telegram suddenly came from Kotlas stating that comrade Kogan, chief of all the penal camps in the U.S.S.R., newly appointed by Moscow, was on his way to Ust-Sysolsk accompanied by the plenipotentiary of the OGPU in the Northern area, comrade Shiyron.

The unexpected guests were to arrive the next morning and nothing had been prepared for their reception. Vaskov raced from one department to the other, shouted and cursed, not knowing what to do. The prisoners instinctively felt that ominous clouds were gathering over their heads.

The next day I watched the pompous reception from the window of our warehouse. A detachment of armed guards stood at the pier in formation. Vaskov and the high commanders of the camp were waiting, dressed in their best clothes with their boots brightly polished. A brass band was in readiness.

As the steamer approached the pier the band struck up the "International," not without discords. Vaskov quickly ran up the gang-plank, only to come back at a still faster pace. He frantically motioned to the band to stop and as the leader continued to wave his baton he poked him in the ribs. The band took flight in all directions. This beginning was not promising.

A short plump man in an OGPU uniform came down the gang-plank carefully, holding on to the railing. He had several red stripes on his collar and his chest was decorated with several medals on red ribbons. His pale, slightly powdered face, and his disdainfully pursed lips expressed disapprobation of the proceedings, as if to say that he had not expected quite such an exhibition of idiocy. His pudgy nose hung a little heavily over his clean-shaven upper lip. After him came the familiar figure of Commander Boksha and several other men. All of them carried brief-cases.

Boksha motioned to the guards, who quickly disappeared. Vaskov was embarrassed and whispered something into Boksha's ear. The important personage slowly proceeded from the pier to the mainland and in another minute the whole group was sitting in droshkies on their way to town. The triumphal reception was a flat failure.

At our office everybody was excited. The great man, after a cursory inspection of the work post, was going to make the rounds of all departments.

At the work post an even greater embarrassment awaited our commanders than at the pier. A large number of prisoners, who had for various reasons not gone to work, were playing football in the yard.

Sashka, a woman prisoner who had gone insane, kept step with the inspecting high commanders. She was the first to meet them at the work post's gates, shouting at the top of her voice: "Ah, the chief executioner is here!"

"What is this I hear?" asked Kogan, red with anger.

"An insane prisoner, comrade commander," answered the commander of the work post.

"Well, why do you leave her at large? You should isolate her," said Kogan angrily.

"She is the quiet kind, comrade commander, she does no harm. We have several of them here, they are all good workers."

Kogan lost his temper. "It is an outrage," he said. "And why aren't these prisoners at work?" He pointed to the football players.

"They are sick, comrade commander," muttered the scared commander of the work post. He immediately realized his blunder.

"These men sick? Do you take me for an idiot? I'll have you arrested, then you'll see what it is to get sick. This is a Luna Park and not a work post of the OGPU!" Kogan, now really enraged, turned to Boksha: "What the hell is the matter with all of you here?"

He quickly crossed the yard and went into the barracks to inspect the buildings and talk to the prisoners.

"What are you in for? What term? Any complaints?" came the usual questions.

At the women's barracks a peasant woman asked to have the prostitutes removed from the barracks. The high commander only snorted and walked on.

At their noon-day meal the commanders discussed the question of the eighteen newly-born infants and the thirty more that were expected. The camp regulations contained no instructions fitting the case and a decision had to be made without delay. Should the infants be left with their mothers or should the mothers be sent on to remote district camps and a sort of camp creche be organized for the care of the infants? The latter decision prevailed.

At two o'clock the high commander began inspecting the departments. His attention was first drawn to prisoner Moskovsky, a former Denikin officer, who now worked at the secretariat. Bukhaltzev, recently arrested and presumably under lock and key, occupied a room at the secretariat and enjoyed perfect freedom, walked about town and came to the administration's dining room for his meals.

"A White officer guarding a criminal!" he cried out when he was told about it. "This requires imagination! Put one of them back at manual labor, the other one in prison. Do this immediately."

After this Vaskov felt quite sick and went home to drown his sorrow. Boksha, with a forlorn expression on his face, continued to accompany the high commander. Kogan stopped at the desk of each clerk and asked him the usual questions while his secretary made notes of the answers. The prisoners did not know the purpose of these notes, but as usual hoped that they would bring some change for the better. Not wishing to stand at attention before the chekists, I had made a timely exit and gone to the store-rooms. When I came back I was told that the names of seventeen clerks had been included in a special list. Later in the evening their fate was announced. The high commander had ordered all of them to be transferred to manual labor, since they were all serving terms on charges of counter-revolution.

This order put confusion into the ranks of the OGPU commanders themselves who were chiefs of the various departments. They were deprived of the services of valuable men who actually did all the work. All the work of the administration was done by the counter-revolutionaries. Vaskov calmed them all down the next day, promising to return the prisoners to their old jobs as soon as Kogan departed. True enough, after four days they were all back, including Bukhaltzev. What a puppet-show!

CHAPTER SEVENTEEN: BACK TO NORMALCY

On August 8, 1930, a list of names of eighty-two prisoners was made public. The eighty-two had been ordered to be shot on various charges, such as sabotage, attempts at escape, agitation against the authorities, refusal to work, etc. The list carried a note to the effect that the order had been executed. It was signed: Kogan.

We combed the death-list. I noticed the names of some of my former friends. The amiable and amusing Petkin, who had been arrested suddenly some three weeks before Kogan's arrival, headed the list. My cell-mate from the Lefortovsky prison, Timofeyich, was among them for having twice attempted to escape from the Uftug timberworks. So was my former pupil, the Lettish officer Baltrusevich, who had stubbornly refused to do any kind of work ever since his arrival and until the day he was shot.

Simultaneous with the publication of the list, there appeared a decree promulgated by Kogan on the day of his departure. The decree brought another fundamental change in the penal camp regulations. All the recent reforms were scrapped, and the effect was to restore the old order of things. True, the prisoners still had the right to refuse to work at their assigned tasks, but they were then accused of sabotage; only in the most exceptional cases had doctors and medical assistants the right to release prisoners from work, and they were personally responsible for any abuse of this privilege; the assignments of work were to be in accordance with the new schedule, but were always to be interpreted so as to mean the maximum. It was proposed that during the holidays the prisoners should be kept busy at some useful tasks.

This was both unexpected and serious. The decree was very effective, the former working schedule was re-established, and the exploitation of prisoners continued. The death-list made it clear that the right to issue personal orders for the execution of prisoners was now conferred on the chief commander of all penal camps and on the plenipotentiaries of the OGPU in the various districts.

Before Kogan's arrival the daily decrees rarely mentioned the names of the prisoners shot. The administration preferred to shoot them quietly and though we all knew that many were shot, it was never publicly announced. During the month and a half of the reform status there had not been a single execution and we had grown accustomed to a feeling of security. Therefore, the execution of the eighty-two men came as a shock to us. That order was followed by more of the same kind, and thereafter names of executed men were published daily both in the decrees and in the camp's news-leaflet. Life had returned to normal.

At Archangel the prisoners of our camp district were employed at various tasks, but chiefly in loading timber for export. All export timber was loaded on the ships by prisoners. Reports came from Archangel concerning fabulous escapes of prisoners. Prisoners tried to communicate with the outer world by means of inscriptions on the exported timber, calling attention to the fact that it was produced by convict labor, and to their dire living conditions.

Reports from Solvychegodsk gave the number of prisoners who died every day from sickness and exhaustion following the liquidation of the timber-works. Penug reported the completion of trestles and the progress of earthworks along the railroad track. The highway construction division reported results and demanded shovels, more and more shovels. The shovels were of such poor quality that they had to be scrapped after a week's use and there was always a shortage of shovels at all work posts. The geological expedition to Vaigach Island reported the finding of lead; an expedition to Ukhta started drilling for oil. The work went on, the prisoners died, the clerks at the administration wrote, telegraphed, figured, and filled untold reams of paper.

My personal fate was indirectly affected by Kogan's visit. My living conditions became less tolerable. The secret intelligence department of the camp had started an experiment in "rebuilding men." It was decided that prisoners with a reputation for not being in sympathy with the existing Soviet regime were to be given the worst living conditions in camp, that they were to be forbidden to use the employees' dining room, were to sleep on dirty shelves in the general barracks, come out to the roll-call in the morning, shout "zdrah," etc. The influence of Zakhariantz again made itself felt. My record was not good and I was included in the list of prisoners to be "rebuilt." I was transferred to the barracks of the First Work Post, to eat from the common pot, fight the vermin, and enjoy the full flavor of life in a squadron.

Just about this time a popular prisoners' song hit was imported from the Solovetsky camp. The melody was sad and each verse ended in the refrain:

"Why should we hope? Our lives are wholly blasted,

"And all of us are damned by destiny!"

Whether it was because the refrain expressed so faithfully the mental condition of the prisoners or because of its strain touching the hungering soul, the song spread like wildfire over all the work posts of the penal camps and could be heard everywhere.

Perhaps the song had an enervating effect, for just at that time an epidemic of suicides struck the camps. It was clearly a case of psychosis. The administration was alarmed and issued orders forbidding prisoners to sing that particular song, offenders to be thrown in the dungeon. The watch at the barracks was increased and loud-speakers were installed to divert prisoners' thoughts from sad reality. An urgent order was sent to Moscow for guitars, mandolins and balalaikas, which were then distributed at the work posts.

In August 1930, a fresh epidemic of typhus broke out. Instead of improving sanitary conditions at the camps, the authorities decided to shave the prisoners' heads and bodies regardless of their sex or age. The order was to be executed within three days.

The work began. All the barbers were busy from morning till night, clipping, lathering and shaving. It was a simple procedure. The prisoner entered the room and stripped, whereupon he was shaved clean. As there were no women barbers, all women prisoners were shaved by men. Some peasant women bitterly resisted the order, but nothing helped. They cried and they wept, but in spite of all remonstrances they were dragged out of the barracks, had their clothes torn off them, were lathered and shaved. The Lett Ozol, who was the warden at our work post, insisted that it was his duty to be present at the shaving of women and told them not to mind him, as he was "not a bourgeois."

The unfortunate priests wept as they parted with their luxuriant hair and beards. They exhorted the commanders and sent them petitions explaining that their religious order forbade them to cut off their beards. It was to no avail, all of them were shaved clean, and deprived of their marks of distinction from other prisoners.

At the end of August there was a sudden change in the personnel of our high command, by order from Moscow. Boksha and Vaskov were replaced by the former commander of the Vologda OGPU, Sienkevicz, a carpenter by trade, and by Shkele, formerly of the secret intelligence service. At the same time Zolotarev was appointed the new head of the supply department.

Zolotarev, alias Goldman, was a man of forty and a chekist of a different order. His kind had become more numerous in the OGPU during the last few years. He was always clean-shaven, washed and neatly dressed; his hands were scrupulously clean and his manicured nails covered with rose nail-polish. He spoke in a high voice, in an effeminate undecided manner, was very polite, and understood nothing of business. But, as a matter of fact, his system was good — he did not interfere with the real workers in his department.

During two months the supply department had had several chiefs. First, the engineer Grinstein was replaced by Volkov, a veritable idiot. He in turn was replaced by another chekist, then a third, and so on, at an average rate of one chief a week. During this game of leap-frog, the workers of the department were busy preparing a supply plan for the penal camps.

Penal camps, like all other institutions in the U.S.S.R., were furnished their supplies directly by Moscow, according to a plan prepared in advance. The plan was prepared in minute detail and calculations were based on certain quotas. For calculation purposes, the constantly varying number of prisoners in the Northern penal camps in 1931 was estimated to average sixty thousand men.

The preparation of the plan for food supplies was easy. It was not so with the requirements of the technical department, considering the uncertainty as to what construction work would be undertaken during the ensuing year. After three weeks of hard work the detailed plan was ready. It showed not only the rails, tools and machinery required, but also included sewing needles, lamp-wicks, etc., giving their exact price and the total amounts. The plan was duly prepared and the supplies ordered, but neither I nor any of my associates expected to receive even the tenth part of them, as we knew the deplorable condition of the home industries. The plan was sent to Moscow and earned praise from high quarters which was later of some service to me. From that time on I was an "invaluable" worker of the administration, and my position was much more secure. Indeed, but very little is needed to deserve commendation in the U.S.S.R.

Just about this time the entire organization of penal camps in the U.S.S.R. took final form. The "Administration of Penal Camps" had its seat in Moscow and was headed by Kogan. He was put in charge of all the camps in Soviet Russia. At the end of 1930, the prisoners numbered about two hundred thousand, but the organization of new camps progressed rapidly and in 1931 this number was doubled.

It was a centralized organization of the military type and the camps were all managed direct from Moscow. All the district administrations were replicas in miniature of the Moscow head-office. Moscow transferred prisoners from one district to another whenever necessity demanded and supplies were distributed accordingly.

The fact that the OGPU system was in importance second only to the war department did not seem to help the organization of supply. All goods were of poor quality and sent with great delay.

Kogan's appointment to the high post coincided with the birth of grandiose plans for new construction in the North. It was decided to begin building the railroad from Kotlas to Kem, which had long been under consideration. This new project caused the railroad line already under construction by our camp to lose all importance.

True to form, the Soviet government started on a new enterprise before finishing the old. In connection with the new project it was decided to enlarge our camp greatly, bring the number of prisoners to a hundred thousand, transfer the administration to Kotlas, and recommence the exploitation of timber in the Uftug and Archangel districts.

It was easy to order the large number of prisoners working in the administration to be transferred to Kotlas, but it was a different matter to find housing facilities for them. But the OGPU does not boast in vain that it knows no obstacles. The main thing was the decision, the details would take care of themselves.

The architect with whom I had spent my first days in Kotlas was urgently called to Ust-Sysolsk. He was ordered to Kotlas at once by a river boat, and while en route he was to make a rough draft for the construction of a settlement to house the three hundred administration workers. A thousand prisoners of his own choosing were placed at his disposal. He was ordered to work day and night and to finish the ten buildings by the first of November. Tools and materials were to be furnished him promptly.

Nothing could daunt the architect. He readily guaranteed completion on time, but not the quality of construction. However, nobody was interested in the latter and he went ahead full speed immediately upon receipt of his instructions. All the local organizations were ordered by the district OGPU to place all available building materials at his disposal. High-handed tactics were used to secure the necessary timber. Detachments of guards stopped the rafts of timber en route to Archangel and groups of prisoners rolled them ashore and brought them to the building site.

These timber rafts belonged to "Severoles," but all the protests of the latter were of no avail. The OGPU was too strong. All the building materials going to the autonomous territory of Komi via Kotlas were held up and unceremoniously diverted to the building site. Good progress was made and by the end of October the main buildings were ready for occupancy.

The administration started to move to Kotlas. One man from each department was to stay at Ust-Sysolsk and finish the business on hand. The choice in my department fell upon me. I was loath to remain, for I wished to get back to Kotlas as quickly as possible, since it was from there that I hoped to carry out my plans for escape.

As luck would have it, there was a shortage of brick and boards at Kotlas. I received a telegram: "Urgent. Ship immediately all brick remaining from railroad construction. Buy and ship minimum two hundred standards of sawn timber."

It was easier to write such a telegram than to execute it. There were about one hundred and fifty thousand bricks at the railroad, but they were stored three kilometers from town, the roads were softened by the rains, and a horse could haul not more than seventy-five bricks per load. All the horses of the penal camp were busy on earth-work construction which could not be stopped. But the telegrams came thick and fast — the brick was urgently needed and all hopes were centered on me. I had to use a well-known trick and entice teamsters away from work for other Soviet organizations. To do this I offered a bonus of a package of tobacco for each load hauled.

The announcement of the bonus spread like wildfire and the next morning bricks were being hauled to the pier at full speed. Then came the problem of transportation, as the local office of state navigation refused to furnish barges. I used Bukhaltzev's method and generously distributed some luxury goods such as cigarettes, preserves, chocolate and tea. Instantly some barges were found and brought to the pier. Tobacco bonuses were also used for the loading of brick and similar tactics helped in the purchase and loading of sawn timber.

Finally all the brick and half the timber were loaded and ready to leave. But suddenly a change of weather set in; it turned very cold and in the morning we found the river frozen and the closing of navigation was officially announced. The tugs were taken to the docks and were guarded to prevent us from ordering them out in spite of the ice. Our barges remained at the pier.

I was quite aware of the danger confronting me. If the barges remained there for the winter, I faced dire consequences. I had many chekist well-wishers such as Zakhariantz, and it would be easy for them to portray this occurrence in a light that would make it appear I had intentionally planned it. I could be accused of sabotage and "wrecking," could be arrested again, and sentenced to the usual punishment meted out for such grave crimes. My only chance was for warm weather which would melt the ice. Two days passed in anxious expectation. The ice was getting firmer.

During these two days I received an untold number of telegrams and was constantly called to the office of Shkele, the assistant commander of the camps, who had remained at Ust-Sysolsk. The conversation was always the same: "Well, how about the river?"

"It is still frozen."

"And the brick and the timber?"

"Awaiting shipment."

"When are you going to ship them?"

"As soon as the ice thaws."

"What makes you think that it will thaw?"

"It is bound to thaw."

"But why is it bound to?"

"Because it must."

"All right. You may go."

I would leave, only to be found within the hour by an urgent messenger who demanded that I come to the chief's office at once. Then the same conversation was repeated.

Under the influence of the continual radio messages from Kotlas, Shkele's tone of voice abruptly changed toward the end of the second day. True chekist that he was, he was already looking for the goat on whom to pin the guilt and the thought was ripening in his head that the blame for the ill-fated shipment could be heaped on my shoulders.

"How about the river?" he kept asking, now with anger and a hidden threat in his voice.

I knew that if the cold weather persisted I was lost. Everybody was excited and demanded that the barges be unloaded immediately, but I stubbornly insisted on patience and I won. In the evening of the second day the atmosphere at the office was so tense that I asked for a last respite until morning, assuring everybody that the barges would leave with sunrise.

My assurance was not entirely due to a blind trust in luck. I had a strong pain in my injured knee and this to me was a sign of a definite change in the weather. On my way back from the bathhouse to the barracks I was delighted to note that my barometer had not deceived me. A warm wind was blowing in my face. In the morning rain and wind helped to break up the ice and our barges left triumphantly.

Now I was impatiently waiting for orders to leave for Kotlas, but they did not come. I had no more work and not wanting to spend my time in the barracks, I wandered about town and the cemetery, where the priest daily said morning mass in an empty church. He thought himself quite alone and sang the service in a beautiful, inspired voice which resounded clear as a bell from the listening walls. In the perfect silence of the temple his voice rolled and lulled, then grew again, filling the church with reverberations and penetrating the innermost recesses of the soul. I closed my eyes and gave myself up wholly to the charm of it, forgetting for a moment that I was a prisoner.

The telegram calling me to Kotlas came two hours before the departure of the season's last steamer. I left Ust-Sysolsk hoping never to see it again. The journey was as melancholy as the clouded sky. On the second evening the lights of Kotlas greeted me in the darkness and at ten o'clock I entered the building of the EKO office, where our supply department had made its headquarters.

CHAPTER EIGHTEEN: THIN ICE

In Kotlas the construction of buildings for the administration was progressing rapidly. The prisoners working on them lived in tents at the site of construction. The entire area reserved for the administration settlement was already surrounded by a barbed-wire fence. There was an acute shortage of all other building materials, but barbed wire was always plentiful.

The large new two-story office building was ready except for the window-panes; the barracks reserved for the office staff were also not quite completed and the staff was temporarily housed in the military barracks at the station. They were cold and dirty, with a floor of packed earth. I spent five days in one of these barracks. As usual there was neither room nor facilities for sleeping, but, being hardened in this respect, I found a berth on top of some wooden boxes and slept on them without murmur.

In Kotlas I met again my old prison companion, Pevny. Within these nine months he had changed from a man of Herculean build to a feeble stooping old man with sunken eyes and a bad cough, the result of an assignment of work in the forest. My other companion from the Lefortovsky prison, the financial inspector Granovsky, had been transferred to Ust-Vym and died there of consumption in October. Only forty of my fellow passengers in the prison-train that had brought me to Kotlas, remained there. The great majority had been assigned to the Uftug timber-works and had perished there.

The once dreaded Grigoriantz had been caught in some misdeed and reduced to the position of camp messenger. He swept the floors of our supply department and was sent by us on errands. His broad cheek-bones now distended in a servile smile instead of the former insolent one. Slavishly he endeavoured to please the commanders, the wielders of power. He ran ahead of them to open the door, helped them on with their overcoats, took off his cap and bowed low. A little while later he became a sort of personal butler to Zolotarev, the manicured commander, and his star began rising again.

The work in our department proceeded as usual. We had our meals in the mess-room which had formerly served as stables for the fire department. By agreement with the fire department the stables were altered to house the mess-room. Stoves and boilers were installed and tables moved in. When it was all ready, the city militia announced that it needed the building and ordered it cleared. When its demands were rejected, it occupied the building by force and ejected its occupants and their equipment. Sienkevicz, the energetic commander of the administration, was called to the rescue and immediately took decisive steps. He ordered a detachment of armed guards to chase out the militia, by force if necessary, and then to report to him. Seeing the determination and the greater number of the enemy, the militia took to their heels and at three o'clock the regular dinner was served.

Five days after my arrival ten of the more responsible members of the managing staff rented a large room in town and moved into it with all their belongings. But our vanquished enemy, the militia, eager for revenge, did not leave us in peace. It procured the necessary legal documents from the city authorities and ejected us in turn from our new quarters. We moved to another place and were again put out. Our commander Sienkevicz was impotent in the matter as all formalities had been complied with. Six times we were chased out, until at last the new barracks were ready for us and we settled there for good.

The walls of the barracks were hastily put together and admitted plenty of fresh air. We had excellent ventilation, but as winter was advancing, it was rather cold. My bunk was near the window and in the morning I would find my pillow covered with a fine spray of snow and frozen to the wall. But life was more comfortable than at Ust-Sysolsk and I did not carp at fate.

The enterprising radio operator had constructed a receiving set and installed a loud-speaker in the corridor of our barracks. After midnight we could hear the broadcasts from abroad. Officially it was forbidden to listen to any of these, but the commandant in charge of our barracks loved fox-trot music, did not enforce the regulation, and was the first to come to the midnight concerts. At the first sounds of dance music large numbers of prisoners came into the corridor from their dormitories in search of momentary solace and oblivion.

They came out heavy with sleep, hastily dressed in overcoats and felt boots. It was a curious-looking assemblage. In order to forget the sad realities, they covered their eyes with their hands and stood or sat around listening to the splendid orchestra from the Savoy Hotel in London. The audience in the corridor mentally flew to the source of the music, sighing and trembling with excitement when they heard the applause of the people who were actually present, and free to dine and dance. Then, as soon as the music started again, they were instantly still, drinking in the melodious tunes. Some of the younger prisoners were even inspired to do some dance steps on the coarse cold floor, in spite of their heavy felt boots. The dim light of a kerosene lamp fell upon our nocturnal revel; it was pathetic and grotesque.

The other buildings were nearing completion. All that was wanting was the electric lighting. There was no wire or appliances. Sienkevicz, who overcame all difficulties with the directness of a carpenter, issued orders to the supply department to procure all the necessary material in two weeks' time. Upon signing these instructions, he promptly left for Archangel.

Zolotarev, the chief of the supply department, was in a quandary. He could not get the materials required except in Moscow or Leningrad. He decided to send there one of his employees, and his choice fell upon me. I was to be furnished a certificate commissioning me to do purchasing in Moscow, and, upon fulfilling my mission, was to return to the penal camps.

It seemed that luck was favoring me. The administration itself was facilitating my escape, giving me a certificate for an unmolested passage to Moscow by rail. Detailed plans for escape formed in my head.

I packed my things, received food and money for my journey, and went to get the certificate, outwardly calm but trembling with anxiety.

"Going to Moscow?" asked a fellow clerk. "Wait a minute, I'll prepare your certificate."

He wrote it out and took the priceless document in for signature. His department was run by Breitbard, a newly appointed, young and reckless chekist. He quickly signed the certificate and took it into the private office of the commander of the administration. During the absence of the stalwart carpenter-commander, the Lett Shkele took his place. My heart fell as I thought of it. Shkele, with his distrustful eyes! He would not sign the certificate, he knew me too well. But, a miracle might happen; I clung to the hope that he would sign it.

Breitbard came out of the office. I saw that there was no seal on the certificate. Alas, no luck!

"Tell the chief of the supply department that I signed it but Shkele vetoed it," said Breitbard. No further comments were necessary.

My department chief was in a rage. He was ordered to procure certain materials without fail and when he tried to do so obstacles were put in his way and his man was refused a certificate. What the hell did they think they were doing? He grabbed the telephone receiver.

"Comrade Shkele? What's the matter? Why do you refuse to sign?"

A pause.

"I have positive instructions from Sienkevicz and you oppose them."

A pause.

"Ah, so that's the case. But I accept personal responsibility. Can't be done? Why?"

Impatiently he rapped the table with his fingers, looking at me and frowning.

"Tomorrow you will leave under escort," he said finally, hanging up the receiver.

This was immaterial to me. It would be an easy matter to give my escort the slip, once I was in Moscow. It was important to get outside the zone of the penal camps.

But I was again doomed to disappointment, for an electrician, a stool-pigeon, was recommended for the job by the secret intelligence department and left in my place the next day. Once more I was thwarted. My only compensation for the disappointment was the food which had been furnished me for my journey and which served as the piece de resistance for a supper with my room-mates. One of them even brought vodka to console me.

With the advance of winter, watchfulness was increased to forestall escapes. Sentries patrolled the barbed-wire enclosure and there was a guard at the gates who let prisoners out only if they had a special permit. I had such a permit and frequently went to town trying to re-establish my old connections. But even during my short absence, most of my friends had been either arrested and exiled or transferred to work in remote provinces. The peasant who had been willing to drive me to Viatka had been arrested for seditious propaganda. A year ago when there was a chance for escape I lacked the necessary money; now, when I had the money, there was nobody to help me. Escapes in the Uftug district were more frequent now that the swampy ground was frozen, but on the other hand we, members of the office staff, knew that most of the fugitives were caught and that only one in fifty of the attempted escapes succeeded.

About the middle of September 1930, a telegram from Moscow advised our office that some equipment for the Ukhtinsky Geological Expedition was stuck at Archangel and that it was impossible to ship it up the Petchora River, as originally intended. Our camp was instructed to arrange for the transportation of this material over the winter route.

Immediately a conference of engineers and transportation specialists was called. The shipment weighed about five hundred tons and consisted of steam boilers, well-drilling machinery, electric motors, etc. It had to be delivered to the Ukhtinsky-Petchorsky Camp, as the geological expedition was called, at Uhkta, some seven hundred and fifty kilometers from Kotlas. All the engineers at the conference agreed on the impossibility of transporting the material in the ordinary manner. The peasants' sleds had a capacity not exceeding half a ton, while some of the machines weighed over five tons. The deep snow and bad roads made doubling up of horses impossible. After a long conference the transportation specialists came to the conclusion that the shipment could be moved only with the help of tractors, pulling specially constructed sledges. It would first be necessary to construct a roadway of packed snow and ice.

A long telegram was sent to Moscow in which it was pointed out that a special roadway over the ice would have to be constructed and that the job would require several thousand prisoners and would take several months. The telegram remained unanswered for a long time and we began to think that the project had been abandoned. Then Moscow suddenly informed us that the materials would be transported by means of tractors as we had suggested, that twenty-five tractors were being shipped to Kotlas, that the geological material had already left Archangel bound for Kotlas, and that "Comrade Sidorov," a special plenipotentiary, was leaving Moscow for Kotlas, to take charge of the transportation from that point on.

It was clear that the enterprise was doomed to failure if the icy roadway was not built. Plans for the latter were urgently taken in hand and the main details worked out, comprising the installation of fuel stations and of repair-shops en route, the establishment of communication relays by mounted messengers, etc. The plan was presented to Sidorov on his arrival.

Sidorov was tall and slender, looked energetic, had a red nose and sunken gray eyes. He would have nothing of our plans.

"What is all this for?" he questioned. "An icy road-way, indeed! Not at all necessary, we shall move it over the river-bed, simply. Oh, don't worry, the ice will hold it all right. Where there's a will, there's a way. Let's have less discussion and more action. We'll send a special snow-sweeper ahead of the tractors. You don't know a thing about it. These methods have been used in Canada, and if the bourgeois can do it, we shall surely succeed in doing it even better. What we need, citizens, is whole-hearted cooperation and less sabotage."

The last phrase accentuated the underlying realities. "Less sabotage!" So that's it. All the assembled "citizens" had had plenty of experience in these matters at the time of their cross-examinations by the OGPU.

Sidorov's equipment consisted of a large supply of energy, self-reliance, and ignorance. No obstacles existed for him.

"We must get the materials to Ukhta without fail," he announced in a tone allowing no contradiction. "It is a matter of paramount importance to the state. Preliminary investigations show the existence of tremendous supplies of oil in the Ukhta district. It will be a second Baku. More than that, it is destined to become the world's greatest oil-field. It is physically beyond the reach of foreign intervention. And in the face of all this, you make cumbersome plans. Enough! We'll take it over the ice. First over the Vychegda, then over the Vym River. Understand?"

The arguments and manner of talking were quite familiar to the engineers. But since the absurdity of the idea made ultimate failure inevitable, our transportation specialists composed a detailed report outlining their recommendations. They predicted the failure of Sidorov's plan and stated that they were ready to obey orders, but refused to accept the responsibility.

Sidorov was incensed when he saw the report.

"Oh, you are ready to obey instructions, are you?" he cried. "You go to the devil, all of you. I shall manage without you."

He was one of those ignorant, headstrong workmen who had made a career in the communist system. He followed his own fixed idea blindly, in spite of all obstacles. Some of the important Moscow chekists had evidently perused the report of the engineers and had understood its main point to be that tractors were required for the transportation. Not bothering about further details, they entrusted Sidorov with the execution of the plans. He was of Northern origin, knew local conditions and was the very man to handle the matter.

The engineers and transportation specialists whose help had been rejected, breathed a sigh of relief. Sidorov would manage without them. Wonderful! They had not expected such good luck.

Sidorov started work the next morning. He found a tractor specialist at the Kotlas Transfer Station shops, Ralenko, a young Ukrainian engineer who had been sentenced for his open criticism of conditions at the Kharkov Tractor Works, after he had returned there from his educational trip to the Ford plant in the U.S.A.

Ralenko was about thirty-five, an able worker and quite an expert on tractors. As a doctor makes his diagnosis after examining the patient, so he inspected tractors, listened to them working, and then made an unfailing analysis of their defects.

Sidorov entrusted Ralenko with the inspection and repair of the incoming tractors and himself began to select a large staff of workers. He organized and dispatched a detachment of surveyors, selected sites for the storage of fuel, appointed foremen. The very first tests showed that the kerosene was of such bad quality that gasoline would have to be used. Gasoline and lubricating oils were urgently requisitioned from Moscow. The arriving tractors were in very bad shape: they were poorly assembled, partly broken and had no spare parts. They were repaired and reassembled at Ralenko's shop, which kept working day and night. Five of the tractors were sacrificed in order to replace defective parts of the others.

At the same time fifty tractor sledges were built, as well as a special snow-plow of Sidorov's own design. The sledges were large and heavy, reinforced with strips of iron. As to the snow-plow, the engineer who was put in charge of its construction vainly tried to convince Sidorov that it would turn over and break, and would hold up the tractors rather than help them. Sidorov stubbornly insisted that he was right and ordered the "wonder-sweeper" constructed strictly in accordance with his design.

Bad news came from the surveying detachment. The ice on the rivers was thin, and covered with deep snow-drifts. The detachment went ahead slowly as half the men were frostbitten.

"Get on ahead," wired Sidorov. "Give your men alcohol to keep them warm."

Being himself a good hand at drinking, he found a worthy disciple in Likhachev, who was in charge of the surveying detachment. The latter arrived at Kotlas with his assistant, young Count Tatishtchev, immediately upon receipt of Sidorov's telegram. They left Kotlas that same evening, their sleigh loaded high with large containers of alcohol. Faster progress was reported from that time on, to the delight of Sidorov, who was driving things ahead with all his might. Our engineers continued their sceptical attitude toward his endeavors and were busy figuring what the idea would cost the government.

"Hundreds of thousands of roubles will be lost," said the old engineer P. indignantly. "And besides, you may be quite sure that part of the tractors will break through the ice and go down."

He had been sentenced to the penal camps for insisting on the necessity of maintaining a normal speed of work instead of forcing things ahead. Here at the camp his advice was again ignored and he predicted an estimated loss of half a million roubles, in keeping with the famous Bolshevik "forced tempos" — probably the worst "wrecking" factors in Soviet industry.

Thanks to the unceasing efforts of Ralenko, the tractors were ready in the middle of February 1931, and the loading of material began. Steam-boilers and machinery were lowered on ropes from the high bank to the river. Heavy and cumbersome cases were loaded with great difficulty on the special sledges. The ice had been cleared of snow all around the loading zone; it creaked slightly. The entire five hundred tons were loaded by February 20th and the tractors, with the sledges behind them, awaited the signal to start. The procession was headed by a "Cletrac" pushing an American snow-plow; then came a second "Cletrac" with the "wonder-sweeper" of Sidorov's design. After the "wonder-sweeper" came a column of "Cletracs" and after them the heavy and unwieldy "Communars" of the Kharkov Tractor Works. In the rear were three trucks, one housing a travelling repair-shop, one carrying food supplies, and one a van to serve as sleeping quarters for the drivers. Each tractor pulled two or three sledges. Twenty guards escorted the caravan.

All the commanders of the penal camps and the officials of town offices came to see the procession start. A large crowd of people surrounded them. It was thirteen degrees below zero.

Sidorov made a speech, standing on top of the little red Monarch tractor which went with the caravan for maneuvering purposes. The speech lauded Soviet achievements, described the wealth of the Ukhta oil-fields, went to great lengths stupidly describing the inefficiency of the Czar who had not given his people any tractors while the Bolsheviks were producing large quantities of them at their own plants.

A thin voice from the crowd interrupted his speech. "Stop romancing," it cried, "there were no tractors at all before the war." Sidorov's enthusiasm was checked. The anti-Soviet agitator was dragged out of the crowd forthwith and proved to be a boy of fourteen, son of a railroad worker and a pupil at the local school. He was properly scolded and released.

The bookkeeper went up to Sidorov and facetiously recommended that he postpone the start for a day, as Friday was an unlucky day. The head of the local Soviet made a little speech and the caravan started forward. In another half-hour it had disappeared, leaving only loose boards and ends of rope on the ice of the loading zone.

At three o'clock it was already reported that the American snow-plow was not powerful enough for the Northern snow-drifts and had to be assisted by a crew with shovels. The next day brought the news that the "wonder-sweeper" was a total failure and had been abandoned en route. Then came a period of waiting. From time to time messengers arrived from the expedition and their reports gave us a fairly clear picture. The tractors had abandoned the road-way staked out by the surveying detachment and were following the peasants' sleigh-road over the river. They were making about fifteen kilometers a day. The American "Cletracs" worked satisfactorily, but the Soviet "Communars" were constantly breaking down and their repair held up the caravan. Sidorov fed the drivers alcohol to keep up their spirits and mobilized all women and girls from the villages on the river to come help shovel snow in the way of the caravan. He walked about gun in hand and threatened to shoot anybody doubting the success of the enterprise. The drivers froze, and drank inordinately. The creaking of the ice was quite menacing at times. In case of success, the arrival at Ust-Vym could be expected by the middle of March. From there on it would be easy to continue to Ukhta'over the highway under construction.

Daily reports were sent to Moscow describing the progress made. "Why so slow?" Moscow answered. "Increase the pace!" Telegrams of a like character came in almost every day.

For a whole week Sidorov's reports were short and laconic. Then came a three-day silence, followed by a confidential telegram, the contents of which immediately became known to everybody in the office. Sidorov begged for help. The ice had cracked and two tractors and six loaded sledges were at the bottom of the river. They had gone down in a shallow spot and could be recovered.

Immediately upon receipt of the telegram, a party of secret intelligence officials left for the place of the accident. It was accompanied by the captain of the camps' tug with hoisting and salvage equipment. After several days the salvage operations were brought to a successful end, all the materials were recovered, and the caravan again started forward, accompanied by the captain with his tackle.

Two days later there was a second catastrophe, this time unfortunately at a deep spot. A "Communar" tractor with two sledges and cases containing the most valuable materials went to the bottom of the river for good. All efforts to recover them proved unsuccessful. After that Sidorov decided to abandon the plan of transportation along "the natural tractor highway over the river ice," and to continue via regular country roads. The caravan was about halfway to its destination. It was a rolling country; the road had been built before the advent of automobiles and wound its way, descending to the banks of the river and then again leading right over the tops of the hills. Breakages were now frequent. Couplings gave way repeatedly and loaded sledges broke away and slid downhill. Engineer Ralenko hurriedly left Kotlas and went to the rescue, but even his presence could not help matters. The roads were not suitable for this mode of transportation, the caravan stopped and the unloading began. Parts of the shipment proceeded forward, the balance was to await the opening of navigation. By the end of the winter, only four tractors out of the twenty reached Ust-Vym, one was sunk, and the rest waited to be loaded on barges and to be returned to Kotlas. The plan ended in a total failure and the estimated loss was about six hundred thousand roubles.

The bookkeeper met Sidorov on his arrival. "You shouldn't have started on Friday," he said, "but you ignored my advice, and now you see what it got you."

CHAPTER NINETEEN: "THERE IS NO CONVICT LABOR!"

In February 1931, we were transferred to the new barracks where the temperature hung around the freezing point. At night it fell below freezing, and engineer A. once awoke in the morning with a frostbitten ear. The moment we reached the barracks, we climbed into our bunks, keeping on our felt boots and overcoats and covering ourselves with every available blanket or piece of clothing.

Members of the office staff lived comparatively well, but the lot of the ordinary prisoners was quite otherwise. They were still kept in tents and barracks fit only for cattle. They were given excessive working assignments, and became worn and ill with fatigue. The reports from the timber-works were deplorable. There the rate of mortality was as high as before, and scurvy, typhus and other diseases were taking their toll. The work was far behind schedule.

Analyzing the results of 1930, the administration came to the conclusion that the plan had failed as far as the construction of the railroad and the highway was concerned. The bad living conditions and undernourishment of the workers were clearly to blame. But as usual the blame was placed where it did not belong. The "directors" of construction were accused of inefficiency, lost their positions, and were sent to field duty. It was decided to continue building the railroad, but without a large staff of engineers: only one engineer, Alpers, was left in charge. Sienkevicz, the carpenter, took matters in his own hands. Drastic orders were sent to all superintendents to insist on the fulfillment of the planned objectives, threatening court-martial in case of failure. The prisoners immediately felt the brunt of the new order. Sienkevicz also instituted the practise of assembling the prisoners for conferences in which plans and improvements were discussed. On one occasion the office staff was called to attend one of these conferences. Attendance was obligatory.

On the night of the conference, all the office workers assembled in the large administration hall. Our stalwart carpenter-commander sat at a table covered with green cloth, surrounded by his retinue. Speeches were made by chekists and by prisoners in favored positions who were making their way upward in the penal camps administration. The latter were especially zealous and proposed a high-sounding resolution to the effect that "prisoners failing in the efficient execution of their duties should be branded with shame." In his opening speech Sienkevicz had announced that all prisoners would be permitted to express their thoughts freely, without fear of consequences, but the prisoners sat there with an impassive expression on their faces, listening in silence to the loud utterances of the hypocrites.

Quite unexpectedly Wahl, the former chief clerk of the EKO office, rose from his seat to make a speech which proved a veritable sensation. It astounded us especially that it was he, of all prisoners, who had resolved to express the hidden thoughts of us all. He was usually so subservient to his chiefs and so mean to those fellow-prisoners who were dependent on him. And now he was the only one who had the courage to speak his mind. It was hard to tell what actually prompted him, as he must have known what the consequences would be.

Wahl started his speech by the statement that he had been a prisoner for over four years and that he had six months more to serve until the end of his sentence.

"I worked hard from the very first day of my arrival. I shall not pretend that I did this because I wished to be of the greatest service to the penal camps..."

Indignant exclamations came from the ranks of the chekists and the presiding officials whispered to each other.

"... No, I did this because we were given a solemn promise of commutation of part of our sentence if we worked well. But what have we now? I have worked efficiently in this camp for over a year and a half. Have I come any nearer to the commutation of my sentence? It is not even mentioned any more. You ask us honestly to perform our duties. To what end, we would like to know? For the success of socialism? It is foreign to us and we do not believe in it. All we want is our freedom. Announce definite rules governing the commutation of sentences, improve living conditions and your success is assured! If not, you are doomed to failure. You may publish a dozen resolutions a day, but that will not improve things. How can you demand that prisoners work efficiently if you do not feed them? Besides ..."

"Enough!" cried Sienkevicz, jumping up and hammering the table with his fist. "You are a mercenary wretch, pris-oner Wahl. We do not need men like you. We'll put you in the dungeon, and there ..."

"I know what's there," shouted Wahl, pale as a sheet. "You asked us to say all that we thought, freely. Everybody here is of the same opinion as I, but they are afraid to speak..."

"Silence!" thundered Sienkevicz, furious and red in the face. "Get out of here at once."

Several chekists started towards Wahl. Without waiting for them, he quickly went out of the door. An awkward pause followed. The officials whispered among themselves, giving vent to indignant exclamations. Threats to punish Wahl for his insolence were heard. The prisoners remained silent.

Half an hour later the assembly unanimously passed the resolution "branding selfish mercenaries with shame" and expressing devotion to the cause. As usual in the U.S.S.R., the unanimous vote was achieved by the expedient of asking the dissenters to raise their hands. There was none. Then those not voting were asked to raise their hands. Again no hands were raised. Under the conditions which exist in the U.S.S.R., there is no sense in exposing oneself to the danger of dissenting from communist resolutions. This explains why the amazing number of resolutions, be they for home consumption or for effect on foreign public opinion, are always carried unanimously. No one familiar with life in Soviet Russia wonders at it, but politically-minded citizens of the Western democracies are surprised and come to the conclusion that the population of Russia is unanimously in accord with Bolshevik rule.

Three days after his memorable speech Wahl was attached to a group of prisoners being sent to the new penal camp at Syzran. When he arrived there, he was caught in a trifling transgression, thrown into the dungeon, accused of agitation against the Soviets, and sentenced to an additional five years in the penal camps.

Korolkov furnished another instance of breaking discipline, but he fared much better than Wahl. He had been commissioned as a specialist to accompany the penal camps' delegate to the district agricultural convention. He made certain proposals, but found opposition from the delegates of the Komsomol — Young Communists — who posed as peasants, but knew next to nothing of agriculture. Korolkov defended his theories, and then, turning to the Komsomol delegates, said: "As for you, my Komsomol comrades, all I have to say is that as farmers you would make good shoemakers," and he added an apt but obscene pun.

This gave rise to a veritable furor. The Komsomol delegates were indignant; the women demanded the immediate ejection of Korolkov, the peasants laughed heartily; the chairman frantically rang the bell, trying to restrain his mirth; the delegate from the penal camps howled with laughter. The conference was speedily adjourned.

The next day Korolkov was officially reprimanded. The pun made a big hit with the commanders and Sienkevicz repeatedly called Korolkov to his office and asked him to tell the story in his own words. Each time he was rewarded with the commander's Homeric laughter. Shkele was also present on one occasion and he proposed putting Korolkov in the dungeon. "Oh, no," laughed Sienkevicz, "no dungeon for him. Give him a reprimand, that's all."

In January, the supply department got busy securing materials for the repair of its tug-boats. Moscow was furnished the necessary requisitions, but did not send the materials and answered all our telegrams with promises, the worth of which we knew only too well. The camp's fleet consisted of four tugs, and three of them were in very poor condition. The fourth tug-boat had been transferred to the Vychegda River from the Volga, and a prisoner, sea captain K., was placed in command.

Imagine his surprise when he went to the tug to take command and recognized it as his own tug which had been taken from him by the Bolsheviks and nationalized in the early days of the revolution. He had not seen it since, and during the intervening years its name had been changed several times. It was now called the "Ufa," a name quite different from "Krasotka" (Little Beauty) which he had originally given it. Still, since Providence had brought it back to him, he took a proprietor's interest in it, which accounted for its good condition.

Special boiler plates were needed for the repairs. They could be obtained only in Archangel. I met with unexpected resistance when I explained to Zolotarev, the manicured chief of our department, the necessity of immediate purchase of the boiler plates.

"Why should we buy them?" he replied. "We have enough of our own iron."

"We have no such iron," I pointed out.

"This goes to show how you work! You don't even know what you have on hand. You have all the iron you need."

"I am sorry, but we really have none in stock."

"I am telling you that we have," he said, getting a little excited. "I have just received the stock-list. Here, you may see for yourself. One and a half tons of broken cast-iron kettles; this should be sufficient for the repairs; let the captain select a suitable piece..."

This was too much, and I burst out laughing. It reminded me of Mark Twain's story of the editor of a provincial agricultural magazine and his unique advice to farmers. Life in the penal camps had its comic side.

From that time on my relations with my immediate boss were spoiled. He could not forgive my laughter. I explained why his suggestion could not be carried out. He turned crimson and did not lift his eyes from his polished nails. "You may go," he said.

Probably this incident would have had no further consequences had I not recounted it to my friends that evening. It was too good a story to be left untold, but one of the stool-pigeons reported it to his superior, and the next day I lost my position as head of the technical department. My friend, the engineer Tselikov, replaced me and I was made his assistant. Zolotarev began to take his revenge. My salary of fifty roubles a month was cut in half, I lost the privilege of taking my meals in the dining room reserved for the managing staff, my permit for free passage about town was taken away from me and, had it been possible, I would have been sent to do hard labor in the forest. Two considerations prevented this; first, I was indispensable to our department as a worker, and second, such a drastic measure entailed the risk of the incident becoming known to the higher authorities.

Zolotarev was ambitious. He had worked in the cheka and then in the OGPU since 1920, and was trying to attain the rank of an "Old Chekist." This honor was conferred upon chekists who had served the OGPU faithfully ten years or more. It opened the way to a more rapid advancement, a higher pension in case of disability, and other privileges. All the workers of the OGPU proudly called themselves "chekists" and were ambitious to become "Old Chekists."

Early in 1931 the Soviet press began printing more and more articles dealing with the agitation in New York and London against the importation of Soviet goods produced by penal or forced labor, particularly in the lumber industry. The Soviet papers had never once admitted that penal labor was actually employed. The government cared little that the employment of penal labor cast a shadow on its reputation, but was concerned with the threat that Europe and America might forbid the import of Soviet timber. Such an embargo would seriously affect the foreign exchange balance, needed to pay for the machinery bought abroad for the Five-Year Plan.

In the beginning of February, the situation became acute. An embargo by the Western countries on the import of Soviet timber and other products seemed imminent. The tension was transmitted to our camps. We could feel that important changes were impending.

Toward the end of the month a general meeting of all the administration office workers was called and the assistant commander Shkele read a report dealing with the unprincipled agitation of the Western-European press against the U.S.S.R.

Shkele read his speech with a strong Lettish accent. He repeatedly referred to the sacred "Five-Year Plan in four years" and stated that the Soviet Union would not tolerate any interference in its internal affairs, that the agitation was carried on by Russian Whites living abroad in order to prevent the Soviets from finishing the construction of the railroad and the highway. He never mentioned the timber-works and loading of timber at Archangel, as if this did not even exist. We looked at each other askance: "What was he driving at?"

After the speech a resolution prepared in advance was read to us. The resolution referred to the shameful and baseless agitation against the Soviets, stated that the prisoners were satisfied with their living conditions, liked their food, were well treated, and were eager to give all their strength to the country so that it might successfully complete the Five-Year Plan. Again there was not a word concerning the timber industry; the arguments were confined to the railroad under construction. Shkele raised his hand.

"Tomorrow, citizens, this paper will be handed around for your signatures. Tonight we shall vote on it. Let anyone who opposes the resolution raise his hand. Nobody. It is carried unanimously," he solemnly declared. "Has anybody abstained from voting? Nobody again? That's fine."

With a look of importance, as if a real vote had just been taken, Shkele sat down and kept staring at the assembled prisoners with a self-satisfied air.

As we were told later, the meeting had been called in accordance with instructions from Moscow, but we did not know for what purpose. Similar meetings took place at all the work posts, identical resolutions were read, voted on, signed by the prisoners, and returned to Moscow, to serve as positive proof, if occasion required.

A week after the meeting had taken place the real explanation of the existing tension was given. A secret code telegram was received from the head-office in Moscow instructing us to liquidate our camp completely in three days, and to do it in such a manner that not a trace should remain. Moscow faced the probability of having to admit a foreign investigating commission and had decided to erase all evidence of the existence of penal camps.

A veritable panic ensued. The usual Bolshevik methods were employed for the liquidation. After a short conference in Sienkevicz's office, telegrams were sent to all work posts to stop operations within twenty-four hours, to gather the prisoners at evacuation centers, to efface all external marks of the penal camps, such as barbed-wire enclosures, watch-turrets and signboards; for all officials to dress in civilian clothes, to disarm the guards, and to wait for further instructions.

In reply to these instructions, many telegrams were received stating that it was impossible to execute the orders in so short a time, that there were not enough horses to effect the evacuation, that the sick would have to be left in the forest, etc. Sienkevicz answered that whoever failed to execute his orders within the stipulated time would be shot.

Pandemonium broke loose. At the Kotlas Transfer Station the double barbed-wire enclosure was speedily removed, the shop equipment was packed. The crowded barracks were filled to overflowing by the influx of prisoners evacuated from the Uftug forests. At Solvychegodsk Karjalainen, the Finnish carpenter who had recently been appointed commander there, exhibited wild energy, the result of a triple ration of alcohol. He ran into the toy-making shop, which was manned by invalids, remonstrating at the slowness of packing there, shooting at the ceiling and yelling so loud that the scared invalids took to their heels and ran out of the building.

"I'll kill you," yelled Karjalainen at the superintendent of the shop, waving his revolver. "I'll kill you if you don't have everything packed in an hour."

From all sides the forest-workers were marching in groups to Solvychegodsk. They carried government equipment in addition to their own belongings. Those seriously ill were crowded on teamsters' sleds, the sick who could still walk followed in the rear. Some of the sick died en route and were buried in the forest.

The situation at Archangel was even worse. The evacuation of the thirty thousand prisoners working there required eight hundred railway cars.

None was available and the prisoners were loaded on old discarded freight and flat cars. Trains picked up groups of prisoners at the stations to which they had been forced to march from their remote outposts. While waiting for the trains, they spent several nights in the forest, hungry and freezing. Prisoners suffering from fever, scurvy or tuberculosis formed no exception, and endured the same privations. Many men died during the mad rush of the evacuation. There were also many attempts to escape, but the cordon of guards had not yet been lifted and most of the fugitives were caught.

In order to show his zeal and to merit praise by his superiors, Okunev, the commander of the Archangel camp peremptorily ordered all prisoners to leave the barracks, removed the barbed-wire enclosure, reversed the signboards and painted new names on them, calling the old penal camp buildings schools, clubs, rest-rooms, etc. His ingenious plan cost the lives of many prisoners. They spent many days in the open waiting for cars near the railway station and suffered great privations. At the end of the year, it was learned that the evacuation of Archangel and Uftug cost thirteen hundred and seventy lives.

The administration itself moved its offices to Solvychegodsk in the record time of twenty-four hours.

We, the privileged staff of the administration, hired a large sleigh, got into it all together and set out about noon. We quickly passed the little gray houses, the yard for scrap iron, the half demolished mill, the shutters of the sausage factory run by the local cooperative which had remained closed for several years because of the shortage of raw material.

We stopped for a meal at Yakovlevskaya. Our peasant host, not seeing any men in uniform among us, brought out vodka. We spread our supplies of lard, preserves and fish, and went to it. Through the window we could see the unending line of prisoners marching and chekists driving by.

The administration office workers marched without escort. They were dressed in new uniforms which had been designed by Sienkevicz himself and consisted of black overcoats with an unnaturally high waist-band, and black caps made of the same material. Sienkevicz had grown tired of seeing poorly dressed people in his office and had ordered the new uniforms just before receiving orders for the evacuation. To save time the tailor shop had cut all the uniforms to one size, for medium height. Therefore the tall and the short prisoners looked very funny in their ill-fitting coats. The black figures looked like scare-crows silhouetted against the white snow.

Sleighs loaded with camp equipment followed groups of prisoners. Food, hay, boxes of all description, were all loaded together helter-skelter. Two little white cribs, belonging to Filippov, the second assistant commander, looked very incongruous, placed on top of a load of hay. The Kotlas Transfer Station was transfigured. The harshlooking barbed-wire fence had disappeared, the old sign over the gates was replaced by a new one, telling the visitor that he is approaching the dormitories of "Severoles" workers. The new sign on the warehouses designated them as "Warehouses of the Penug-Syktyvkar Railroad Under Construction"; to all telephone calls the Transfer Station's office responded: "Railroad construction office talking."

A telegram was received from Archangel stating that the evacuation had been completed on time as ordered and that no outward sign of a penal camp remained. The transformation was thorough and complete both at Kotlas and at Archangel. A commission of foreign investigators could now be freely admitted. In exactly the same manner the evacuation was carried out at the Solovetsky camp, both on the islands and on the mainland. All the timber which had been cut was abandoned in the forests.

During the evacuation of the Kotlas hospital, three of the typhus patients who had recently had fresh charges of anti-Soviet agitation in the penal camps brought against them, were dragged out into the nearby forest and there Nazarov, chief of the secret intelligence department, personally shot them. They were immediately buried in a pit which was dug at the place of execution.

Several days after the evacuation the newspapers brought the report of Premier Molotov's speech. Stalin's right-hand man expressed the indignation of the Soviet government at the calumnies spread by its enemies, to the effect that the government was using penal labor in the preparation of timber in the Northern area. He categorically denied this.

"There are no prisoners employed in the timber industry of the Northern area," said Molotov. He did not deny that penal labor was employed for other purposes, such as road construction. But even in the United States roads were built by prison gangs, so where was the argument? Molotov concluded his speech with the announcement that though the Soviet government would not admit any foreign investigating commission to its territories, it would not oppose visits to the Northern area by foreign consuls or newspaper correspondents.

Molotov did not lie. At that moment the evacuation continued and the exploitation of penal labor in the timber-works nearest the railroad line had stopped. He was very careful in his phraseology. He never once mentioned that the work at the timber-bases of the penal camps had been discontinued only a week before.

The foreign consuls knew the real condition of affairs and none of them visited our territories. Several foreign correspondents came to the Archangel region, where they were shown the camp buildings adorned with the new signboards designating them as "schools," "clubs," etc. These reporters were satisfied that all the reports about convict labor in Soviet Russia were false. They stated in their newspaper articles that the penal camps did not even exist and that no prisoners worked in the forests. The deception was complete.

In the same speech Molotov mentioned the wealth of the Ukhta oil-fields, from which large quantities of oil were being exported. He offered this as proof that the statements concerning the ruthless exploitation of oil in the Baku region were unfounded.

The prisoners of the Northern penal camps were well aware of the absurdity of this statement. The equipment for the eleven oil-wells to be drilled at Ukhta was still on the way; the failure of the attempt to transport it by means of tractors was already evident and part of the equipment was irretrievably lost in the Vychegda River. Until all the equipment arrived the eleven oil-wells mentioned by Molotov could not be begun.

As a matter of fact, only one oil-well in the Ukhta region was producing and the production was so small that it barely sufficed as fuel for the single Diesel engine of the Ukhta penal camp.

Two weeks passed. None of the prisoners were allowed in Kotlas, for there was still fear of a foreign investigation. When this danger was past, all the former conditions were gradually restored, the Transfer Station was again surrounded by a double fence of barbed wire and though the signs still described the buildings as ostensible boarding houses of free workers, the men behind the wire were prisoners who were daily dispatched from the Transfer Station to their new destinations in the penal camps of the Southern and Central regions of the Soviet Union.

CHAPTER TWENTY: THE EARTH BELONGS TO ITS CHILDREN

The OGPU faced a dilemma. On the one hand, it was not allowed to send prisoners to the timber-works, while on the other hand, a large quantity of timber had been prepared for export and its abandonment in the forest would result in a serious financial loss. Moscow gave much thought to this problem. Finally a solution was found which served the interests of both the wolves and the sheep. It was the so-called "voluntary colonization" movement.

In his splendid book on the Soviet Union, the American professor, Calvin Hoover, states that he saw trainloads of peasants deported into exile, who told him that they did not know where they were being taken. These were the prosperous peasants or "kulaks" who were to be "exterminated as a class" and who were being taken to the remote regions of the U.S.S.R. as "voluntary colonists."

When the Central Committee of the Communist Party had decided to exterminate the "kulaks" as a class, it entrusted the OGPU with the execution of the plan. The latter immediately realized that extraordinary methods would be necessary, since approximately four million peasants, not counting their families, had to be arrested and sent into exile.

The whole business had to be done quickly and the OGPU did not bother about formalities. Mass arrests of peasants began simultaneously in all parts of the Union. In actual practise the procedure was as follows: the district agent of the OGPU collected his information from the village soviets and made out lists of "kulaks." He then announced that all the peasants named in the lists were under arrest and must prepare to leave their village within one hour. The OGPU agent had at his disposal the militia and special detachments of the OGPU guards to overcome any resistance. Wives were ordered to follow their husbands, and likewise the children if there was no one with whom to leave them. As the mothers did not want to part from their children, they almost invariably took them along.

The arrested peasants strapped their most necessary belongings and some food supplies on their backs, formed in a column and marched under escort to the nearest railroad station. Each was obliged to take along at least one needful farming tool.

The houses, cattle and all the belongings of the arrested were either transferred to the local Kolkhoz (collective farm), or auctioned off, the proceeds going to the government. The old parents of the "kulaks" were chased out of the houses and ordered to leave their native village for good.

No specific charges were brought against the "kulaks" and no sentences were pronounced. They were simply exiled forever into remote regions of the Union.

On arrival at the railroad station, they were packed in freight cars and in this appalling manner transported to distant parts of Siberia, the Komi territory, Murmansk or the Northern area, where they had to march to their final destination.

Before 1931, exiling of the "kulaks" was entirely without system, but after that it was carried out strictly according to plan. The procedure was officially incorporated in an agreement of the OGPU with the colonization office in Moscow, dealing with the settlement of several million colonists in the remote regions, to be carried out by the OGPU. The exiled "kulaks" were designated as "voluntary colonists" and the OGPU assumed the duties of organizing settlement centers in distant localities, furnishing food to the colonists while they were en route, and supplying the necessary tools and materials after their arrival.

Of course there could not be even a semblance of a regular supply of the colonists' needs, considering the speed with which they were exiled. It is impossible to describe the privations and sufferings to which they were subjected. They were transported to their new territories like cattle. Upon their detrainment they and their families, including little children, had to make several hundred kilometers on foot. They carried their heavy bundles on their backs and were fed nothing or only scant rations of bread. Upon arrival at their destination they were told to clear some land in the forest and to build themselves huts. Their arrival was registered by the local soviets and as "voluntary colonists" they were listed as part of the population.

As soon as the "voluntary colonists" had completed the construction of their new homes, they were assigned work in the forest, to be performed in payment for their transportation and food. Refusal to do the work assigned was punished by arrest, separation from family and a charge of sabotage.

By orders of the local soviets it was obligatory for all members of the local population to do their share of work in the forest.

The formal listing of the exiled peasants as part of the local population was required by the OGPU. The reason for this was simple. The foreign press had protested the import of timber produced by penal labor. Part of the prisoners from the Northern timber-works were transferred to penal camps in Southern and Central regions. The cut timber remained in the forest and the OGPU had no workmen to complete the job. Timber exports had to be continued, as it was part of the Five-Year Plan, but it had to be handled in a way to avoid foreign criticism. No inducements were sufficient to make free workers move into the Northern timber region.

It was these considerations that led to the ingenious plan for the exploitation of the labor of "voluntary colonists." In point of time it coincided with the adoption of the policy of extermination of the "kulaks" as a class.

The scheme was diabolically clever and effective. On the one hand, it replaced the hundred thousand prisoners employed in the winter of 1930-31 with two hundred thousand "voluntary colonists" and thus stopped foreign protests. On the other hand, it helped to exterminate the more prosperous peasants as a class.

Among these exiles were also some parties of German colonists, of whom much was written in the German press and on whose behalf the German ambassador at Moscow had intervened, but in vain. They were descendants of the German farmers invited by Catherine the Great to settle in Russia on a grant of land provided for them on the Volga. They formed a prosperous colony and preserved their language and customs down to the time of the Bolshevik revolution.

I was in Solvychegodsk when navigation opened. Long caravans of barges went up and down the Vychegda River, some carrying winter supplies for the Komi territory and some loaded with sawn timber for export via Archangel. Many barges carried transports of "voluntary colonists," once well-to-do peasants who had been deprived of their land and possessions and deported from the central regions. Thousands of these unfortunates went by, men, women and endless numbers of pale, sickly children.

In addition to the natives, a goodly number of families of exiled German colonists from the Volga lived in Solvychegodsk. The families were crowded into little rooms which often quartered as many as ten people, the floor affording barely enough sleeping room for them. In spite of the crowded conditions, German cleanliness and accuracy was fully in evidence; the patriarchal customs of the colonists had been preserved through all their trials.

The head of each family, "der Vater," was loved, respected and implicitly obeyed by all its members. Everybody worked hard, the women laundered and embroidered, bringing all their earnings to the father, who spent the family cash as he saw fit. There were never any quarrels in these families. They were a substantial, hard-working, thrifty people.

Some of us who spoke German were always welcome guests in these families. In spite of their poverty they asked us to come in for a glass of beer and opened their hearts to us. "Wir wollen heim," they constantly repeated, telling us of the bounty of their Volga colonies, of their fine horses, cows, pigs and the well-cultivated soil.

"Not a single boulder in my fields," boasted one of them.

"People came from afar to look at my horses," sighed another.

"Mine was the best house for fifty miles around," said the third.

"Wir wollen heim," came the general chorus.

"Why did they deport us? What harm did we do them? We worked quietly, did not interfere with anybody, did not riot or oppose the Reds, paid our taxes promptly. Why then were we exiled? True, we did not want collective farms. We colonists are not in favour of it; no good comes of it; and therefore we did not join the Kolkhoz. Then an OGPU commissar drove us out of our homes, made us get into railroad carriages with our wives and children, and here we are. Our houses and belongings were confiscated, our cattle transferred to the collective farms. We have lost all we had. We had no time to take anything with us, for we were given only twenty minutes to get ready. Our children were used to milk and wheat bread; now we have not even enough black bread to feed them. Oh, how many of them have died! Look at those little ones, don't they look miserable?"

Indeed, the thin sickly children with swollen bellies were a pitiable sight.

The colonists lived in harmony and followed events back home through correspondence with their former fellow-villagers. They hoped against hope for early repatriation. "Wir wollen heim," and nothing else would suit them. Make a new start in the North? Here, on this land? And then have it again taken away in a few years? No, no. "Wir wollen heim," they repeated stubbornly, with tears in their eyes, "wir wollen heim."

Already in Kotlas I had often observed these so-called "voluntary colonists." There they lived at the "colonists' transfer station," which was situated on an island in the river, some six kilometers from town, and consisted of a hundred barracks designed as quarters for two hundred men each. These barracks were always overcrowded. The station generally sheltered more than forty thousand colonists with their families. Almost daily large parties of them came and went. The colonists were strictly forbidden to go outside the barbed-wire enclosure. As the only well in camp was emptied to the bottom quite early every morning, the colonists got most of the water they needed from the river, going there twice a day, escorted by guards. It was forbidden to fetch water without an escort, but no announcement to this effect was posted. It was only after nine colonists had been killed by the sentries on watch because they had crawled under the barbed wire to obtain water to quench their thirst, that the authorities decided to provide a better supply of water and to post an announcement forbidding anybody without escort to pass beyond the barbed wire.

When our penal camp was transferred to Ust-Vym, we found one of the "voluntary colonists'" stations of the Komi territory situated next to our barracks. It consisted of a number of large tents erected in an open field. They adjoined each other and were surrounded by a barbed-wire fence. Guards were constantly on watch in two turrets erected for this purpose. Within the enclosure a multitude of men, women and children swarmed about. They were never let out of the enclosure and all day long they moved about aimlessly in the limited space. The women sat in groups nursing their babies, the men talked to each other or sat about forlornly, while the boys and girls ran about and tried to play games.

The colonists were given four hundred grams of rye bread daily and nothing else. There were no stoves, so that those who had their own supplies could not prepare any kind of food. They subsisted on bread and water alone.

The station was under iron discipline. At seven in the morning the commander arrived, accompanied by the doctor's assistant. The women and children were driven into the tents and the men stood in line for inspection. The commander stopped here and there in front of the lines and from time to time we could hear his shouts and unprintable swearing. Then he would enter the tents and instantly the air would resound with the shrieking and howling of women and the crying of children. The doctor's assistant would carry out of the tents the bodies of children who had died during the night, the crying mothers would follow him to the gate where the cart was waiting. Some of them frantically grabbed the doctor by the arms, tore their hair, fell on their knees, begged, implored and, when they were finally dragged away by the guards, threw themselves on the ground and gave way to heartrending sobs.

The men stood in line a little way off and did not move. The slightest resistance was considered rioting and was punished by shooting. They knew it.

After the inspection tour the children's bodies in the cart were covered with burlap and were carted away, accompanied by the doctor's assistant, the weeping and shrieking mothers, several colonists armed with picks and shovels and by some armed guards. They were taken to a place about half a kilometer from the station. Quickly a hole would be dug and a little mound would appear next to the others. There were a great number of these little mounds in the field and from our window they looked like a natural undulation of the ground. The children died like flies.

Adult deaths were less frequent. When a husband was buried, the wife accompanied the cart up to the mound-covered field, the colonists dug the grave and lowered the body into it, covering it up quickly. The soldiers would forcibly remove the crying woman from the grave. When a woman died, the husband did the digging himself. No coffins or ceremonies of any kind were permitted.

It was strictly forbidden to go outside the barbed-wire enclosure, and sentries shot from the turrets without warning. In spite of this, many of the unfortunates were driven by hunger to brave the danger. During the night the exhausted faces of bearded peasants and the pale faces of their poor wives appeared at our windows and they would beg for a bit of food, "in the name of Christ." We shared what little we had. Alas, it was but a drop in the ocean.

Large parties of "colonists" were sent to the North regularly. Loaded with their packs, they trudged along heavily, the children clinging to their mothers' skirts. It was an appalling sight. These parties had to walk hundreds of kilometers, into the very depth of the Zyryan forests, where they had to break ground and start life afresh.

Judging from the letters received by the prisoners, conditions in the U.S.S.R. showed no improvement. There was widespread peasant opposition to the collectivization campaign, followed by the policy of the "extermination of the kulaks as a class." The Russian peasants without exception, be they of the "poor," "middle," or "kulak" classes, share the view common to peasants or farmers of all lands. They have always regarded the land as belonging to them, as their absolute property. They could not reconcile themselves to the communist land program, i. e., to the principle that the land is the property of the state and that those who cultivate it have only a temporary privilege to make use of it.

Already in Lenin's time the Bolsheviks had been forced to yield on this point in order to maintain themselves in power. Hence Lenin introduced the NEP and encouraged the peasants to "enrich themselves." After Lenin's death the NEP was abolished and the well-to-do peasants were gradually stripped of their property either by "lawful" taxation or by arbitrary confiscation.

When Stalin had firmly established his power, the Communist Party returned to its former platform and a long struggle with the peasant class ensued.

The communists believed that they were waging a successful battle but in reality the attempt to subdue the peasant was hopeless and brought about difficulties in the matter of food supply which threatened, in a few years, to take on the proportions of famine. It is difficult to wage a war against eighty percent of the population.

When the collectivization of the peasants' property was begun, strictly in accordance with the estimates of the Five-Year Plan, the well-to-do peasantry took a definite stand against it and opposed it in every way. The extermination of the "kulaks" was undertaken, but the results of their opposition soon became evident: almost all of the breeding livestock belonging to the "kulaks" had been slaughtered, and common livestock had diminished to such an extent that there was a shortage of fertilizer.

The peasants joined the collective farms in spite of the fact that they were opposed to collectivization. They did this chiefly because they had no other alternative and because they had decided on the most effective form of opposition, passive resistance.

CHAPTER TWENTY-ONE: PLANNING

At the time of our arrival at Solvychegodsk this lovely little town was still in its winter garb. Roofs were covered with deep snow which had not been removed since autumn. Boys coasted their sleds down the steep banks on to the river ice; here and there men on skis were to be seen, evidence that winter sports had penetrated even these remote provinces.

There were no factories in the town. The institutions included the local soviet, a technical school, two cooperative stores, the OGPU, the fire department, the government vodka warehouse and dispensary, and the electric power station.

The local landmark was the little house in which Stalin, the present dictator of the U.S.S.R., had lived before the war as an exile. The owner of the house was a young man of swarthy complexion, with the features of a native of the Caucasus, contrasting sharply with those of his blond Northern fellow villagers. The local party headquarters had just sent him to Moscow, where a brilliant career probably awaited him.

Weeks went by; the snow began to melt. Spring was coming. In the camp hospital ten to fifteen prisoners died daily. Dr. Jacobson, in charge of the hospital, shook his head sadly. He considered all of his patients doomed and referred to them as living corpses left behind by the February evacuation.

On the first of June the driving of logs down the rivers of the Northern areas began. Usually logs are driven in rafts, but on account of the shortage of anchors, chains and other equipment, and for want of experienced raft drivers, both "Severoles" and "Komiles," the two timber trusts of the North, decided to float the logs to Archangel without making rafts of them.

A plan was carefully prepared providing for several million logs to be slid into the waters of local streams. The entire population was to be mobilized and everybody without exception was to help. The authorities issued a decree closing navigation for a month and special booms and pockets were constructed near Archangel to catch the logs.

As usual in the U.S.S.R. the calculations on paper were quite precise. The exact time of the logs entering the rivers and the exact time of their arrival at the booms were determined, the number of logs floated and the speed of the current as well as other important details were taken into consideration. But as usual, the existence of unforeseen, accidental circumstances was ignored and the advice of experienced timbermen was overridden. Timber specialists remarked that it was better to drive fewer logs and be sure of catching them, but this was considered to border on sabotage. After that, the specialists remained silent.

The driving of the logs began on the night of June first. Logs floated down the swift current of the Vychegda River past Solvychegodsk. They turned and twisted, shoved each other, stood on end, climbed on top of each other. They looked alive in their movements and resembled a school of gigantic fish forcing their way down the river. The pressure behind the logs was tremendous and it was hard to imagine how such a mass could be dealt with at Archangel.

An old man, who had worked in the timber industry all his life, sat on the bank of the river and looked at the logs sadly.

"Another week, and it will all be in the White Sea. How do they figure they can stop this onslaught? They've overdone it again and have shoved all the logs into the water at the same time. It takes imagination! So much valuable timber thrown away, so much work wasted in the cutting of it! Oh, the power wielded by fools!"

The logs drove by in an unending mass all day and all night. On the second morning disquieting reports were received of strong rains in the regions of the two most important log rivers, the Sysola and the Vym. It was reported that a much greater number of logs had been shoved into the rivers than the plan provided. The Komi territory had overplayed its hand by mobilizing the population and distributing alcohol among the workers. Now the tremendous mass of logs was driven by the swollen waters of the rivers and made one fearful for the results.

But of course the mischief once started could not be stopped. Reports started coming in from Archangel to the effect that the logs had begun to arrive, were caught and pocketed according to plan. The originators of the idea of driving the loose logs were triumphant. But the old man on the bank of the river quietly chuckled.

A week passed and suddenly the catastrophe came. An urgent telegram from Archangel reported that the main boom had given way and that the logs were carried into the ocean. It was ordered that the entire population be again mobilized to stop the floating logs.

It was easier to send the telegram than to execute it. But measures were taken at once and the entire population was mobilized for the work. All the old men, women and children were sent to the river together with the men. All the prisoners were ordered out.

There were no boat-hooks. Therefore we undressed, got into the water and fished out the nearest logs as they passed us, dragging them out on the bank. The main mass of logs proceeded unhindered in the middle of the stream. We could not reach them. We worked hard all day and late into the evening; it was pleasanter than sitting in the office. A large number of logs was saved, but in comparison with the main mass it was a drop in the ocean.

On the following day we resumed the work; the number of logs in the river gradually diminished. On the third day we were back at the office, but the mobilized population continued working. The attempt to drive the logs without tying them into rafts was a total failure. More than a million logs had gone out into the ocean!

However, the driving continued. Thousands and thousands of logs passed Solvychegodsk daily, floating down the river in unending succession. The damaged booms at Archangel were hastily repaired, the communist in charge was replaced by another, and his technical adviser, an engineer, was arrested and thrown into jail.

Toward the end of the log-driving operations, we were again sent to the river, for the water-level had fallen to such an extent that many logs remained on the banks and had to be shoved back into the water. Together with the mobilized population we were kept busy at this for another three days.

On June thirtieth the log-driving operations were officially declared completed and navigation was reopened. A narrow ribbon of logs in the middle of the river was all that was left, but tugs again made their appearance, dragging barges with supplies for the Komi territory and with "voluntary colonists."

Then came the reports of the results. About forty percent of all the logs had been lost in the ocean.

About this time a telegram was received from Moscow containing important instructions. The Northern penal camps, transferred to the village of Ust-Vym, in the Komi territory, were to be called the Ust-Vym Corrective Penitentiary Camp. The new camp was charged with finishing the highway construction between Ust-Sysolsk and Ukhta and with keeping the half-finished Syktyvkar-Penug railroad line in repair. A liquidation commission was to remain in Solvychegodsk.

A new commander arrived and took charge. It was the chekist Dikiy-Dymoff from the Caucasus, who had been caught in some transgression but had been pardoned and made commander of the new camp. This swarthy little man was not still for a moment and stirred up everybody with his superabundant energy.

He remained in Solvychegodsk only half a day, but visited all the departments of the camp, rushing from one to the other on horseback, canceling old orders and issuing new ones. In the evening he took the river boat for Kotlas, examined the warehouses, gave some new instructions and left for Moscow. Most of his orders were impracticable, but he had descended upon us like a tornado and brought some life into the monotony of our daily existence. In another week he was back from Moscow with an order to complete without fail the construction of the highway before winter. Special speed-shifts of prisoners were to be put to work and the highway was to be turned over to the inspection committee by November first.

Two days later we left by steamer for our new destination. We passed the remainder of the floating logs. They came down loose and in rafts, some small rafts of six hundred logs and some enormous ones of eight to ten thousand. The crews consisted of men and women apparently in the best of spirits. They built fires and cooked their food right there on the rafts. Like confirmed nudists they played and swam, dived and climbed back on the floats; the lads pursued the lasses, grabbed them and tumbled into the water with shouts and laughter.

Towards evening our steamer stopped to give way to a caravan of rafts. Bathers swam in the narrow space between the rafts and the steamer. The play and shouting on the rafts continued. The lads were getting drunk and often the girls screamed with genuine fright. Our captain was on his bridge, cursing loudly. The surface of the water was quiet like a mirror.

Suddenly a strange figure of a swimmer appeared at the edge of a raft. He was floating face down, his arms and legs drawn under, and just his round back protruding out of the water. Just at that moment the sportive nudists on the raft dragged a flushed and disheveled girl to the edge and tried to push her into the water.

"Don't, comrades, I can't swim," she howled.

The back of the strange floating figure came alongside.

"Push her in," someone shouted and the yelling girl was thrown into the water. She scrambled and splashed, swallowing water and grabbing hold of the body floating past her. She flung her arms around it as it turned about in the water, facing her, and only then did she realize what it was. She was looking into the blue swollen face of a drowned man.

For a long time the yell of the terrified girl rang in my ears. She let go of the body and went under, came up to the surface again and mechanically seized the body once more. Then she gave another yell, even shriller than the first, and went down again. She would have surely drowned, had it not been for an old man from the raft who jumped in after her and dragged her out.

The whole show took only a couple of minutes but it left an unforgettable impression. The body had again turned face downward and continued floating down the river alongside the raft. Our captain shouted something through the megaphone to the men on the raft. "Pick him up yourself," they answered.

"It's a bad omen," said the superstitious assistant warden of our camp. He was a gloomy Pole, serving his term on a sentence for espionage. It was strange that he should have made his way up to the position of assistant warden, considering the crime he was charged with. His belief in omens was confirmed in this instance, for two months later he was killed with an axe in a drunken brawl.

On the following day, at noon, we arrived at the village of Ust-Vym. Our camp was small and the buildings were closely grouped together. An old church stood on a slight elevation in the very center of the camp. The camp had removed the antique grilled-iron fence that had surrounded the church and had turned the iron into bolts and nuts and the brick into stoves for the camp buildings. The old fence was replaced by a barbed-wire enclosure. It was the only church in the village where services were still held. On Sundays the villagers came here to worship. The doors of the church remained open and the singing could be heard outside. The few prisoners who were not at work gathered around the barbed-wire enclosure and listened to the singing. They were not permitted to enter the church but no objection was made to their standing around and listening.

About two hundred yards away there was another church built in the sixteenth century and standing on a hill. It was exceptionally beautiful. The old cemetery had been situated between these two churches until the penal camp took possession of the property. Now it was all dug up, the monuments and the crosses were removed and "more useful buildings," as Dikiy called them, had taken their place. At the time that one of these "more useful buildings" was being built there was a shortage of boards for flooring. Dikiy then ordered, with his usual ingenuity, that the floor be made of the antique ikons stored in the third church, which was now occupied by the dining room, kitchen and the repair shops of the camp.

The ikons were nailed to the floor-beams and a sort of parquetry resulted, but it was so insecure that eventually boards had to be nailed over the ikons. Thanks to this sacrilege many priceless ikons were buried, perhaps for a long time to come.

The grandiose plans for the Northern construction were all scrapped. The building of the railroad and the industrial central settlement at Kotlas, as well as all other projects, were abandoned half-way. The only thing left in the program was the highway. Its construction was rushed with all possible speed. Twelve thousand prisoners were concentrated in twenty-four work posts along the line and worked unceasingly. In the winter months these prisoners were to be transferred to work in the forest, cutting timber in accordance with a contract made with "Komiles," an exporting organization. This contract had not been canceled, for the Moscow planners shrewdly surmised that even if foreign investigating commissions did arrive, they would never reach these remote regions.

Usually earthwork labor was easier than timber-cutting, but in this particular case the prisoners were doomed to disappointment. Moscow had given definite orders for the completion of the highway by the first of November and had found an exemplary executive in Commander Dikiy to see the plan through.

A mad rush began. Shock detachments were organized at every work post. They consisted chiefly of young criminals who were won over by promises of a partial commutation of their sentences. With this inducement in view, they went to it tooth and nail, working fourteen to fifteen hours a day and even exceeding the planned quotas. Workers of these detachments received increased rations of porridge or soup and were paid five roubles a month in cash.

The shock detachments of the various work posts competed with each other in speed; all other workers were also involuntarily drawn into the tempo of the speeding-up and soon the work along the entire line presented a picture of a huge socialistic competition in achievement.

However, in spite of these very effective methods, by the end of August it was plain that the work was behind the schedule set by the plan. Early in September a telegram was received from Moscow with instructions to have the highway ready for delivery to the inspection commission ten days earlier, i. e., by the twentieth of October. It was imperative to force the work to an even greater speed.

The administration commanders sent menacing telegrams to the construction bases and every evening all superintendents were called on the telephone and admonished with threats, curses and abuse. It was a sort of daily doping. But the doping did not help much and the work continued to lag behind the requirements. Then the hunt for scapegoats began. The superintendents blamed circumstances beyond their control and above all the shortage of shovels.

One day I was quite unexpectedly called to the secret intelligence department. The commander, Nikolayev, a drunkard and a libertine, greeted me with a frown:

"Why are there no shovels? You are in charge of the technical supply department for the camps and you have done nothing about it. You are to blame for the stopping of the work. Why are there no shovels?"

I had foreseen the shortage of shovels long before. Not putting any faith into promises from Moscow and contrary to the regulations of the Moscow supply department, I had been purchasing all available shovels in the surrounding country for several weeks past. Shovels were coming in from all sides, and still there was a shortage. It was the quality that was to blame. Shovels produced by the Soviet industry had never been good, but they had become considerably worse during the last year.

I explained to the commander that I had sent twice the number of shovels to the highway construction bases that was specified by Moscow. Knowing the bad quality of the shovels, I had done this on my own initiative. If he wished to accuse me of anything it should be the furnishing of supplies in excess of specifications, but in this instance I had acted with the written consent of Camp Commander Dikiy.

"We'll check up on that, you may go," he growled. The case was not followed up because there was nothing to follow up. But had there been any cause for complaint, these shovels would have surely cost me an additional sentence of at least three more years.

It is part of the system to try to find culprits in every case of failure, even if there are none. At the same time the OGPU daily committed crimes that should be classed as "wrecking." I shall cite but a few instances.

The "Komiles" Company had a tractor-base adjoining our camp; in it were four "Cletrac" tractors that had to be overhauled, but there were no spare parts and their shop equipment was not adequate. They sought help at the OGPU penal camp.

"You wish them overhauled. Certainly. Send them over here."

The next day the tractors were brought in. The tractor mechanic inspected them and reported that by taking one tractor to pieces he could produce three tractors in perfect working order.

"Three? Why three? Let there be two," the camp commanders decided and "Komiles" was given the alternative of taking back their four tractors needing repair or of receiving in exchange for them two tractors in perfect order, the spare parts not used in the repair to remain the property of the camp.

"It is highway robbery!" Komiles retorted, but they had to agree, as there was no other way out. The dismantling of tractors was strictly forbidden by the central supply organizations and constituted a crime, not to speak of the hold-up action of the OGPU. It was a clear case of "wrecking," but as the OGPU itself was the "wrecker" nothing further was done about it.

Then there was the case of the cows. The local peasants, owners of the cows, had to sell to the government a considerable portion of the milk they received, and the keeping of cows became unprofitable, as the money received would buy but little real goods. Consequently the owners of the cows all wanted to get rid of them. But the slaughtering of a cow was a crime punishable by five years in the penal camps. On the other hand there was a shortage of fodder. The OGPU found a way out of this vicious circle.

Members of the administration had their meals in a special dining room operated for their benefit. The chef complained of a shortage of meat, which he could not buy anywhere in spite of the fact that the country did not lack in cows. But — it was unlawful to kill the cows and they could be purchased only for dairy purposes. The administration immediately began buying cows for its own dairy, which actually did not exist, and issued corresponding certificates to the sellers. Cows were offered from all sides, the chef selected the best of them, and they were promptly slaughtered. Nobody said a word about the OGPU committing a crime. The local soviet knew all the details, but kept its mouth shut and accepted without question the certificates of sale brought in by the peasants.

The highway was finished by the middle of October. During the last two weeks work was continued through day and night. All available man-power was thrown into the fray. Work was rushed with all possible speed.

Though it was proposed to have the highway ready for inspection and acceptance by the fifteenth of October, the damp rainy weather threatened to make this impossible. All hopes were set on the change in the weather. Both sides, our administration as the builders of the highway, and the inspecting commission, had agreed at a special session that the highway should be accepted by the fifteenth, but both sides knew that it was impossible to accept it unless cold weather set in and froze the ground. Therefore a change in the temperature to below the freezing point was awaited like a gift from heaven.

On the fifteenth of October the rain still continued. Moscow demanded that the acceptance take place and would not accept any excuses as to "circumstances beyond control." Another few days passed. It rained and it

Then, very conveniently, the chairman of the inspection commission fell ill. The sick man sat in Dikiy's private office and himself penned the telegram describing his illness. Judging by the text of his telegrams, he got worse on the second day, though he spent the entire day playing billiards with Dikiy. On the third day he reported a temperature of 104°, but on the fourth day, as it grew colder outside, he stated that he was feeling better. On the twentieth of October we woke up feeling chilly, looked out of the windows and saw a coating of frost on the ground. We stepped out and found that the ground was frozen. Now the highway could be accepted.

All the high commanders of the administration, all members of the inspection commission and several prisoners holding responsible positions set out in four trucks. The trucks ran beautifully over the frozen ground. Divisions of the highway were accepted one by one, the members of the commission never bothering to leave their comfortable arm-chairs which had been installed for them on the trucks. The division just completed by the "shock detachments" was in dreadful condition and the most ignorant inspector could not reasonably be expected to accept it. Still, after a good luncheon with vodka, served en route, even this division was accepted with expressions of praise and gratification.

Whom were they trying to swindle? The highway was not only not ready, but if it had not been for the frozen ground, it would have been impossible to drive a car over it.

Still, upon arrival at the final station, Ukhta, the accepting documents were duly signed and a rush telegram to this effect was sent to Moscow. Everybody was happy. The business was satisfactorily finished and a well-deserved rest could now be enjoyed in the domains of Comrade Moroz, Commander of the Ukhtinsky-Petchorsky penal camps.

Quite unexpectedly a telegram was received from Moscow instructing our camp to resume the construction of the railroad.

The work had been abandoned in the spring; the work posts were in disuse; we had only one tenth of the number of prisoners needed for the task; all the foremen and technicians had been transferred to other camps. How could we resume the construction work?

But an order is an order. Engineer Alpers was the only one of the technical management of the former construction who was still with us. He was commissioned to work out a plan for the resumption of work, and in another week fresh detachments of prisoners began arriving at station Penug.

Two special commissions to investigate the condition of the abandoned construction left simultaneously from both ends of the line. A sad picture awaited them. The earthwork fills, built on swampy ground and left without top reinforcement of a track, had settled and washed out; some of the trestles had shifted out of line and would have to be rebuilt; all loose property of the work posts had been stolen by the peasants.

The chairman of the commission, a chekist, did not trouble to inquire into the causes of the deterioration, but decided offhand that it was due to the work of "wreckers." Upon his return from the inspection tour, he immediately caused four engineers and twenty foremen and technicians of the former construction force to be arrested and brought back to the penal camps.

Upon their arrest, the "wreckers" were kept in jail for seven weeks and then sent to hard labor, while a report of their cases was forwarded to Moscow. They pleaded not guilty, which was of course indisputable. Nevertheless they were quite sure that additional sentences would be imposed on them, and this would undoubtedly have happened, had they not been saved by the intervention of the Commissariat of Ways and Communications.

After the highway had been completed and delivered, the prisoners who had worked there were transferred to the railroad line under construction. The former superintendents of the work posts were now put in charge of the construction on the line. Our commander thought them quite competent for the job. They had managed to construct a highway, so why shouldn't they be able to build a railroad? Our engineers protested and tried to argue.

"Much you understand about it," answered Dikiy. "Those boys are smart fellows, let them go to it, they'll manage it all right."

The smart fellows went to it. The engineers were in despair.

Luckily for the socialistic construction and for the smart fellows, a fundamental change soon took place.

Moscow had decided to transfer all hands to a new project, the construction of the White Sea Canal, "Belmorstroy," connecting the Gulf of Finland with the White Sea. One hundred and fifty thousand prisoners were to be employed there and the canal was scheduled to be completed in three hundred and sixty days.

All the prisoners of our penal camp were to be sent to the canal, as well as all prisoners from the Svirsky and the Solovetsky camps. This large number of prisoners was to be augmented considerably by additional transports from the OGPU prisons. The construction of the canal was rated as a matter of the very first importance and Kogan himself, the head of all penal camps, took charge of the work.

Just as suddenly as the railroad construction work had been resumed a little while earlier, it was now terminated. Columns of prisoners marched from all work posts to Penug station. The order for the transport of man-power was followed by another order, instructing that all food supplies, clothing, tools and equipment be shipped to the new penal camp, Belmorstroy.

And then came an order to dismantle the twenty kilometers of railroad track which had been completed, and to ship the rails and ties to Belmorstroy at once. This meant nothing else but that Moscow was abandoning the idea of completing the Syktyvkar-Penug railroad line. Tens of thousands of prisoners had worked on this line for two and a half years, fifteen million roubles had been expended and the railroad was half completed. The new decision meant that the results of all labor and fifteen million roubles were to be scrapped. But why bother about such trifles as this? The canal was more important, the canal had great economic significance. Therefore let the railroad perish and long live the canal! The usual occurrence was again repeated. The Bolsheviks were reaching out for new achievements and scrapping the old before they were completed.

The administration which had always executed all Moscow orders with military promptness, hesitated for the first time. The idea of sacrificing all this labour and the fifteen million roubles expended made them think twice. Finally our commanders sent a long code telegram to Moscow pointing out the inadvisability of the proposed action. The Komi territory was also aroused. The long promised and much needed railroad was to be taken away from it.

The answer to our telegram came promptly. Moscow demanded the immediate execution of its orders and warned us that any delay would be punished by the board of the OGPU. The work of dismantling the railroad line began that very evening.

I made my computations from all incoming reports and daily sent an urgent telegram to Moscow giving details of materials shipped. Our supply department had to bear the brunt of all work connected with the evacuation and we again had to work sixteen to eighteen hours a day. For over two weeks the offices of the administration were a veritable madhouse; then the evacuation was finished and things got back to normal.

We soon began to receive letters from the prisoners who had left for Belmorstroy. They all said that life there was a repetition of the worst days in the early history of the penal camps. Prisoners had no place to sleep, and were cold and hungry. The barracks were filthy and the assignments of work required utmost exertion.

"Pray to God," they all said, "that they do not send you here."

However, prayers did not help, and one by one transport columns of prisoners were formed and left for the new camp. They first had to walk some four hundred kilometers to Kotlas, from which place they were transported by rail to the canal zone in the wilderness of northern Karelia.

CHAPTER TWENTY-TWO: IN THE SPIDER-WEB

In the women's barracks the prostitutes were herded as usual together with the peasant women and with the women of the educated class. Among these latter there was a Jewess with prematurely gray hair and sad brown eyes staring out of a young face. Her name was Eva Taitz.

She was a laundress and her daily assignment was fifty pairs of shirts and drawers. Her coarsened hands still preserved their shapely form. I recalled the name of Taitz. David Taitz, the jolly Moscow jeweler, was my cellmate in the Butirsky prison. I asked her whether he was a relative of hers.

"He was my husband," she answered.

The congenial Taitz, who had added so much to our amusement in prison by his funny stories, had been shot. She was declared his "accomplice" and was given a five-year sentence. As she told me her story, her large eyes grew even sadder than before. "So you knew David, my good, kind David, always so tender and thoughtful." She began to weep.

"I haven't spoken to anybody for a long time," she murmured through her tears, "I am not liked in the barracks. You see I am a Jewess, and they say that the Jews are to blame for everything. It is too bad that David is not here, he would have told them who is to blame. The Jews to blame, indeed! No, the Russians are to blame and the Jews only took advantage of the situation; they would have taken advantage no matter what form of government we might have had..."

She caught me by the sleeve. "Please, tell me more about David, tell me more of the hours you spent together with him in prison. What was he like during that time, how did he act? Tell me, please tell me everything you know..."

I talked with her for a long time and told her everything that I could recall about Taitz. I assured her that Taitz had often thought of her and spoken about her, that he would lose his cheerfulness and grow dejected only when he worried about her and the hardships she was probably enduring. She listened to me and cried bitterly.

In the early autumn the widow of prisoner Granovsky suddenly arrived, in search of her husband's grave. I met her on the street by accident and conducted her to the cemetery.

"The grave is around here, somewhere," said the watchman. "You can't expect me to remember where each prisoner is buried, too many of them die in these regions."

The many oblong mounds on the ground made walking difficult. Granovsky's body was under one of them. But where? There was not a cross, not an inscription on any of them. "Around here, somewhere," said the watchman.

She stood there in despair, staring at the mounds. She stayed at the camp for a long time and every day stopped prisoners in the street, trying to find those who had buried her husband. It was wasted labor — those prisoners had been transferred to other camps long since.

Ukhta, a little provincial Northern town, or rather village, was run entirely by the OGPU. The local soviet existed here only in compliance with the law. Everything was under the rule of the camp commander, Comrade Moroz.

He was a portly man of about forty-five, one of the important chekists of the South, who had been found guilty, together with our commander Dikiy, of excessive drinking, thieving and a few other unsavory crimes. Both of them were sent to the North for correction.

His energy, strong will and powerful friends helped his rapid advance to the position of commander of the Ukhtinsky Geological Expedition, which was later reorganized into the penal camp. This camp was charged with the exploitation of the resources of the northern part of the Komi territory. Formerly this huge area was almost entirely uninhabited, but now over twenty thousand prisoners were working here, in the Ukhta oil-fields and Petchora coal-mines.

Commander Moroz was a wilful, ignorant, insolent chekist. He firmly believed that as he was the commander of the camp, he knew everything better than anybody else in it. Once, while showing us the camp buildings, he noticed that one of the shops had no electric lighting. A new power station had just been erected at Ukhta. Moroz was very proud of it and boastfully switched on the lights in every building he showed us.

"Why is there no light here?" he cried. "Tell Kish to come here immediately."

In a few minutes Kish came in, all out of breath. He was an electrical engineer, about forty, one of those Hungarian prisoners of war whom the Soviet government would not allow to return to their native land.

"Why no electric light here?" yelled Moroz at him.

"We have no electric wire, citizen commander," answered Kish humbly.

"What are you telling me? There's more than enough wire."

"Sorry, citizen commander, but there isn't any."

"I'm telling you there is. Just use your brains once in a while, you bonehead. You have two strands of wire everywhere. Why such luxury? Unwind some of it and use single wires instead, you will have plenty and to spare. Have it all done by tomorrow, understand? Ha, ha, such ignorance, and he calls himself an engineer!"

Some stood there with wide-open mouths, not believing their ears, others turned away trying not to laugh. Kish was bewildered and stunned. To unwind the double strand of wire? It was too unreasonable, even for a chekist. Moroz had cut the Gordian knot.

"This is impracticable, citizen commander," finally said Kish, smiling. "There would be no light anywhere, if we did that."

"Don't talk nonsense and do as you're told. Have it done by tomorrow, understand? My, what an engineer!" repeated Moroz.

This was too much. Somebody burst into a snicker. Moroz turned around and understood from the expressions of our faces that something was wrong. He blushed and blood rushed to his eyes. He stared at Kish, who still stood there waiting.

"Get out of here and throw him into the dungeon for ten days, the bonehead, the idiot!" he suddenly shouted.

Things were getting serious. Commander Dikiy took Moroz by the arm and led him away. We followed. The incident with the wiring was closed. It reminded me of Zolotarev's advice to use broken cast-iron kettles for the repair of boiler plate. All these chekists were appallingly alike.

The incident of the wiring was already known in the engineers' barracks where we visiting prisoners had been invited to have tea.

"Do you think this is an exceptional case?" said engineer E. with a laugh. "Far from it, we are quite used to it and have to adapt ourselves to work with these fellows."

While at Ukhta, I saw again my old friend Dr. S. from Kotlas, with whom I had once made the memorable trip to the Pitsky base of the Uftug timber-works. He had just returned from Petchora. We shook hands warmly, glad to see each other.

"You are still alive. Thank God!" was the exclamation with which he greeted me.

The doctor told me of conditions at Petchora and frowned sadly. Bad, very bad, just the same as we had seen elsewhere. Scurvy, typhus, general exhaustion and loss of resistance. Men died and were replaced by new arrivals. "We have more prisoners than we need," was the insolent comment of the chekists. "They'll all have to die sometime. Let them croak doing useful work."

The only positive mark that distinguished the Ukhtinsky-Petchorsky penal camp was the absence of barbed wire around the work posts. It was impossible to escape from those regions, and barbed wire was dispensed with as a matter of economy.

There was ample evidence in Ukhta disproving the reports of industrial development there. The production of oil was five barrels a day, coal was being mined, but could not be shipped for lack of means of transportation. Things looked very different on the spot from what they did from a distance. All the boasts of production there could have been made only with the expectation that nobody would ever go to that remote region to check up on it. Even so, it took extraordinary imagination to make official statements concerning the enormous exports of Ukhta oil, as Premier Molotov did.

Ukhta. Oil, coal, rich resources. What a farce!

A surprise awaited us upon our return to Ust-Vym. Eight prisoners of the office staff, former officers of the army, had been arrested. The ninth member of their group, who had accompanied us on our trip, was arrested as he was leaving our automobile.

Two weeks later we were told that they had been arrested on suspicion of organizing a group for counter-revolution. They had been watched as they assembled at the house of a peasant. The examination showed that they had as a matter of fact frequently gathered there, but for drinking and not for plotting. As far as drinking was concerned, they were really guilty of great excesses, but there was obviously a difference between drinking and counter-revolution.

Nikolayev, chief of the secret intelligence department, saw the point immediately. He took the examination into his own hands and, being a confirmed drunkard himself, had a fellow feeling for the offenders and freed them. All they got was a reprimand for drunkenness.

Nikolayev was a former Leningrad chekist who had been sent to the penal camps for correction. He showed a kindly consideration exclusively for those prisoners who shared his fondness for drink. He was also benevolent to good-looking woman prisoners who were frequently called to his apartment, presumably for household tasks. The prostitutes went there willingly. The four educated women prisoners were not sufficiently attractive. His chief interest, however, centered on young peasant girls, daughters of "voluntary colonists" who had tried to run away from exile and as punishment had been sentenced to a year in the penal camps. There were many of these and Nikolayev did not pass by any of them.

The greater number of these girls were assigned duties as waitresses in the administration's dining room. They wore little aprons and regular waitress' head-dress, and were trained in their duties by the superintendent of the dining room, Kevorkov.

Whenever Nikolayev fixed his attention on a new victim he instructed the superintendent to send up his dinner to his house and pointed out the waitress who was to bring it over. He invariably got what he wanted, by persuasion or by force.

He was a ruddy man with a short neck and rather repulsive in appearance. His little gray eyes watered, there was a disdainful expression around his bulging lips and his head was thickly covered with grayish-black curly hair. He smelt of vodka, even in the early morning hours. He was a bachelor and a libertine. We called him "the sensual baboon."

Among the women prisoners there was Elizabeth, a very attractive tall and slender blonde with a beautiful figure and lovely lips. At first she was modest and shy, but changed radically when she saw herself pursued by the attentions of prisoners, chekists, Nikolayev and even Commander Dikiy himself. She began neglecting her duties and her manner became fresh and overbearing.

She was the cause of many quarrels among the chekists. When Nikolayev became infatuated with her, he began banishing Elizabeth's other admirers one by one to remote work posts. But when Commander Dikiy became one of the competitors, things took a different turn. Nikolayev was given a leave of absence and never came back. Our commander was not to be trifled with.

It seemed as if Elizabeth's career were assured. But one day she overstepped the bounds of discretion and was insolent to Dikiy in everybody's presence. The following morning she was deported to the most remote work post, where she went from bad to worse, became infected with venereal disease and finally hanged herself.

One of the last steamers of the 1931 season brought a new group of prisoners to our camp. Their destination was Ukhta, but they were in such condition that the doctor temporarily detained them at Ust-Vym on the ground that they were unable to march the long distance to Ukhta.

It was a small group, about fifty men, all former Red Army officers arrested in Odessa on a charge of plotting counter-revolution. Almost all of them had received ten-year sentences. They were dreadful to look at. Their faces were gray and puffed, their eyes tired. In comparison with us, old timers at the camp, they looked like miserable survivors of some awful terrors of another world. They walked with difficulty; for some reason they all had swollen feet. We inquired as to the cause, but it seemed as if they were sworn to silence and none of them would tell. For a long time they evaded all questions, looked at us with suspicion and gazed around furtively as if afraid of being watched. But in the end they gave in and told us "in sacred secrecy" that their swollen feet were the results of methods practiced at their examinations in Odessa.

Colonel R. showed us his calves and feet, with broken blood-vessels and dreadfully swollen. Then he told us the whole story.

All of them had been employed in the Odessa military district, mostly as instructors. In the early summer of 1931 many arrests were made among the former officers of the old regime and they were charged with plotting counter-revolution against the Soviet government. First the prisoners were put in solitary confinement, then they were thrown into dungeons and fed bread and water. When these measures failed to bring confession, the tactics were changed. They were all put together in a dungeon and their guards were instructed not to let them sit down. It was dreadful torture. Men were made to stand there for hours and days, without rest, without food or sleep. Those who fell down were beaten with rifle-butts and prodded with bayonets. The chekist inquisitors, who worked in relays, sat at the table and urged the officers to confess.

"What's the use," they said. "Sooner or later you'll have to confess. Can't you see that we mean business? We'll make you stand here until you confess."

There was nothing to confess, for there was no plot and they did not know what they could say. Had there been any kind of plot some of them would surely have weakened and confessed, such was their suffering.

The dungeon was dimly lighted by electric bulbs. There were no windows and they could not tell day from night. The colonel thought that he stood there for eleven days. It was hard to believe, but his legs and feet were good evidence that the torture must have lasted several days at least, for weeks had gone by and their feet were still awful to look at.

The inquisitors still urged them to confess and relieve not only their own suffering, but also that of their arrested wives. Time went on and the torture became unbearable. Men fainted, water was poured over them and they were again made to stand up. The guards were losing patience and grumbled.

Then the wife of one of the officers, Colonel G., was brought into the dungeon. She was in such a dreadful condition that her husband frantically threw himself upon his guards, shouting at the top of his voice. "Let her go, for God's sake," he cried. "I'll sign anything you want me to, just let her go." The examining chekist led her out, followed by the colonel and guards. Two more hours passed.

Then the prisoners were called out one by one and were shown the signed confession of Colonel G., giving the details of the plot, with names, etc. The prisoners were asked to add their signatures to the confession or to return to the torture in the dungeon.

Only half of the prisoners chose to return to the dungeon. Those who had pleaded guilty were eventually shot, the others were kept in the dungeon a little while longer and were then confined to solitary cells. Several weeks later the board of the OGPU passed sentence on them. Those who had not been shot received sentences of ten years in the penal camps.

Among the prisoners who arrived with the group of officers was the gifted Soviet poet Prince Baryatinsky, who is known under the nom de plume of Lidin. Concerning him the administration had received a telegram from the Commissariat of Public Education, asking that the talented young man be placed in living conditions conducive to creative work. He was therefore assigned to our barracks for privileged workers.

Under the influence of the more normal living conditions the young poet soon regained his fervor and used his hours of rest to write to the camp commander a forty-page protest against the Odessa OGPU and the methods employed there.

He read it to me when it was ready and I tried my best to dissuade him from sending it. Couldn't he understand the uselessness of it and didn't he know with whom he was dealing? But all my arguments were wasted, the protest was handed in. Two days later the young poet was dispatched to Ukhta under special convoy.

The case of another prisoner had the savor of an anecdote. It concerned an humble, elderly man, a bookkeeper. He was highly religious and, grieving over the persecution of his church, had written an appeal to no other than ... the Pope in Rome. He signed his full name and mailed the letter in the regular way. Since in the U.S.S.R. all suspicious looking mail is read by the censor, the envelope addressed to the Pope at Rome was opened and its conscientious author arrested. His account of the examination that followed was told and retold among the prisoners and caused much merriment.

It was a good story but almost cost the poor man his life. He was charged with appealing for foreign intervention and was sentenced to be shot. He assured us that only the hand of God had saved him at the last moment. After some deliberation, the board of the OGPU declined to confirm the sentence. A man who openly wrote letters to the Pope could not be considered a very dangerous plotter and it was not necessary to shoot him. He got off with a ten-year sentence in the penal camps, for correction. He accepted his fate with resignation, grieved for his religion and slowly wilted. Looking at him one felt sure that he would not live to serve even half his sentence.

The relations among the prisoners themselves were quite friendly. Only the Ukrainians quarreled with each other on the sore subject as to which form of government was best suited to the Ukraine. None of them doubted the ultimate independence of the Ukraine and without exception they advocated complete secession from Russia. The petty bourgeoisie stood for government by the Rada (parliament), the peasants — for the Hetman. The adherents of the Rada idea were hard pressed, as the great majority of prisoners were for the Hetman. This majority had had its fill of experiments, they didn't even want to listen to any arguments in favor of the Rada. Only a Hetman could bring order into the chaos and they pinned all their hopes on Hetman Skoropadsky. They had no use for communists or any other socialists. "It is these party politicians that brought ruin to the Ukraine," they said. "The Ukraine does not need men who prefer their party to their country. They ought to be chased out of the country for good."

At the barracks my neighbor to the right was the draftsman Petrov, a typical lost sheep, morally delinquent. Once he went out in the evening, going in the direction of the camp of "voluntary colonists" and when he came back he told me that he "had had a woman for a kilogram of bread."

He assured me that many prisoners, especially those from the unprivileged barracks, went out evenings to meet women. Possibly this was quite natural, for but few prisoners were given permission to have their wives visit them, and many wives could not come on account of the distance or the lack of money. As to the bachelors, they had no recourse at all.

"That's why we take it where we can," he said. "You say that it was vile, that I should have given away the bread without asking anything in return, but I tell you that I cannot live this way. I am a murderer and a scoundrel. Well and good. But I cannot live the life of a hermit." He glowered at me, his jaw trembled and his hands contracted. Only two years before, he had strangled his fiancée, the girl he had grown up with, with these very hands.

He related to me the story of his life and crime. He had become an orphan during the revolution, when he was ten years old. A gang of rowdies broke into his house, raped his mother in front of him and then finished her off with a knife. His father had his eyes struck out and cried like a madman until he was killed. The boy had no relatives, so he joined a gang of homeless children. He wandered all over the Caucasus with them, killing cats and selling their fur. Finally he was picked up and placed in a children's home. The memory of the murder in his house never left him. He liked to torture and strangle the cats. "You have to catch them this way," he said, "and then you strangle them with two fingers, like this."

"Olga and I had a little quarrel," he continued, telling me about the murder for which he was sentenced. "I told her to shut up but she went right on scolding me. So I took her by the throat, like a cat... I did not want to strangle her, but I couldn't stop; I was aroused and my fingers contracted in a cramp. Right to this minute I am not sure whether she put up any resistance or not. When I came to, it was all over, she had stopped breathing. I called the militia and gave myself up. Thanks to my good attorney and a doctor's certificate they gave me eight years instead of ten, knocking off the two years for my youth and the voluntary confession."

It cannot be said that a fellow like that was a comfortable sleeping companion, but I had been sufficiently hardened in this respect by the experience of the last few years. Petrov was not more dangerous than that Chinaman who had slept next to me in the Butirsky prison. That fellow had quarreled with his partner about a three rouble note, had killed him, cut him up in small pieces, boiled those, put them up in aspic and sold them in the market-place. The Chinaman got off easy, with a five-year sentence, probably because of his proletarian origin.

My neighbor to the left was a middle-aged German railroad man from the Ukraine, who was serving a five-year term. He was the victim of the OGPU policy seeking to prevent the possibility of counter-revolution or intervention in the Ukraine in the future.

About a year before he had been invited to the OGPU offices and requested to become a secret informer on his associates. He refused and was promptly arrested. Since it was difficult to find a charge against this conscientious employee and exemplary family-man, the young examining chekist asked him what he would do if Kiev were to be occupied by an invading army. Would he remain on his job at the railroad or would he leave the town together with all other Soviet institutions. He answered that he would act in accordance with instructions from his superiors. The examining official was not satisfied with this answer and continued pressing his point, asking the man what his personal decision would be if his superiors had left no specific instructions.

"In that case," answered the German with frankness and simplicity, "I would stick to my job. I was born on the railroad and shall die on it too."

"Oh, no, my good man, that's where you're wrong," laughed the contented chekist. "You will die at the penal camp of the OGPU where we shall send you. I'll guarantee you a minimum of five years for your frank answer."

The bunk next to the railroad man was occupied by a young man who was perfectly gray and who was sentenced by the court to a term of eight years because his wife had committed suicide. In spite of the fact that the wife had left a note asking that nobody be blamed for her death, he was convicted on the neighbors' testimony that they had often heard the couple quarreling. The mistake made by the court was so evident that the upper tribunal refused to confirm the sentence and cut his term in half. Had he been a workman or a peasant he would certainly have been acquitted, but as he was a former officer, the court gave him the maximum sentence.

Next to this man was the bunk of an engineer "wrecker," sentenced to five years. Then came a German colonist, a Lutheran clergyman, a Don Cossack, an Armenian baker, an old veterinary surgeon. On the other wall of the barracks were the bunks of the Ukrainians; next to them slept a Chinese murderer, several former officers, two priests, an agricultural expert and several peasants who were watchmen at the administration. Almost all these men were serving terms on so-called political charges of the OGPU. All of them of course were antagonistic to the Soviet government, but few had ever openly done anything against it. The OGPU could have chosen others to take their places with equal justice, picking them out with their eyes closed from at least three quarters of the total population of the U.S.S.R.

CHAPTER TWENTY-THREE: "THE LAST OF THE MOHICANS"

Once, upon my return to the camp from an inspection trip, I was told that Prince Oukhtomsky had been transferred to Ust-Vym.

In my four years spent in Red prisons and penal camps, I had encountered no figure among the prisoners equal to the spiritual titan who bore the name of Prince Constantine Erastovitch Oukhtomsky. He was a law unto himself in the Soviet prison world.

I first met Oukhtomsky in the Lefortovsky jail in Moscow. A tall and slender old man, with gray hair and a waxen complexion, there was a peculiar fascination about him which had a disarming effect on all.

Oukhtomsky combined deep culture with vast erudition. His voice was low. His gray eyes looked alert and keen from behind a pair of pince-nez. His long slender fingers were shapely. He was unusually modest and never spoke of himself, but all prisoners knew of everything occurring that concerned him.

He had been in prison more than nine years. Formerly he had served as a cavalry officer in the World War, was a landowner, and had owned sugar refineries in the Province of Kiev. He was an open foe of the Bolsheviks and did not disguise his hostility to them even in prison.

During the retreat of Denikin's army he was badly wounded and was captured by the Bolsheviks. He escaped execution only because of his wound. After he recovered, eight months later, he was sentenced to be shot. He refused to defend himself, declaring that he knew what his sentence would be and that it was beneath his dignity to beg for pardon. His behavior and courageous declaration in court made such an impression on the judges that they petitioned the TSIK on their own initiative to commute his sentence to ten years' imprisonment.

One year later he was offered his liberty and the command of a division in the Red Army in the Polish campaign. He declined the offer, declaring that he would never serve in the Red Army as he had sworn allegiance to His Majesty the Czar. As a consequence, he was transferred to the Viatka Isolation Prison and there subjected to an exceptionally severe regime.

In another three years he was again offered liberty and the post of instructor at the Academy of the Red General Staff. He again declined and said that he considered the Bolsheviks traitors and destroyers of his country, that he remained hostile to them and faithful to the oath of allegiance to the Czar.

Soon afterwards Oukhtomsky was transferred to the Lefortovsky prison in Moscow and had remained there for years. Here he had been visited by Voroshilov, Budenny and other chiefs of the Red Army, who offered him liberty in exchange for his services in the Red Army, but all their offers met with unswerving refusal.

Nearly ten years of imprisonment had not broken the old man's spirit. Ulrich, the President of the Military Tribunal of the Supreme Court, wrote a special article for the press devoted entirely to Oukhtomsky's courage. He recognized him to be an enemy of the Soviet government and considered it necessary to continue to keep him in confinement, but said that men with such strong convictions deserve unqualified respect.

At our prison the Prince was given the nickname of "The Last of the Mohicans." Whether it was due to the visits of influential personages, or to Ulrich's article, or to the strength of his personality, he was favored with quite exceptional treatment by the prison authorities. Contrary to the general rules, Oukhtomsky was not required to do any work and could dispose of his time as he saw fit. He spent his leisure hours in writing notes on the history of the World War.

Outside of the few roubles per month he received from the Red Cross, he had no income whatever. Nevertheless he declined the offer of the State Publishing House to pay him ten thousand roubles for his notes on the World War. He said in reply that his work was not intended for them.

Oukhtomsky lived very poorly and existed exclusively on prison fare. His allowance was expended entirely on cigarettes. All of his years in prison he had spent in solitary confinement. He had never permitted any of the visiting delegates to enter his cell and they were only allowed to get a glimpse of him through the observation opening in his door. The only man whom he admitted to his cell was a monk who was serving a five-year sentence for concealing some church treasures.

What nobility, will-power, and dignity of character! But he did not escape the fate which awaited almost all of us, prisoners of the Lefortovsky Isolation Prison. He was one of the first contingent sent to the penal labor camps.

I remembered running into him upon our arrival in Kotlas. It was shortly after the examination of my belongings which had been scattered in the snow. Oukhtomsky was dressed in a large and worn fur coat and was accompanied by two convoy soldiers. Behind them came two more soldiers carrying his baggage. When he came near me, he winked at me, pointing to the soldiers and explained that they were his "porters," furnished him after he had refused to budge from the railway carriage unaided; camp commander Monakhov had then gone in personally to see him, had provided this escort, and arranged for a special sleeping-shelf for him in the barracks. Every time that I came in contact with this "last of the Mohicans" I admired more and more his steadfastness and the determined line of conduct which he unswervingly pursued.

Oukhtomsky was taken to the privileged barracks. He was placed in a building occupied by office workers and foremen. I did not see him for a long while. Then, when I returned from my inspection trip with Zakhariantz, I ran into my old friend again at the Kotlas Transfer Station. Oukhtomsky was idle, for an order direct from the camp administration had just put a stop to the work assigned him, namely, to deliver instructive lectures to the prisoners. Oukhtomsky laughed as he told me about it and said that the order was signed by the omnipotent Vaskov himself, and bore his own notation: "You dumbbells, inviting the goat into the vegetable garden. Stop it immediately."

After the execution of the eighty-two, when I was demoted to the status of a common convict, I again met my old friend Oukhtomsky at the First Work Post. He had been transferred to Ust-Sysolsk together with the socialist-revolutionary sailor with whom I had become acquainted at the Sixth Work Post. Both of them lived in the old stables which had been changed to barracks and both showed remarkable determination. Oukhtomsky was in bad health, but as a matter of principle never asked the authorities to improve his living conditions. He ate the common food and slept right under the ceiling, on the third tier of shelves.

A group of disciples had formed around him, consisting of the widest variety of human beings. There were many peasants and priests, as well as a large number of criminals who were devoted to him. He was obeyed like a father, his advice was always sought and he merely had to start speaking to cause all noise around him to cease.

Prisoners were particularly impressed by the report of his conversation with Vaskov, the omnipotent camp commander. Upon his arrival the Prince was summoned to Vaskov's office and a conversation took place, which was faithfully reported to the prisoners, though the Prince had not said a word about it upon his return. Vaskov greeted the Prince and offered him a position as sanitary helper at the camp hospital, on condition that the latter abstain from political discussions.

"We do not need any monarchists," said Vaskov. "You should be sent to do manual labor, but, taking your age into consideration, I shall not do this. Will you give me your word of honor that you will not carry on discussions which are not suitable for penal camps?"

Oukhtomsky refused. No, he could give no promise which would limit his freedom of thought.

"If this is the case you will be banished to one of the most remote work posts, where nobody can listen to you," said Vaskov. "I would like to warn you that we shoot people for agitating against the existing regime. Bear this in mind. You have been prisoner for over nine years, soon your term is up. Do you really think that we shall let you go if you continue your seditious propaganda against us?"

"I know very well, citizen Vaskov," replied Oukhtomsky, "that I shall be released only when your communist song will be ended. Then we shall change places, though we shall probably treat you differently."

"You mean you will shoot us?" asked Vaskov, smiling.

"Oh no, we shall hang you," calmly answered the Prince.

"Take prisoner Oukbtomsky out of here!" cried the infuriated commander, but the Prince's courage made such an impression on him that he was given a job at the hospital just the same.

The story made a sensation among the prisoners. Men came up to the old man to thank him "on behalf of all." They sent him cigarettes, tobacco, sugar, anything they had to offer, to show him deference and devotion. He immediately divided all the gifts among the needy of the barracks and sat on his high shelf unperturbed, continuing to work on his notes of the World War.

The sailor was stunned. "If Russia had had more men like Oukhtomsky," he said, "we would not have had the revolution."

The sailor was quite distressed by the fun poked at him by the prisoners.

"Our high respects to the socialist," was the greeting he invariably received. "How is the Constituent Assembly? How about the Ukrainian Rada? Oh, you, deluded revolutionary, now you are reaping what you have sown."

He took all the abuse stoically, but winced under the accusation.

My last two days at Ust-Sysolsk were made pleasant by the treat of again seeing Prince Oukhtomsky, who was sent back to the work post. His fate had also been greatly affected by the change of administration. He was relieved of his duties in the sanitary department and was now being sent to one of the most remote posts of the camps. He took the blow stoically, as usual. He had experienced such depths of misery during the last ten years that nothing affected him any longer. He had three months left to the end of his term. Anyone else in his place would have waited impatiently for the moment of release and made plans for the future. Not so Oukhtomsky. He was convinced that he would not be set free in three months, nor in three years.

"They will never let me go," he replied to my query, "never. I know it and do not dream of freedom. I do not know when I am destined to die, but I am certain that I shall die in prison."

He spoke with a smile, occasionally biting the end of his long gray moustache. He still lived in the same reconditioned stables and slept on his old shelf near the ceiling, where he was exposed to wind and rain penetrating through a large crevice in the wall. I had my last glimpse of him as he was leaving for his destination. He sat in the carriage wrapped in his old reindeer coat and wearing his military cap with the red ribbon. He waved to me as he disappeared through the gates of the camp. Alas! The world had but few such men as Oukhtomsky.

And now, at Ust-Vym, the path of Oukhtomsky crossed mine once more. I learned that upon his arrival, in my absence, he had been called to the private office of Commander Dikiy and had stayed there over an hour and a half. It did not become known at first what the two had been talking about, but after the interview the old Prince was taken straight to the dungeon.

The dungeon was in the administration building and it was forbidden to send food supplies to prisoners confined there. But we used our influence with the guards and saw to it that the old man was furnished enough food and tobacco to last him a week. A week later he was transferred to the isolation prison on the other bank of the Vym River. The chekist in charge there maintained strict discipline and further transfers of food became impossible.

Oukhtomsky was kept very strictly, which seemed to have no effect on him whatever. He remained the same unswerving, uncompromising hero. Later on we were told the reason for Dikiy's disfavor.

The Prince's ten-year sentence had come to an end, but, as he had foretold, he was not given his freedom. From the chekists' point of view release was out of the question, but on the other hand, a man could not be held forever without at least an ostensible reason. Since some show of legality has to be followed even by the chekists, the OGPU had decided to trump up a new charge against the Prince.

During their long talk Dikiy had offered the Prince his freedom on condition that the latter proceed to write the history of the civil war under the supervision of the local OGPU and "in a vein desired by the Bolshevik Government." Oukhtomsky refused point blank. No, he had served his ten-year term and demanded his release. He would never write history "in any desired vein," especially under the supervision of the OGPU. He had already finished the history of the World War and had refused to have it published by the government, though he had been offered ten thousand roubles for it. His writings were intended for posterity, therefore, should he ever write the history of the civil war, he would do so impartially and not "under dictation."

The conversation had continued on similar subjects and when it ended Oukhtomsky found himself arrested and was led away by the guards, while a new charge of counter-revolution was preferred against him. After he had been confined in the isolation prison for some time, Dikiy called on him there and repeated his offer, but met with the same staunch refusal. At the isolation prison the Prince promptly aroused the ire of the chekist in charge and in the way of punishment was placed in a cell with the most desperate criminals and bums. As usual the charm of his personality was so great that even these lost souls surrounded him with care and exalted him like a god.

I was not destined to see Oukhtomsky again. Some months later I left the penal camps and the U.S.S.R. for good, but the memory of the heroic old man will live with me forever.

CHAPTER TWENTY-FOUR: THE ROAD TO FREEDOM

Almost four years had passed since the day of my arrest. The ordeal sent me by fate was nearing its end and I began counting the days as the expiration of my term approached.

All the efforts of my relatives to have me freed or to obtain my release in exchange for some communists arrested in Finland had proved fruitless. The Soviet government always answered no. As for myself, I had never appealed to the government for pardon.

I had witnessed scores of prisoners writing petitions, hoping and waiting ... only to receive a postcard some six months later with the printed form message that "The Presidium of the TSIK (Central Executive Committee of the Soviets) after due consideration of your petition for mercy, has decided to take no action." The postcards were not even signed.

Seventy days were still left when the first ray of sunlight came, the first in four years. Moscow had finally decided to adopt a system of commuting the sentences of deserving prisoners. The chief requirements were: good behavior in the penal camps for at least one and a half years, conscientious execution of all tasks, and loyalty to the Soviets.

As far as the first two requirements were concerned I was well qualified for a commutation, but as to the last, there was plenty of room for doubt. Therefore, some strings had to be pulled to attain the desired results.

Theoretically, commutations of sentence were decided by a special commission headed by the camp commander, but actually everything depended on the secretary of the commission, a young communist embezzler who had been sent to the camp for correction. However, the hopes for his reform were vain. The young scamp got drunk with me on several occasions, accepted a valuable present, and twice borrowed a few Chervontzi (ten-rouble notes) "to be repaid tomorrow." After that he took my case in hand and successfully completed it. In recognition of my two years of service in the responsible position of manager of the supply department of the entire Northern penal camp, I was granted a commutation of twenty-eight days of my sentence.

Only forty-two days were left. The days dragged, the nights seemed never to end. My little dog, Rosa, whom I had saved when a Zyryan boy wanted to kill her, seemed to feel my coming departure, nestled close to me on my sleeping-shelf, yelped a little and licked my hands. She looked at me with her intelligent dark eyes, seeming to ask whether I really intended leaving her. My dear, devoted Rosa!

I had had a lot of trouble with Rosa. It all began when I saw a Zyryan boy making preparations to hang her, as the natives did, in order to make himself a cap from the shiny black fur. The little dog emitted the saddest howls trying to free herself. After long negotiations the boy agreed to give me the dog in exchange for some money and the promise of a cap. Rosa was as thin as a skeleton under her luxurious coat of fur. She was a greedy little dog and it cost me a considerable effort to reconcile my neighbors in the barracks to her presence there, as she had promptly bitten some of them. Two weeks later she had become sweet-tempered, plump and well-fed. Rosa had her admirers and two months later the shrill voices of several puppies were added to the disturbing noises coming from under my shelf. Twice I had to make up for the nuisance by offering vodka to the warden and twice I had to pay damages for shoes injured by the pups, but to the very last day in camp nobody could persuade me to leave my little dog.

When finally the last day came and I held my release paper in my hand, something seemed to break within me. Nothing seemed of importance. Neither the whining of little Rosa nor the cheers and congratulations of my fellow-friends in adversity seemed to touch me.

"You lucky man," said my friend, engineer A., shaking me by the hand. "Are you really conscious of the fact that soon you will hold in your arms all that is dearest to you? You will kiss your little daughter. Oh, how fortunate you are! And I have four more years to go."

Soon I shall kiss my little daughter. When I left my house on that memorable night my daughter was asleep, covered by her tiny quilt. What would she be like now? "Soon you will kiss her." Was it really possible? My head reeled.

On the day of my release I received the flattering offer to remain in the free employ of the penal camp.

"We shall give you an apartment with heat and light, the rations of a Red commander, and three hundred roubles a month. Make up your mind."

To remain working for the OGPU? They certainly were on the wrong tack.

"No, thank you very much, but this does not suit me," I answered.

"But why not? How about four hundred, or five hundred roubles ..."

"Not even for ten thousand a day would I work for you," I said, looking him squarely in the face. I was free now and did not have to mince words, within certain limits of discretion, of course.

"Ah, I understand what you mean. Well then, good-bye, but you may keep in mind that it will not take much to bring you back here, what with your ideas."

I closed the door behind me and regretted that I could not have spoken my mind freely. Oukhtomsky would have done it. But ... not being Oukhtomsky, I could not.

The grateful penal camp was not generous enough even to provide means of transportation for me to the railroad station. According to the regulations, I should have been furnished a horse to Kotlas and a railroad ticket from there to my home town. They gave me the railroad ticket, but as to the horse they said: "We are sorry, but you will have to wait a week or so for the regular teams to leave; they may take your things and you can walk alongside."

I rented a room in a peasant's house and on the eve of my departure my friends gave me a farewell supper there, not wishing to see me go without due honors. In spite of the abundance of vodka and beer, there was little cause for cheerfulness, but the situation was saved by the unexpected arrival of my friend of the Kotlas Transfer Station days, Prince Karamanov, who had befriended the Turcomans.

He had obtained his release six weeks before and was now en route for Kotlas. He had frostbitten cheeks and nose, but had not lost his courage and his sense of humor. Like all released prisoners, he was left to his own resources to reach the railroad. And he did it. During the six weeks he had covered eleven hundred kilometers. Sometimes he got a lift by reindeer teams going his way, but mostly he walked. He could not hire a horse for money and had no tobacco or food to offer in exchange for such services. The government did not permit the purchase of a horse, so the only thing left was to walk. And so he journeyed as best he could.

Karamanov brought cheer into our sad gathering, told a few "newest" stories which had a pre-war flavor and made us drink a great number of toasting cups. As a result our Zyryan host did a jig, a guitar was produced and engineer A. sang some gipsy songs. It all ended with a general chorus of "Our last jolly day together," and then the prisoners one by one left me and returned to the camp, while I laid myself down to sleep — a free man for the first time in four years.

On the following day we succeeded in making arrangements for transportation with a Kolkhoz caravan that was taking eight bales of rabbit-skins to Kotlas. The caravan consisted of five sleighs. We asked why so many sleighs were needed for the transportation of eight bales of furs and were told that some of the sleighs were loaded with oats and hay for the horses, as no feed could be had anywhere for a distance of four hundred kilometers. In former days two sleighs would have been ample, but since the advent of collective farming, two sleighs could never have reached their destination. Collective farming did have some curious results.

We sat on the hay and were warm and comfortable. The Zyryan system of transportation was that thirty-five kilometers of travel were followed by five hours of rest, irrespective of the time of day. The Northern day was so short that we mostly travelled in the dark. The journey was pleasant but fatiguing.

Four Zyryan teamsters dressed in large reindeer coats and mittens, fur outside, either ran alongside their sleighs or climbed on top of the hay for a snooze or a smoke. The head-team was driven by a middle-aged Zyryan woman dressed in several coats and skirts, her head covered by a multitude of kerchiefs. She was so round on all sides that it was hard to tell which way she was facing. At the stopping places she was taken off her perch by combined efforts and on departing was lifted on again and sat there motionless like a Buddha during the whole journey.

This bundled-up woman had an angry disposition and her commands were implicitly obeyed. Not only her husband and son, but also the other two teamsters, serious and solid-looking bearded men, had the greatest respect for her. All the teamsters were calm and silent, like real Finns, and in endurance they were a match for their horses.

We asked them why they had joined the collective farm if it brought them no good and their answer invariably was: "Can't help it, fellow, it's better to live a little worse in the collectives than to have it all taken away from you. That's it, fellow." The Zyryans called all men "fellows," regardless of their age.

At every stop-over I was furnished fresh evidence of the poverty into which the population had sunk. No household, for instance, had any chickens in its yard. It did not pay to keep them, said the collective farmers. The taciturn Zyryans only repeated: "Yes, fellow, it's a hard life nowadays." As a consequence of the government's tax collections, which had preceded the collective farming edict, the peasants had slaughtered all their livestock. Now they had neither cows, nor pigs, nor sheep, nor even goats.

At all stop-overs Karamanov invariably took the seat under the ikons, next to the samovar. He had a long neck, which looked shriveled from the long exhausting journey and on it sat his little head with sharp eyes and an abnormally long nose. Zyryan women from other cottages came in especially to get a glimpse of the huge frostbitten beak with a hump on it and stood there staring at it. Karamanov was bald and had a grayish beard. He resembled a faded eagle. Tea did not seem to satisfy him. He held that "water is good to run under the bridges," and always opened negotiations for a bottle of vodka. It was usually produced and Karamanov changed in an instant, joked and made merry. Half an hour later he would be sound asleep.

During the six days of our journey we did not undress, sleeping on benches in the cottages or dozing on top of our hay. While we were on Zyryan territory our teamsters had no concern for the safety of their teams during the stop-overs. They were quite sure that nothing would be stolen. But when on the third day we crossed the border into the Northern area populated by Russians, our Zyryans took an entirely different attitude. They kept a constant watch near the teams and paid no attention to our hosts' assurances that this was not necessary.

"Bad folks here, fellow, thieving folks. Can't leave anything unwatched," they said and advised us to look out for our own things. They were right. On the very first stop-over on Russian territory somebody broke the lock of my basket, which I had left in the hall, and got away with some of my supplies.

All the villages of this region were crowded with the wives of peasants exiled from central Russia. Their number greatly exceeded that of the natives. It was hard to tell how they made a living, for the poverty all around was appalling. Young mothers with babes in their arms looked especially pitiful. They were evidently half-starved and as a result they lost their milk and the children died of hunger. These little living skeletons stubbornly struggled for existence and spent their last bit of strength screeching for food. Their little hands eagerly reached for the bottle, grabbing it and sucking the sugar-water greedily. We left all our supply of sugar in these regions.

At Kotlas we had our first regular sleep and the next morning we boarded the train for Viatka. Before departure and during the journey our travelling documents were checked over three times. Finally the train started and through the windows we got our last glimpse of the memorable infernal Kotlas Transfer Station, where two years before we had been drilled and humbled, starved into submission and made to stand in the icy cold or trot to the pleasure of our masters.

The Viatka station was full of people waiting for transportation. They were crowded like sardines. We were stopped twice and asked to show our papers. Viatka was the last post of the penal camp guards on the lookout for fugitives. Here Karamanov and I parted. He was going south via Moscow, while I was bound for Leningrad.

I was given a warm welcome at the Finnish Consulate. A lovely room, a bath, a spring mattress, sheets as white as snow, and warmth — how foreign all of this had become! It seemed unnatural to sit down to a nicely appointed table and eat properly. But, alas, there were only few such oases as our consulate in Leningrad.

During the two weeks which I had to spend in the city, waiting for my visa to leave the country, I called on some of my former friends. Only a few of them were still there. Many changes had taken place during the four years. Some were dead, others had left and others again had been imprisoned or exiled. A new generation was growing up. Boys had grown into youths, girls into young ladies. How irretrievably I had been robbed of my time!

I found one of my former very good friends lying on his bed with his feet held up in the air by a rope attached to a hook in the ceiling. It was only three days since he had returned home after three weeks in the OGPU prison in the Gorokhov aya. For twenty days he had had to stand in a room that was so crowded with people that it was impossible to sit down. Seventy men and women were kept in a small room which was barely large enough for ten. One after the other they were called out for examination. They were all suspected of concealing foreign exchange — "valuta."

"Tell us where you keep your valuta."

"But I have no valuta."

"That's all! Take the prisoner back, bring on the next!"

And so it went. They were allowed to leave the room only for purposes of examination. In the corner of the room was a sanitary receptacle which both men and women had to use in front of everybody. The air was frightful. People fainted and were taken out into the corridor where they had water poured over them. Then they were immediately returned to the room again.

If it had not been for his swollen feet suspended from the ceiling, I would have suspected my friend of exaggeration, though I had known him for a truthful man. But facts spoke for themselves. He mentioned two mutual friends, formerly rich men, who had been confined with him in the same room. On the following day I visited them and secured further confirmation of the outrage.

Came the last day, the last hours. I was taken in an automobile to the station. There was a short railroad trip to Bieloostrov, adjoining the Finnish border. There was a perfunctory customs examination. And then a whole hour of waiting for the train to start.

I crossed the little Sestra River, dividing the U.S.S.R. from Finland, and my arms reached out for Luba, my child, and freedom.

POSTSCRIPT

Who can tell the full story of the Soviet prison and exile system? Perhaps it will never be told in its true dimensions. Who can count the prisoners' graves scattered, often without any outward signs, from the borders of Turkestan to the shores of the Arctic Ocean? Perhaps the records will never see the light of day. And as for the noble human spirits blasted, as for the souls damned, the minds broken on the wheel, the children's dreams shattered in captivity, what pen can at this day do them justice?

There have been changes since I left the U.S.S.R. But nothing has really changed there. The OGPU has been absorbed by and made a part of the commissariat of the interior. This has happened before, in 1921, when the cheka was renamed the OGPU. But the terror remains the same. The same men are in charge, the same policies are in force.

The prisons and penal camps are still there. The human fodder is still being poured into the same inhuman mill. The treatment has not improved, the food is still bad and insufficient, the sanitary conditions are atrocious. The wolf has merely changed again into sheep's clothing.

I was one of the "invaluable workers of the administration staff," and as such my living conditions were vastly better than those of ordinary prisoners. The privations of the latter are best illustrated by statistics from the records of the penal camp administration itself. They showed a rate of mortality for the year of 1929-30 of twenty-two percent of the total number of prisoners employed at hard labor in the timber camps. In addition to the dead, twenty percent of the prisoners were reduced to total disability and thirty percent to partial disability, before completion of their terms. But statistics do not always tell the whole story. On checking up on the fate of the three hundred prisoners who came to the penal camps together with me in December 1929, I found that only forty were still alive in February 1932.

The rulers of the U.S.S.R. have not given up their policy of the exploitation of penal labor on a gigantic scale. In 1929 there were six penal camps in the U.S.S.R., in 1932 there were thirteen, with a total number of four hundred and fifty thousand prisoners. At the present time the number of prisoners exceeds half a million. To this figure should be added scores of thousands confined in Soviet prisons, and millions of exiled "kulaks," the so-called "voluntary colonists."

In February 1932, there were the following penal camps in Soviet Russia:

1. Karelo-Murmansky Camp (Karmurlag): 20,000 prisoners.

This is the new name for the old Solovetsky camp, except that the prisoners were no longer kept on the Solovets Islands, but on the mainland, at Kern, on the western shore of the White Sea. They were employed at fishing, roadwork and in mines.

2. Belmorstroy OGPU: 150,000 prisoners

Prisoners were employed in the construction of the canal that is to join the White Sea and the Gulf of Finland.

3. Svirsky Camp (Svirstroy): 24,000 prisoners.

Prisoners were employed on the construction of a dam and power station on the Svir River, between Lakes Ladoga and Onega.

4. Ukhtinsky-Petchorsky Camp (Upitlag): 22,000 prisoners.

Situated in the Komi territory on the Ukhta River. Prisoners worked in the Petchora coal mines and the Ukhta oil-fields.

5. Ust-Vym Camp (Uvitlag): 20,000 prisoners.

Situated on the Vym River. Prisoners worked on highway and railway construction and in the winter were employed in the timber industry.

6. Vishersky Camp: 15,000 prisoners.

Situated at Usolie. Prisoners worked at the new chemical plants and salt mines.

7. Vaigach Geological Expedition OGPU: 1000 prisoners.

Situated on Vaigach Island in the Arctic Ocean. Prisoners were employed in lead mines.

8. Temnikovsky Camp: 25,000 prisoners.

Situated at Potma, on the Moscow-Kazan Railroad. Prisoners worked on the cutting of fire-wood for Moscow.

9. Novosibirsky Camp: 25,000 prisoners.

Situated at Novosibirsk (formerly Novo-Nikolayevsk).

10. Khabarovsky-Vladivostoksky Camp: 23,000 prisoners.

Situated in the Vladivostok region near the Pacific Ocean.

11. Alma-Ata Camp: 50,000 prisoners.

Situated near Alma-Ata. Prisoners were employed on agricultural work on State Farms.

12. Akmolinsky Camp: 60,000 prisoners.

Situated near Akmolinsk. Prisoners were employed on agricultural work on State Farms.

13. Daghestan Camp: 15,000 prisoners.

Situated in the Caucasus, south of Astrakhan. Prisoners were employed in the fishing industry.

Made in the USA
San Bernardino, CA
30 March 2018